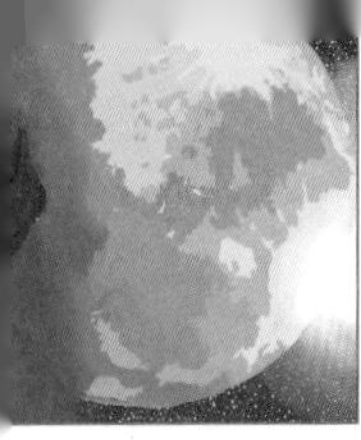

STYX

"HEROES" DAVI

OCOL HARUM

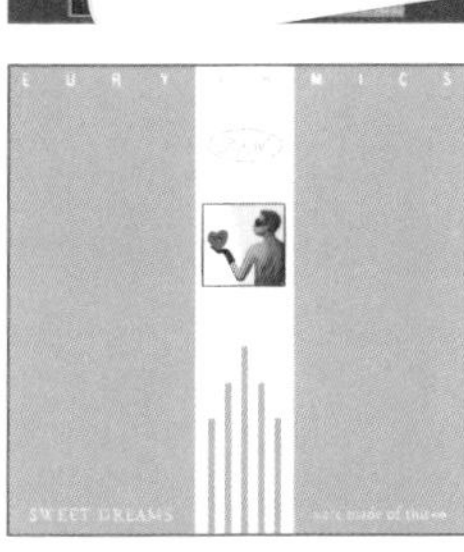
SWEET DREAMS

GREEN
DAY
american
idiot

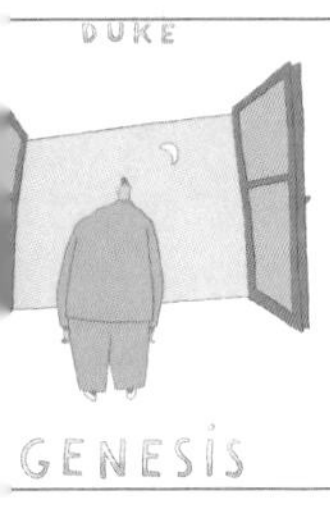
DUKE
GENESIS

BOSTON

LADY | GA

Billy Joel / Piano Man

KILLERS
HOT FUSS

BEAST
BOYS

DEREK & THE DOMINOS · LAYLA

NIRVANA
NEVERMIND

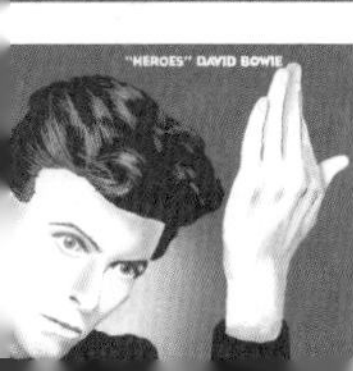
"HEROES" DAVID BOWIE

BLUE OYSTER CULT · AGENTS OF FORTUNE

ORIGINS OF A SONG

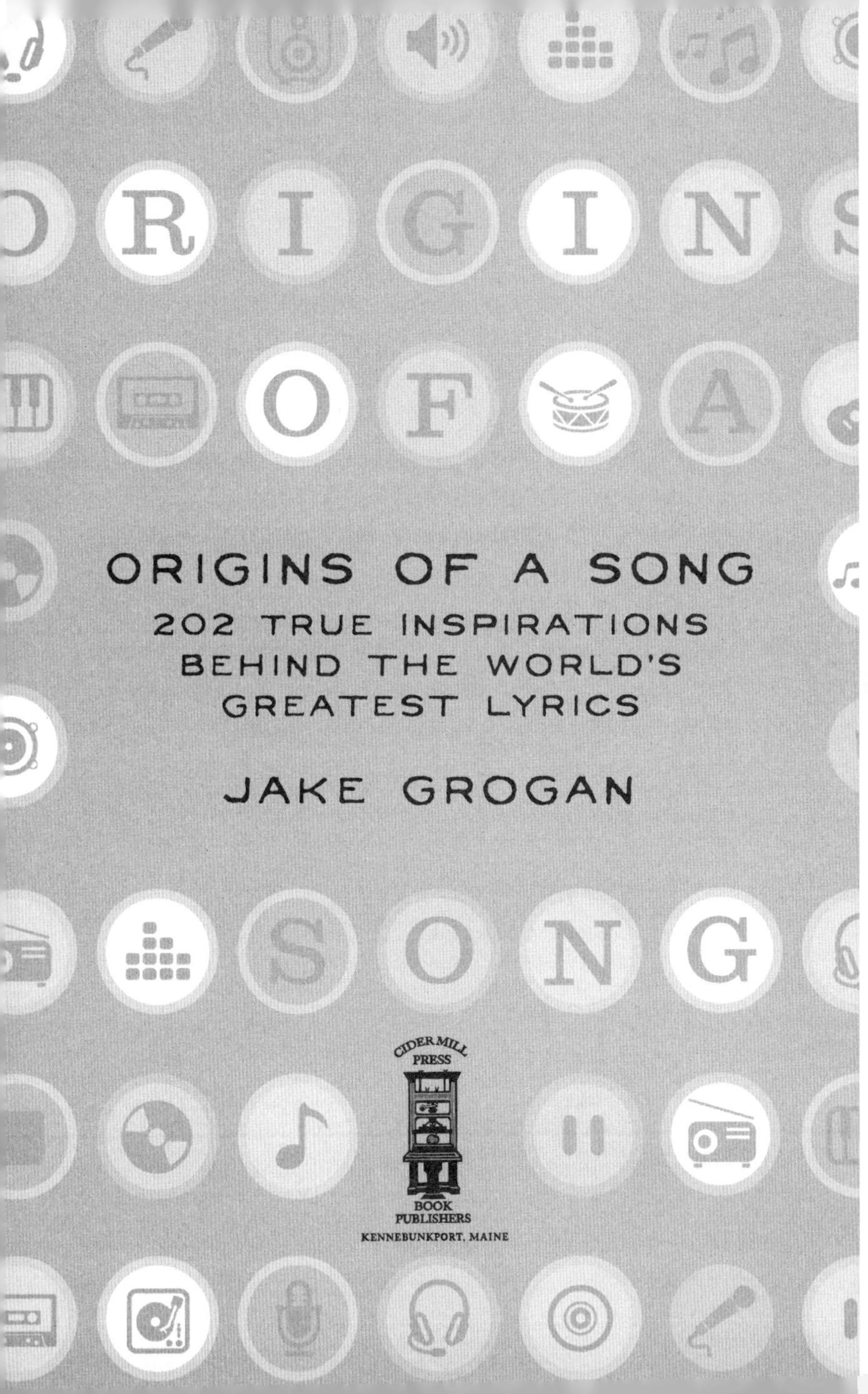

ORIGINS OF A SONG

202 TRUE INSPIRATIONS BEHIND THE WORLD'S GREATEST LYRICS

JAKE GROGAN

CIDER MILL PRESS
BOOK PUBLISHERS
KENNEBUNKPORT, MAINE

Origins of a Song

13-Digit ISBN: 9781604337754
10-Digit ISBN: 1604337753

This book may be ordered by mail from the publisher. Please include $5.99 for postage and handling. Please support your local bookseller first!

Books published by Cider Mill Press Book Publishers are available at special discounts for bulk purchases in the United States by corporations, institutions, and other organizations. For more information, please contact the publisher.

Cider Mill Press Book Publishers
"Where Good Books Are
Ready for Press"
PO Box 454
12 Spring Street
Kennebunkport, Maine 04046

Visit us online!
cidermillpress.com

Typography: Garamond, Policy Gothic, Clarendon

Printed in the United States of America
1 2 3 4 5 6 7 8 9 0
First Edition

Contents

Introduction

I've long been a fan of Electric Light Orchestra; their CDs were a part of my dad's collection and were always available to the delight of my eager ears. Once my brother and I began exchanging Christmas gifts I requested E.L.O. music for two straight years; their three-disc *Flashback* collection and *The Classic Albums Collection* have found their way onto the bookshelves of every apartment and dorm that I've lived in since. Despite owning their entire catalogue, the young are often responsible for validating clichés, and my favorite song was their mega-hit "Evil Woman." In fact, it still is! I know the song backward and forward; the opening piano riff, the backing track, Jeff Lynne's heart-wrenching lyrics, combine to make the song one of my favorites ever. Of course, I didn't know that the song was meant to serve only as a filler on the band's *Face the Music* album. The song was written and recorded in just two days, and was the result of the band finding out that they were short on tracks with little scheduled recording time left.

Uncovering that little piece of information was what attracted me to this project. It's interesting, sure, but it also helps to further contextualize the songs that accompany us throughout our days, years, and lives. Music is so important to so many of us; it has the power to take us back to faraway times in which we get to re-experience past iterations of ourselves. It could have been a song that you listened to last summer, or a staple from your favorite college bar. It doesn't matter if you loved it one year or several decades ago; the point is that a song coming across the airwaves can take you to a place you haven't been for some time. The effect may not always be a positive one, but it's no doubt powerful. I'm lucky, as my positive associations with music far outweigh my negative ones. I'm also lucky that I've always had music in my life. The first song I remember listening to was The Who's "Boris the Spider." I was introduced to Pink Floyd's *The Wall* while in elementary school. Jeff Lynne was my favorite artist growing up, while Lana Del Rey has been my favorite artist for quite some time. I know how a song makes me feel, how I interpret the lyrics, where and who I was when I first heard it. So why not find out how the artist felt while writing it?

That said, providing information that contextualizes a song and may or may not further substantiate your listening experience wasn't my only intent. I've found that a book like this often attracts those in search of creative inspiration. And for good reason! As I researched various novelists for my *Origins of a Story*, I found a variety of stand-alone tales of individuals having their creative processes zapped by an occurrence specific to their lives. While that also happens with some frequency here, I've found that musicians affect each other much more often than authors do. "Today" was in part the result of Billy Corgan being intimidated by Nirvana's success. Paul Simon borrowed the musical stylings of South Africa for "You Can Call Me Al." An alarming number of songs employ Phil Spector's Wall of Sound technique, the earliest version of which was used by The Ronettes on "Be My Baby."

Music is collaborative; techniques are developed, borrowed, and built upon; lyrical stylings are made popular by a few and are then gobbled up by the many; and genres change based on what the artists in that space deem acceptable. Sometimes it's open and obvious, like when David Bowie wrote "All the Young Dudes" for Mott the Hoople. Sometimes it's less open and just as obvious, resulting in the loss of ownership for the performing band. Sometimes it's just a mix of admiration and jealousy, like when Prince wanted a song that would make the crowd react like they did to Bob Seger, and ended up writing "Purple Rain." There's something to be learned from how the inspired got that way, as evidenced by most of the individuals featured in this book.

So, whether you're in search of inspiration or are simply interested in the interesting, I hope you get as much enjoyment reading this book as I got out of writing it.

LIKE A ROLLING STONE

Bob Dylan

-

1965

"It was 10 pages long," Bob Dylan, discussing "Like a Rolling Stone," told Jules Siegel in a 1966 interview. "It wasn't called anything, just a rhythm thing on paper all about my steady hatred directed at some point that was honest. In the end it wasn't hatred, it was telling someone something they didn't know, telling them they were lucky. Revenge, that's a better word. I had never thought of it as a song, until one day I was at the piano."

"After writing that I wasn't interested in writing a novel, or a play. I just had too much, I want to write songs."

Dylan told CBC Radio that the process started as him writing "this long piece of vomit, 20 pages long, and out of it I took 'Like a Rolling Stone' and made it as a single. And I'd never written anything like that before and it suddenly came to me that was what I should do.. ..After writing that I wasn't interested in writing a novel, or a play. I just had too much, I want to write songs."

Dylan said that the song saved him in a 1966 interview with *Playboy*, "Last spring, I guess I was going to quit singing. I was very drained, and the way things were going, it was a very draggy situation....But 'Like a Rolling Stone' changed it all. I mean it was something that I myself could dig. It's very tiring having other people tell you how much they dig you if you yourself don't dig you."

The title was inspired by Hank Williams' song "Lost Highway," while the organ part was written by Al Kooper, who told *SongFacts* that it was among his finest musical accomplishments. "By the amount of emails I receive and the press that I get it is undoubtedly the organ part on 'Like a Rolling Stone,'" he said. "I kinda like the way Martin Scorsese edited my telling of that story in the documentary *No Direction Home*."

(I CAN'T GET NO) SATISFACTION

Rolling Stones

1965

Then known as the Jack Tar Harrison Hotel, Keith Richards' May 1965 stay there saw him waking with the anthemic chorus and the guitar riff for the Rolling Stones' biggest hit in his head. He recorded a few minutes of the riff on his acoustic guitar along with his "snoring for the next forty minutes." A few weeks later, the Rolling Stones had a single.

"It sounded like a folk song when we first started working on it and Keith didn't like it much, he didn't want it to be a single, he didn't think it would do very well," Mick Jagger said in 1968. "I think Keith thought it was a bit basic. I don't think he really listened to it properly. He was too close to it and felt it was a silly kind of riff."

"People get very blasé about their big hit," Jagger recalled in 1995. "It was the song that really made the Rolling Stones, changed us from just another band into a huge, monster band. You always need one song. We weren't American, and America was a big thing and we always wanted to make it here. It was very impressive the way that song and the popularity of the band became a worldwide thing. It's a signature tune, really, rather than a great, classic painting, 'cause it's only like one thing—a kind of signature that everyone knows. It has a very catchy title. It has a very catchy guitar riff. It has a great guitar sound, which was original at that time. And it captures a spirit of the times, which is very important in those kinds of songs.... Which was alienation. Or it's a bit more than that, maybe, but a kind of sexual alienation. Alienation's not quite the right word, but it's one word that would do."

IMAGINE

John Lennon

1971

The back cover of the *Imagine* LP reads "Imagine the clouds dripping, dig a hole in your garden to put them in." The poem, titled "Cloud Piece," was penned by Yoko Ono and served as a source of inspiration for John Lennon's "Imagine."

"A lot of it—the lyric and the concept—came from Yoko," Lennon said, "but in those days I was a bit more selfish, a bit more macho, and I sort of omitted her contribution, but it was right out of *Grapefruit* [Ono's 1964 book of poetry]."

A Christian prayer book given to him by comedian Dick Gregory also helped form the concept of "Imagine." As Lennon told David Sheff in *Playboy* magazine: "The concept of positive prayer. . . .If you can imagine a world at peace, with no denominations of religion—not without religion but without this my God-is-bigger-than-your-God thing—then it can be true. . . .the World Church called me once and asked, 'Can we use the lyrics to "Imagine"?'. . . .That showed [me] they didn't understand it at all. It would defeat the whole purpose of the song, the whole idea."

Though Lennon may have composed the song on an early morning in 1971 from his Berkshire estate, the process of getting a final product out the door was a bit more involved; Phil Spector, legendary producer turned convicted murderer, played a crucial part in the song sounding like it does. Lennon inadvertently underplays it when he says: "Phil doesn't arrange or anything like that—[Ono] and Phil will just sit in the other room and shout comments like, 'Why don't you try this sound?' or 'You're not playing the piano too well.'. . . .I'll get the initial idea and. . . .we'll just find a sound from [there]," but it was Spector who was responsible for deciding where, with what, and who to record to get the sound that Lennon was going for.

The song angered many; from the devout worshippers who took issue with a line regarding the absence of a heaven, to those with capitalist mentalities who didn't want to hear about fundamental communist concepts fresh off of the Vietnam War. The song was more divisive than one about peace and love ought to be. Lennon clarified his political stance when he told *NME* that: "There is no real Communist state in the world; you must realize that. The socialism I speak about. . . .[is] not the way some daft Russian might do it, or the Chinese might do it. That might suit them. Us, we should have a nice. . . .British Socialism." Regardless, the song still managed to reach the No. 3 spot on the *Billboard* Hot 100 and is almost universally thought of as the greatest song to come out of Lennon's solo career. He had even said that he considered it to be as strong a piece of music as anything that he was involved in while with The Beatles.

HELLO

Adele

-

2015

As indicated by the almost five-year gap between releasing *21* (31 million copies sold) and her follow-up record *25* (which had sold 20 million copies as of June 2016), Adele felt so comfortable where she was writing music that she eventually disconnected completely. "What's been going on in the world of music?" she asked Brian Hiatt, who was interviewing her for *Rolling Stone*. "I feel out of the loop!"

"Hello" is a perfect microcosm of that feeling; a masterpiece that is so perfectly Adele that Greg Kurstin, the song's producer and co-writer, didn't even know if it would get finished. "We had half the song written," he told *Rolling Stone*. "I just had to be very patient." She eventually returned to finish the chorus six months after they had last worked on it, wrapping up the piano ballad that was a way for her to reach out to those who are no longer as active in her life. "'Hello' is about wanting to be at home and wanting to reach out to everyone I've hurt—including myself—and apologize for it," she told *US Weekly*. "It's about friends, ex-boyfriends, it's about myself, it's about my family. It's also about my fans as well. I feel like everyone thinks I'm so far away and I'm not. Everyone thinks I live in f*cking America, I don't."

When asked if the inspiration from the song was derived from the same place as her "Someone Like You," Adele responded "That's over and done with, thank f*ck. That's been over and done with for f*cking years."

RESPECT

Aretha Franklin

-

1967

"What are you griping about?" Al Jackson, a drummer, asked Otis Redding as he complained at the end of a long tour. "You're on the road all the time. All you can look for is a little respect when you come home." Jackson's attempt to set Redding straight inspired the latter to pen a song, which he gave to Speedo Sims and the Singing Demons to record. Redding recorded the song himself and put it on his 1965 album *Otis Blue*, once Sims failed after several attempts. The song had shown potential as being a massive crossover hit, as it reached the No. 35 spot on *Billboard*'s Singles Chart at a time when *Billboard* put out a separate Black Singles Chart, where it reached the top five.

Producer Jerry Wexler identified the song's potential and brought it to Aretha Franklin, known for her powerful and impressive voice. "I walked out into the studio and said, 'What's the next song?'" Tom Dowd, session engineer, recalled in the documentary *Tom Dowd and the Language of Music*. "Aretha starts singing it to me, I said, 'I know that song, I made it with Otis Redding like three years ago.' The first time I recorded 'Respect,' was on the Otis Blue album, and she picked up on it. She and Carolyn [Franklin, sister] were the ones who conceived of it coming from the woman's point of view instead of the man's point of view, and when it came to the middle, Carolyn said, 'Take care, TCB.' Aretha jumped on it and that was how we did 'Respect.'"

Franklin added the song's famous chorus, and claims it has no sexual intent. "It was nonsexual, just a cliché line," she said.

There was nothing cliché about the response; the song reached the No. 1 spot on the *Billboard* Black Singles Chart as well as the *Billboard* Pop Singles Chart. The song even climbed into the top 10 in the United Kingdom, achieving a level of popularity that elevated Franklin into rarified air. Redding took the popularity of the cover well, telling the audience at the Monterey Pop Festival that the song was taken "away from me, a friend of mine, this girl just took this song." Despite that, the song still meant a great deal to Redding, who said: "That's one of my favorite songs because it has a better groove than any of my records. . . .The song lines are great. The band track is beautiful. It took me a whole day to write it and about 20 minutes to arrange it. We cut it once and that was it. Everybody wants respect, you know."

GOOD VIBRATIONS

The Beach Boys

1966

"My mother used to tell me about vibrations," Brian Wilson told *Rolling Stone*. "I didn't really understand too much of what she meant when I was a boy. It scared me, the word 'vibrations'—to think that invisible feelings existed. She also told me about dogs that would bark at some people, but wouldn't bark at others, and so it came to pass that we talked about good vibrations."

Wilson, trying to put words to that thought, sought songwriting help from lyricist Tony Asher and songwriter Van Dyke Parks before eventually receiving it from his band mate, and cousin, Mike Love. "It was this flowery power type of thing," Love recalled in a *SongFacts* interview. "Scott McKenzie wrote 'If you're going to San Francisco, be sure to wear some flowers in your hair,' and there were love-ins and all that kind of thing starting to go on. So the track, the music of 'Good Vibrations,' was so unique and so psychedelic in itself. Just the instrumental part of it alone was such a departure from what we have done, like 'Surfin' USA' and 'California Girls' and 'I Get Around' and 'Fun, Fun, Fun,' all of which I had a hand in writing. I wanted to do something that captured this feeling of the track and the times, but also could relate to people. Because I thought that the music was such a departure that who knows how well it would relate to Beach Boys fans at that time."

Love continued: "The one thing that I figured is an absolute perennial is the boy/girl relationship, the attraction between a guy and a girl. So I came up with that hook part at the chorus. It didn't exist until I came up with that thought. . . .It was kind of a flower power poem to suit the times and complement the really amazingly unique track that Cousin Brian came up with."

The song was recorded in fragments and later spliced together because Wilson didn't have a clear idea of what he wanted going into the recording process. As a result of the time it took to record and the equipment with which they did so, the process racked up the largest-ever sum of money spent on a single. Even so, Wilson considered abandoning the project and giving what they had to a blues group, as he wasn't satisfied. He stuck with it, however, and was later rewarded with a No. 1 spot in the *Billboard* Hot 100. "Good Vibrations" was later named the sixth-best song of all time on *Rolling Stone*'s 500 Greatest Songs of All Time list.

JOHNNY B. GOODE

Chuck Berry

-

1958

Though "Johnny B. Goode" evolved from being based on Chuck Berry's pianist Johnnie Johnson to being about Berry himself, the rock and roll pioneer did take some poetic license with his own life story; he was not an illiterate boy from New Orleans, but rather a well-educated beauty school graduate from St. Louis. Of course, the song's titular character was inspired by both Johnson and Berry, as "Johnny" comes from the former's surname, while the Goode comes from the address at which Berry was born, 2520 Goode Avenue. And the "boy" line isn't autobiographical, the original "colored boy" line was, though Berry switched it in fear of his song being banned from radio stations.

HEY JUDE

The Beatles

-

1968

Paul McCartney, recalling how he came to write "Hey Jude," said, "I was driving out to [John Lennon's] house after John and [his ex-wife] Cynthia had gotten divorced. I was just going out to say hi to Cynthia and [John's son] Julian, and I started coming up with these words. In my own mind I was kind of talking to Julian. . . .You know, it'll be alright. So I kind of got the first idea on the way out there with this 'hey Jules' as I thought it was gonna be called. It seemed a little bit of a mouthful, so I changed it to Jude. I liked the song a lot and I played it to John and Yoko. When I finished it all, well. . . . I actually had finished, but I thought there was a little more to go. There's just one bit of words, which was. . .a stupid expression. 'It sounds like a parrot, you know? I'll change that.' [John] said, 'You won't you know. That's the best line in the song you know.'. . .That was the great thing about John. I was definitely gonna knock that line out and he's like, 'It's great.' I could see it through his eyes and go, 'Oh, ok.' So that is the sort of line now that, when I do that song, I think of John and, you know, sometimes get a little emotional.""

SMELLS LIKE TEEN SPIRIT

Nirvana

-

1991

The only song on *Nevermind* to credit all three band members as writers, the album's first track "Smells Like Teen Spirit" was introduced to bassist Krist Novoselic and drummer Dave Grohl a few weeks before recording for the album was set to begin. Then just a main riff and chorus vocal melody, Novoselic suggested slowing Nirvana front man Kurt Cobain's riff down after being forced to play it for 90 minutes straight. Cobain agreed and slowed the tempo down, Grohl started work shopping a drum beat, and the foundation for one of the most acclaimed songs of all time was laid.

"I was trying to write the ultimate pop song," Cobain told *Rolling Stone* in a 1994 interview. "I was basically trying to rip off the Pixies. I have to admit it. When I heard the Pixies for the first time, I connected with that band so heavily that I should have been in that band—or at least a Pixies cover band. We used their sense of dynamics, being soft and quiet and then loud and hard." It worked, as "Smells Like Teen Spirit" has enjoyed as enduring a degree of popularity as any pop song ever performed. The song is featured in the top 10 of most top songs lists, was called an "anthem for apathetic kids" of Generation X, and has been credited with helping alternative rock enter the mainstream. Lyrical interpretation and the search for meaning has been a major part of the song's success, especially in regards to its title. As it turns out, Nirvana's crowning hit was named thanks to indirect inspiration from deodorant brand "Teen Spirit." As Kathleen Hanna, lead singer of the band Bikini Kill and close friend of Cobain, explained: "Since Kurt and I were angry young feminists in the nineties, we decided that we were going to do a little public service that night. We drank our Canadian Club, and he watched out while I went across the street and wrote 'Fake Abortion Clinic Everyone.' I was kinda the pragmatic one and he was more creative so he went over and

"I was basically trying to rip off the Pixies. I have to admit it."

in 6 foot tall red letters wrote 'God Is King'. . . .We ended up in Kurt's apartment and I smashed a bunch of sh*t. I took out a Sharpie marker and I wrote all over his bedroom wall—it was a rental so it was really kind of lame that I did that. I passed out with the marker in my hand, and woke up hung over." Part of the vandalism involved writing "Kurt Smells Like Teen Spirit" on the wall, a reference to Tobi Vail, the drummer for Bikini Kill. She was Cobain's ex-girlfriend and used to wear "Teen Spirit" deodorant.

WHAT'D I SAY

Ray Charles

1959

"I'm not one to interpret my own songs, but if you can't figure out 'What'd I Say,' then something's wrong," Ray Charles said. "Either that, or you're not accustomed to the sweet sounds of love."

That wasn't the first time Charles lauded the song; when he called Jerry Wexler to inform him about his new material, he said, "I don't believe in giving myself advance notices, but I figured this song merited it."

"What'd I Say" was the product of a set that ran too short and an improvisation that ran to perfection. With 12 minutes left at a meal dance in Brownsville, Pennsylvania, Charles told his backup singers "Listen, I'm going to fool around and y'all just follow me." It was December 1958 and the night was perfect; the audience left their seats and danced to Charles' call-and-response with his backup singers. Though audience members inquired as to where the record could be purchased after the performance, it wasn't until February 1959 that Charles recorded his hit. Because of the song's seven-and-a-half-minute length it had to be split into two parts, one on each side of the same record. The song was released in June 1959 and, despite being banned in response to its sexually charged nature, it topped the *Billboard* R & B Singles Chart and reached No. 6 on the *Billboard* Hot 100 just a few weeks later.

MY GENERATION

The Who

-

1965

On the defining hit "My Generation," The Who's Pete Townshend told *Rolling Stone*'s David Fricke in a 1987 interview, "I was very, very lost. The band was young then. It was believed that its career would be incredibly brief. The privilege that I had at the time was to be plucked out of bed-sitter land and put in a flat in the middle of Belgravia with two tape machines. It was private, and I could look out at these people who seemed to me to be from another planet. I remember one of the things I bought when The Who first became successful was a 1963 Lincoln Continental. I was driving with the top down through London, and a woman in a car going in the other direction looked at me. She was wearing a string of pearls, blond hair, very beautiful, about thirty-five. She kind of looked at me as if admiring me in my car. Then her lip curled, and she said, 'Driving Mummy's car, are we?' That one incident, among a series of other key incidents, made me hate those people. I really started to respond to that. 'All right, you motherf*ckers, I am going to have you. I am going to be bigger and richer, and I'm going to move into your neighborhood. I'm going to buy that house next to you, Lord So-and-So.' And I've done it. And I'm afraid I've done it out of a great sickness. I talk to people I really do respect from that way of life now, and I say to them, 'Do you realize why it is I'm so driven to operate within the Establishment? It's vengeance.'"

Supposedly written on a train from London to Southampton, Townshend spent his 20th birthday penning the song with the rich in mind, as he felt they represented and were responsible for building the very establishment that the counterculture of the 1960s sought to tear down. The height of that establishment for the English would have been the Queen Mother, whom Townshend had love and respect for prior to an unfortunate run-in. In a 2000 interview with David Cavanagh, Townshend said, "It was 1964. My manager Kit Lambert felt that I was unduly held down by my art school friends, so he moved me into Chesham Place, the road between Clarence House and Buckingham Palace. I had this Packard hearse parked outside my house. One day I came back and it was gone.

It turned out that she'd had it moved, because her husband had been buried in a similar vehicle and it reminded her of him. When I went to collect it, they wanted two hundred and fifty quid. I'd only paid thirty for it in the first place."

LONDON CALLING

The Clash

1979

In borrowing a phrase that was specific to London during World War II, The Clash front man Joe Strummer invited the listener to consider the state of the country in the late-1970s. "I read about ten news reports in one day calling down all variety of plagues on us," Strummer told *Melody Maker* in 1988. The phrase "This is London calling" was one used by BBC World Service in their broadcasts to Axis-occupied countries during the war; fittingly, that war ended with the ushering in of a previously unknown power, which was a subject of Strummer's concerns in the '70s. Two world powers were engaged in the Cold War, while the worst nuclear disaster in United States history occurred at Three Mile Island nine months before the single was released in December 1979. "We felt that we were struggling about to slip down a slope or something, grasping with our fingernails," he said. "And there was no one there to help us."

The song's chorus is grounded in a fear that the River Thames will flood. "We knew that London was susceptible to flooding," Strummer told *Uncut*, referring to a conversation that he had with then-fiancée Gaby Salter. "She told me to write something about that." The song also deals with police brutality in London and addressed the concerns that the band had regarding the end of the punk boom and what that would mean for a punk band two years after the boom ended.

PURPLE HAZE

Jimi Hendrix Experience

-

1967

Jimi Hendrix' cover of "Hey Joe" reached the No. 6 spot on the U.K. record chart, but it didn't feel genuine. "That record isn't us," Hendrix said. "The next one's gonna be different. We're working on an LP which will mainly be our stuff."

The result was an incredible collection of hits: "Red House," "Remember," "Foxy Lady," and "Third Stone from the Sun" all came out of subsequent trips to the recording studios. Among those that stood out was "Purple Haze," a song that began as a guitar riff that producer and ex-Animals bassist Chas Chandler stumbled upon. "I heard him playing it at the flat and was knocked out," Hendrix recalled. "I told him to keep working on that, saying, 'That's the next single!'"

Drummer Mitch Mitchell recalls nailing his part on the third take, while Chandler claims that the basic track took just four hours to record. As far as the song's actual development was concerned, Chandler and Hendrix constructed it little by little. Chandler recalled: "With 'Purple Haze,' Hendrix and I were striving for a sound and just kept going back in [to the studio], two hours at a time, trying to achieve it. It wasn't like we were there for days on end. We recorded it, and then Hendrix and I would be sitting at home saying, 'Let's try that.' Then we would go in for an hour or two. That's how it was in those days. However long it took to record one specific idea, that's how long we would book. We kept going in and out."

Though the song is interpreted by many to be about psychedelic drugs, the general thought amongst those versed in the subject is that Hendrix' love for science fiction was the inspiration. Hendrix himself said that he dreamt a lot and used those dreams to inspire lyrics. "I wrote one called 'First Look Around the Corner,'" he said, "and another called 'The Purple Haze,' which was about a dream I had that I was walking under the sea." The song certainly seems to have drawn inspiration from the book *Night of Light* by Philip Jose Farmer, in which a planet's purple haze has a psychological effect on the inhabitants.

EARTH ANGEL

The Penguins

-

1954

"Every time the dog barked next door, I'd have to go out and shut him up, and then we'd do another take," Curtis Williams, co-writer of "Earth Angel," recalled. The Penguins were four black Los Angeles teens who introduced the world to doo-wop with their smash hit.

However, the issue of proper credit was the source of much controversy after the song proved to be a major success. The dispute eventually made it into the courts, where Jesse Belvin was asked to sing his version of the song in front of a courtroom. Unfortunately, Cornel Gunter, a member of The Flairs, wasn't awarded any credit despite his contributions. "They had the melody and the harmony but they didn't have the background," Williams told *Record Exchanger* magazine. "This Cornel Gunter got with them and rehearsed them. 'Man,' I said, 'Now we've got something.' In my estimation it had the perfect melody, the perfect harmony and the perfect background which are the three things that it needed." Among those eventually credited for the song's composition were Williams, The Penguins' bassist, Gaynel Hodge, a session piano player, and Belvin, the original composer.

LET IT BE

The Beatles

-

1970

"It will be alright, just let it be," Paul McCartney's mother once told him. She passed away when he was just 14 years old, yet she came to him in a dream 12 years later to help inspire one of The Beatles' last and most impactful hits.

"It was great to visit with her again," McCartney said. "I felt very blessed to have that dream. So that got me writing 'Let It Be.'" McCartney leaves the subject of lyrical intent up to the listeners, though he has said that the reference to the woman who provides him comfort was brought on by thoughts of his mother, not the Virgin Mary.

BORN TO RUN

Bruce Springsteen

-

1975

When asked about a line referencing the potential fear that one's youth has been lost, Bruce Springsteen told *Rolling Stone* that: "The songs were written immediately after the Vietnam War and you forget, everybody felt like that then. It didn't matter how old you were, everybody experienced a radical change in the image they had of their country and of themselves. You were going to be a different type of American than the generation that immediately preceded you. A radically different type, so that line was just recognizing that fact. A lot of my heroes influenced that album. But I realized that I was not them. I was someone else; I was not them. I embraced what made us singular, individual. It wasn't just a mishmash of previous styles. There was a lot of stuff we loved in it from the music we loved, but there was something else too—and that something else was quite a sense of dread and uncertainty about the future and who you were, where you were going, where the whole country was going. That found its way into the record."

"A lot of my heroes influenced that album. But I realized that I was not them. I was someone else; I was not them. I embraced what made us singular, individual."

Springsteen had an uncertain future, though he framed it a little bit differently when he said, "Don't worry fellas—we have no place to go. We're not going away. We're going to continue." All the same, he and his group had a lot riding on *Born to Run*, as their lack of success was beginning to cost them favor with record companies. "Nobody had an investment in me, and we were just slipping through the cracks," he recalled. "I think when *The Wild, the Innocent and the E Street Shuffle* came out it wasn't particularly promoted and I always remember going to radio stations where they didn't know I had a second record out. I remember everybody coming down to watch some promising young band who was opening for us—and then leaving when we came on."

He continued: "At the time, there was a great disagreement over *The Wild and the Innocent*, and I was asked to record the entire album over again with studio musicians. And I said I wouldn't do it, and they basically said, 'Well hey, look, it's going to go in the trash can.' That's the record business, you know."

The song marked a turning point for the artist; Springsteen's future manager and then-rock critic Jon Landau, upon seeing "Born to Run" performed live for the first time, wrote: "I saw rock and roll's future—and its name is Bruce Springsteen." *Rolling Stone* ranked the song 21st on their 500 Greatest Songs of All Time list, while music critic Robert Christgau essentially called it the epitome of Phil Spector's famous Wall of Sound technique.

Talking about the initial inspiration for the song, Springsteen said: "I remember when the riff came into my head. I'd been listening to the record 'Because They're Young' by Duane Eddy, and I'd been listening to quite a bit of Duane Eddy because I was into the twangy guitar sound at the moment. But it was one of those things that I can't completely trace back. I mean, I had these enormous ambitions. I wanted to make the greatest rock record that I'd ever heard, and I wanted it to sound enormous and I wanted it to grab you by your throat and insist that you take that ride, insist that you pay attention, not to just the music, but just to life, to feeling alive, to being alive. That was sort of what the song was asking, and it was taking a step out into the unknown. And that's the big difference, say, between 'Born to Run' and 'Born in the U.S.A.' 'Born in the U.S.A' was obviously about standing someplace. 'Born to Run' wasn't; it was about searching for that place. It was a moment when I was young and that's what I was doing. I was very untethered and you had a rough map and you were about to set out in search of your frontier—personally and emotionally—and everything was very, very wide open. And that's how the record felt, just wide open, full of possibilities, full of fear, you know, but that's life."

LOSE YOURSELF

Eminem

-

2002

Eminem recalled his writing "Lose Yourself" while on set for the movie *8 Mile*, which he relayed to Zane Lowe in an interview on Beats 1. "It was like being a f*cking hamster, and you were just going from one cage, one wheel to the next," he said. "It was a music trailer, and it was the trailer where I gotta learn the lines and, you know, learning the scenes and. . .writing and trying to record, and, you know. Trying to get a little workout in here and there. I was just going from one trailer to the next. Workout trailer, go to the studio trailer, then back to learning the lines. In between takes, I remember writing on my hand because I didn't have a piece of paper at the time. It was fun but it wasn't. It was intense."

The song was released as the lead single from the 2002 film's soundtrack and topped the *Billboard* Hot 100. And the song has staying power—critics continue to say that "Lose Yourself" is among the greatest hip-hop songs ever. The song's lyrics are meant to explain the background and story arc of B-Rabbit, the character played by Eminem in the film.

IT WASN'T ME

Shaggy

-

2000

Who needs inspiration when you have the guiding voice of a higher power? Not Shaggy, apparently.

In an interview with *HuffPost Live*, the Jamaican-American singer/songwriter went into what led him to write "It Wasn't Me," saying, "I actually did write it from the Eddie Murphy movie. I got the whole idea from that," he said. "I was telling somebody yesterday, songs like 'Mr. Boombastic,' 'It Wasn't Me,' 'Angel,' these songs, I didn't write those songs. These songs were written by a higher being. It was just ordained through me." When asked if Shaggy had ever experienced something similar, he responded by saying: "Come on man! I'm too good."

LAYLA

Derek and the Dominoes

1970

"Layla" was supposed to come at the expense of George Harrison, but the Beatle didn't seem to mind. He even played, with Paul McCartney and Ringo Starr, at the wedding of Eric Clapton and his ex-wife Pattie Boyd. According to mutual friend Bobby Whitlock, "I was there when they were supposedly sneaking around. You don't sneak very well when you're a world figure. He was all hot on Pattie and I was dating her sister. They had this thing going on that supposedly was behind George's back. Well, George didn't really care. He said, 'You can have her.' That kind of defuses it when Eric says, 'I'm taking your wife' and he says, 'Take her.'"

Harrison met Boyd in 1964, during the filming of *A Hard Day's Night*, around the same time that he was becoming close friends with Clapton. Each had contributed to the work of the other; Clapton played guitar on Harrison's "While My Guitar Gently Weeps," while Harrison co-wrote Cream's "Badge." The working relationship, while responsible for fostering a friendship, also brought on Clapton's love for Boyd. He wrote "Layla," originally a ballad, with her in mind, a concept that wasn't lost on her at the time. "I wasn't so happy when Eric wrote 'Layla,' while I was still married to George," Pattie told *The Guardian* in a 2008 interview. "I felt I was being exposed. I was amazed and thrilled at the song—it was so passionate and devastatingly dramatic—but I wanted to hang on to my marriage. Eric made this public declaration of love. I resisted his attentions for a long time—I didn't want to leave my husband. But obviously when things got so excruciatingly bad for George and me it was the end of our relationship. We both had to move on. Layla was based on a book by a 12th-century Persian poet called Nizami about a man who is in love with an unobtainable woman. The song was fantastically painful and beautiful. After I married Eric we were invited out for an evening and he was sitting round playing his guitar while I was trying on dresses upstairs. I was taking so long and I was panicking about my hair, my clothes, everything, and I came downstairs expecting him to really berate me but he said, 'Listen to this!' In the time I had taken to get ready he had written 'Wonderful Tonight.'"

Clapton abandoned the ballad concept when Duane Allman, who joined Clapton in the early days of Derek and the Dominoes, composed the song's riff. The piano part came from drummer and "Layla" co-writer Jim Gordon, who Clapton overheard playing a separately composed piano piece. The origins of the piece are murky; Gordon was officially credited for it, while keyboardist Bobby Whitlock said: "Jim took that piano melody from his ex-girlfriend Rita Coolidge. I know because in the [D&D] days I lived in John Garfield's old house in the Hollywood Hills and there was a guesthouse with an upright piano in it. Rita and Jim were up there in the guesthouse and invited me to join in on writing this song with them called 'Time'. . . .Her sister Priscilla wound up recording it with Booker T. Jones. . . .Jim took the melody from Rita's song and didn't give her credit for writing it. Her boyfriend ripped her off."

Regardless of the genesis, that piece of music helped define one of Clapton's most recognizable hits. *Rolling Stone* ranked the song 27th on their list of "The 500 Greatest Songs of All Time." Pattie Boyd put it best when she said: "I think that he was amazingly raw at the time. . .he's such an incredible musician that he's able to put his emotions into music in such a way that the audience can feel it instinctively. It goes right through you."

I WALK THE LINE

Johnny Cash

1956

"I'm going to be true to those who believe in me and depend on me to myself and God," Johnny Cash said of his classic, "I Walk the Line." "Something like I'm still being true, or I'm 'Walking the Line.' The lyrics came as fast as I could write. In 20 minutes, I had it finished."

Cash's song was meant to convey his devotion, specifically to his new wife. "I wrote the song backstage one night in 1956 in Gladewater, Texas," he said. "I was newly married at the time, and I suppose I was laying out my pledge of devotion."

Cash owes some of the song's success to performer Carl Perkins and producer Sam Phillips; the former came up with the name "I Walk the Line," while the latter encouraged it to be a faster song than the slow ballad Cash had originally planned. Phillips told *Uncut* magazine in a 2012 interview that he "wasn't impressed with Cash at first, because I like recordings with class. . . .And Cash seemed rough, but 'I Walk the Line' was a class recording." The audience responded well to the up-tempo song, as well as to the performance that Cash put on while singing it. The demands the song made on his voice were such that he needed to hum in order to make sure he had the key changes down. "People ask me why I always hum whenever I sing this song," he said on his TV show. "It's to get my pitch."

STAIRWAY TO HEAVEN

Led Zeppelin

1971

"I had these pieces, these guitar pieces, that I wanted to put together," Jimmy Page recalled to NPR. "I had a whole idea of a piece of music that I really wanted to try and present to everybody and try and come to terms with. Bit difficult really, because it started on acoustic, and as you know it goes through to the electric parts. But we had various run-throughs [at Headley Grange] where I was playing the acoustic guitar and jumping up and picking up the electric guitar. [Led Zeppelin lead singer Robert Plant] was sitting in the corner, or rather leaning against the wall, and as I was routining the rest of the band with this idea and this piece, he was just writing. And all of a sudden he got up and started singing, along with another run-through, and he must have had 80% of the words there. . . . I had these sections, and I knew what order they were going to go in, but it was just a matter of getting everybody to feel comfortable with each gear shift that was going to be coming."

The song's roots trace back to Bron-Yr-Aur, a cottage in Wales where Plant and Page were staying in 1970. Though Page claimed to have written the music for "Stairway to Heaven" "over a long period of time," that music started at Bron-Yr-Aur. Bassist John Paul Jones remembered having the song introduced to him upon his bandmates' return, saying, "Page and Plant would come back from the Welsh mountains with the guitar intro and verse. I literally heard it in front of a roaring fire in a country manor house! I picked up a bass recorder and played a run-down riff which gave us an intro, then I moved into a piano for the next section, dubbing on the guitars." The song was split into three total sections, each moving at a faster clip than the last. Said Page, "Going back to those studio days for me and John Paul Jones, the one thing you didn't do was speed up, because if you sped up you wouldn't be seen again. Everything had to be right on the meter all the way through. And I really wanted to write something which did speed up, and took the emotion and the adrenaline with it, and would reach a sort of crescendo. And that was the idea of it. That's why it was a bit tricky to get together in stages."

SYMPATHY FOR THE DEVIL

Rolling Stones

1968

"'Sympathy' is quite an uplifting song," Keith Richards said in 2002. "It's just a matter of looking the devil in the face. He's there all the time. I've had very close contact with Lucifer—I've met him several times. Evil—people tend to bury it and hope it sorts itself out and doesn't rear its ugly head. 'Sympathy for the Devil' is just as appropriate now, with 9/11. There it is again, big time. When that song was written, it was a time of turmoil. It was the first sort of international chaos since World War II. And confusion is not the ally of peace and love. You want to think the world is perfect. Everybody gets sucked into that. And as America has found out to its dismay, you can't hide. You might as well accept the fact that evil is there and deal with it any way you can. 'Sympathy for the Devil' is a song that says, 'Don't forget him. If you confront him, then he's out of a job.'"

The search for the song's true origin is thwarted by Mick Jagger's uncertainty, though he's certain that the idea was inspired by French literature, at the very least. "I think that was taken from an old idea of Baudelaire's, I think, but I could be wrong," Jagger told *Rolling Stone* in a 1995 interview. "Sometimes when I looks at my Baudelaire books, I can't see it in there. But it was an idea I got from French writing. And I took a couple of lines and expanded on it. I wrote it as sort of like a Bob Dylan song." The initial direction for the song was towards the folk genre, though Richards thought that the song might be better with an uptick in tempo and a shift towards a samba style of music. "Songs can metamorphasize," Jagger said. "And 'Sympathy for the Devil' is one of those songs that started off like one thing, I wrote it one way and then we started to change the rhythm. And then it became completely different. And then it got very exciting. It started off as a folk song and then became a samba. A good song can become anything. It's got lots of historical references and lots of poetry."

These were helped by the song's mesmerizing beat. "It has a very hypnotic groove, a samba, which has a tremendous hypnotic power, rather like good dance music," Jagger said. "It doesn't speed up or slow down. It keeps this constant groove. Plus, the actual samba rhythm is a great one to sing on, but it is also got some other suggestions in it, an undercurrent of being primitive—because it is a primitive African, South American, Afro-whatever-you-call-that rhythm. So to white people, it has a very sinister thing about it. But forgetting the cultural colors, it is a very good vehicle for producing a powerful piece. It becomes less pretentious because it is a very unpretentious groove. If it had been done as a ballad, it wouldn't have been as good."

"You might as well accept the fact that evil is there and deal with it any way you can. 'Sympathy for the Devil' is a song that says, 'Don't forget him. If you confront him, then he's out of a job.'"

LIGHT MY FIRE

The Doors

-

1967

Jim Morrison came up with a line, drummer John Densmore came up with the rhythm, and Ray Manzarek was responsible for the organ intro. But it was guitarist Robby Krieger who came up with most of what became The Doors' signature track. He told *Uncut*: "I was living with my parents in Pacific Palisades—I had my amp and [Gibson SG guitar]. I asked Jim, 'What should I write about?' He said, 'Something universal, which won't disappear two years from now. Something that people can interpret themselves.' I said to myself I'd write about the four elements; earth, air, fire, water, I picked fire, as I loved the Stones song, 'Play With Fire,' and that's how that came about."

The song was a result of the eclectic backgrounds each member of the band brought to the table. As Manzarek recalls, "Robby Krieger brings in some [flamenco] guitar. I bring a little bit of classical music along with the blues and jazz, and certainly John Densmore was heavy into jazz. And Jim brings in beatnik poetry and French symbolist poetry, and that's the blend of The Doors as the sun is setting into the Pacific Ocean at the end, the terminus of Western civilization. That's the end of it. Western civilization ends here in California at Venice Beach, so we stood there inventing a new world on psychedelics."

The song spent three weeks at No. 1 on the *Billboard* Hot 100 and reached one million copies sold just five months after its release in April 1967.

ONE

U2

1991

"There was melancholy about it but there was also strength," Bono said of U2's anthemic "One."

"One is not about oneness, it's about difference. It's not the old hippie idea of 'Let's all live together.' It is a much more punk rock concept. It's anti-romantic. Like it or not, the only way out of here is if I give you a leg up the wall and you pull me after you. There's something very unromantic about that. The song is a bit twisted, which is why I could never figure out why people wanted it at their weddings. I have certainly met a hundred people who've had it at their weddings. I tell them, 'Are you mad? It's a song about splitting up.'"

"One" was representative of the band's then-dilemma; a split in mentalities on what was wrong with the band and which direction to go in. Bono and The Edge wanted a newer sound, inspired by an increasingly relevant electronic dance music scene. Adam Clayton and Larry Mullen, on the other hand, wanted to stick with what got them to that point. "One" was born during a jam session in which The Edge stumbled upon a chord progression while playing an early version of the song "Mysterious Ways," which was then called "Sick Puppy." "Everyone recognized it was a special place," The Edge recalled. "It was like we caught a glimpse of what the song could be." Bono claimed that they had the foundation for the song within 15 minutes, saying that the lyrics "just fell out of the sky."

The song underwent a number of changes from that point; producer Brian Eno had them remove the acoustic guitar parts, reduced its drag, and added some aggression. U2 dubbed "One" a benefit single upon its release, as all of the royalties generated by the song went towards AIDS research organizations. "The band feels that [AIDS] is the most pressing issue of the day, and we really have to focus people's attention to the AIDS plague that has been with us for 10 years," group manager Paul McGuinness said.

CLOSER

The Chainsmokers

-

2016

"He [producer Shaun Frank] came in and we had been listening to all this Blink-182 and Dashboard Confessional and all these guys that just kind of tell it how it is," The Chainsmokers' Andrew Taggart told the audience at a SiriusXM event in

September 2016. "I liked how he kind of had a very vivid sex scene but didn't really talk about the sex. . .and I was like I want to do a song kind of very visual like that's an unsexy sex scene, and I want to talk to someone that I'm instead of in love with, I'm indifferent to. The song's a culmination of pretty much all my ex-girlfriends and all my old friends."

"Closer" started as a brief collaboration between Taggart and Freddy Kennett of Louis the Child, during which they produced what would become the drop for the song. Taggart then "took the idea, turned it into an entire song and wrote the lyrics with Shaun Frank in one session." The idea to have Taggart sing the male part also came from Frank, who encouraged it despite Taggart having never sung on a Chainsmokers track before. "Shaun was the one who made me believe I could actually sing on a song and showed me how to process and layer my vocals," Taggart said.

The female vocals for the song were originally offered to ex-Fifth Harmony member Camila Cabello, who said that she "loved the song" during an interview on *The Elvis Duran Show*. "I had to turn it down because I was with the group at the time, and we were about to put an album out," she said. "I always tried to do my solo stuff off cycle, so that was super on, and so I had to say no, and then that was the number one song in the world." The lyrics were then offered to Halsey, who enjoyed her first No. 1 single on the *Billboard* Hot 100 as a result.

The Fray's Isaac Slade and Joe King were included as co-writers in the credits of "Closer" after it was pointed out to The Chainsmokers that their hit closely resembled The Fray's

2005 "Over My Head (Cable Car)." "They wanted to work it out before the song came out," Joe King told ABC Radio. "So. . .there was no friction or tension. And I totally get it, it happens a lot, and unintentionally. . .so it's all good."

THE WEIGHT

The Band

1968

Luis Buñuel was described by *The New York Times* as "an iconoclast, moralist, and revolutionary who was a leader of avant-garde surrealism in his youth and a dominant international movie director half a century later." His final film won him Best Director awards from the National Society of Film Critics and the National Board of Review, while his first film, made 48 years earlier, was dubbed "the most famous short film ever made" by critic Roger Ebert. So extensive was his body of work that his inspiring one of the greatest songs ever serves as no more than a footnote in his legacy.

Of course, it was the legend that Buñuel had already established by 1968 that inspired The Band in the first place. As Robbie Robertson, lead guitarist for the group and writer of "The Weight," put it: "(Buñuel) did so many films on the impossibility of sainthood. People trying to be good in Viridiana and Nazarin, people trying to do their thing. In

'The Weight' it's the same thing. People like Buñuel would make films that had these religious connotations to them but it wasn't necessarily a religious meaning. In Buñuel there were these people trying to be good and it's impossible to be good. In 'The Weight' it was this very simple thing. Someone says, 'Listen, would you do me this favor? When you get there will you say "hello" to somebody or will you give somebody this or will you pick up one of these for me? Oh? You're going to Nazareth, that's where the Martin guitar factory is. Do me a favor when you're there.' This is what it's all about. So the guy goes and one thing leads to another and it's like 'Holy sh*t, what's this turned into? I've only come here to say "hello" for somebody and I've got myself in this incredible predicament.' It was very Buñuelish to me at the time."

The lyrics tell a story from the perspective of a southerner who is passing through a town called Nazareth. The town was inspired by Nazareth, Pennsylvania, the home of Martin Guitars. The perspective was inspired by Levon Helm, drummer for The Band and native of Elaine, Arkansas. Though Robertson was from Canada, he frequented the South in the hopes of finding lyrics that would help Helm flourish. "It was right in the heart of America that a tremendous amount of music came out of, like some phenomenon of a 100-mile radius around Memphis and over to where Levon lived [outside of Elaine, Arkansas], and Mississippi," Robertson recalled. "To me, going there was like going to the source. Because I was at such a vulnerable age then, it made a really big impact on me. Just that I had the honor joining up with this group and then even going to this place, which was close to a religious experience—even being able to put my feet on the ground there, because I was from Canada, right? So it was like, 'Woah, this is where this music grows in the ground, and [flows from] the Mississippi River. My goodness.' It very much affected my songwriting and, because I knew Levon's musicality so well, I wanted to write songs that I thought he could sing better than anybody in the world. . . .While I was there, I was just gathering images and names, and ideas and rhythms, and I was storing all of these things—which I didn't realize I was doing—but I was storing them all in an attic in my mind somewhere. And when it was time to sit down and write songs, when I reached into the attic to see what I was gonna write about, that's what was there. I just felt a strong passion toward the discovery of going there, and it opened my eyes, and all my senses were overwhelmed by the feeling of that place. When I sat down to write songs, that's all I could think of at the time."

"It was like, 'Woah, this is where this music grows in the ground, and [flows from] the Mississippi River. My goodness.'"

LIVIN' LA VIDA LOCA

Ricky Martin

-

1999

"Livin' La Vida Loca" revolutionized what successful music in the United States could be, introducing Americans to Latin music and opening the door for the likes of Marc Anthony, Shakira, and Enrique Iglesias, among others.

It also abandoned the conventional method used to record music at the time. As Desmond Child, the song's co-writer, put it, "We were the first to record and mix a record all what they call 'in the box,' on Pro Tools. At the beginnings of Pro Tools. We were the first to go all the way to No. 1 with a song that was 100% non-analog, and that fact made it into *The Wall Street Journal*. One of the things about that new sound of digital, it had a kind of metallic sound, and to compensate for that metallic sound, we made it drier than Latin music had ever been, which is more like ambient dance music, where things were deconstructed and you could hear everything your friend said, instead of the kind of records that sounded as though they were in a hall or with a lot of echo or had a corny kind of Europop sound. So we changed that with Ricky. We got his voice right in everybody's face. It really worked, and from that moment on nothing has ever sounded like it used to sound."

HEROES

David Bowie

-

1977

"I'm allowed to talk about it now," David Bowie, speaking about "Heroes," told *Performing Songwriter* magazine in a 2003 interview. "I wasn't at the time. I always said it was a couple of lovers by the Berlin Wall that prompted the idea. Actually, it was Tony Visconti [Bowie's producer] and his girlfriend. Tony was married at the time. And I could never say who it was. But I can now say that the lovers were Tony and a German girl that he'd met whilst we were in Berlin. I did ask his permission if I could say that. I think possibly the marriage was in the last few months, and it was very touching because I could see that Tony was very much in love with this girl, and it was that relationship which sort of motivated the song."

The song is remembered as one of Bowie's best, despite it not performing spectacularly upon release in 1977. The song was part of The Berlin Trilogy; Bowie, desperate to escape Los Angeles and an "astronomic" cocaine addiction that earned him his Thin White Duke persona, moved to West Berlin and began experimenting with new forms of music. "For many years Berlin had appealed to me as a sort of sanctuary-like situation," Bowie recalled. "It was one of the few cities where I could move around in virtual anonymity. I was going broke; it was cheap to live. For some reason, Berliners just didn't care. Well, not about an English rock singer, anyway." It was during his exploration of German music that Bowie came across *Discreet Music*, a 1975 album by Brian Eno. Eno would go on to collaborate with Bowie, most notably by co-writing "Heroes."

The song focuses on the love between two people; one from East Berlin and one from West Berlin. Considered to have played a role in the fall of the Berlin Wall, Bowie played a concert there in 1987. As he recalls: "I'll never forget that. It was one of the most emotional performances I've ever done. I was in tears. They'd backed up the stage to the wall itself so that the wall was acting as our backdrop. We kind of heard that a few of the East Berliners might actually get the chance to hear the thing, but we didn't realize in what numbers they would. And there were thousands on the other side that had come close to the wall. So it was like a double concert where the wall was the division. And we would hear them cheering and singing along from the other side. God, even now I get choked up. It was breaking my heart. I'd never done anything like that in my life, and I guess I never will again. When we did 'Heroes' it really felt anthemic, almost like a prayer. However well we do it these days, it's almost like walking through it compared to that night, because it meant so much more. That's the town where it was written, and that's the particular situation that it was written about. It was just extraordinary. We did it in Berlin last year as well—'Heroes'—and there's no other city I can do that song in now that comes close to how it's received. This time, what was so fantastic is that the audience—it was the Max Schmeling Hall, which holds about 10–15,000—half the audience had been in East Berlin that time way before. So now I was face-to-face with the people I had been singing it to all those years ago. And we were all singing it together. Again, it was powerful. Things like that really give you a sense of what performance can do. They happen so rarely at that kind of magnitude. Most nights I find very enjoyable. These days, I really enjoy performing. But something like that doesn't come along very often, and when it does, you kind of think, 'Well, if I never do anything again, it won't matter.'"

The song rose to No. 12 on the U.K. Singles Chart following Bowie's death in 2016. Upon his passing, the German government issued a note saying "Good-bye, David Bowie. You are now among Heroes. Thank you for helping to bring down the wall."

BRIDGE OVER TROUBLED WATER

Simon & Garfunkel

-

1970

"He felt I should have done it," Paul Simon recalled, "and many times on a stage, though, when I'd be sitting off to the side and Larry Knechtel would be playing the piano and [Art Garfunkel] would be singing 'Bridge,' people would stomp and cheer when it was over, and I would think, 'That's my song, man. . .'"

The song came to Simon all at once and out of nowhere, to the point where he questioned where the song could have possibly come from. "It came all of a sudden," he said in the documentary *The Making of Bridge Over Troubled Water.* "It was one of the most shocking moments in my songwriting career. I remember thinking, 'This is considerably better than I usually write.'" Feeling as though it would be better suited for Art Garfunkel's voice, Simon suggested he sing it the "white choirboy way." He would eventually sing it solo, though Garfunkel did fight to convince Simon to sing on the song that he wrote. Garfunkel also tried to convince Simon that the song would benefit from a third verse and a big ending, a note that he thankfully took. The song originally had two verses and more of a gospel feel to it, having been inspired by Claude Jeter's "Mary Don't You Weep."

Garfunkel came up with one of the song's most famous lines thanks to Simon's wife, who had recently noticed her first few strands of grey hairs coming in. Simon, according to *Rolling Stone*, was never a fan of the line. The vocal style was inspired by "Old Man River" by The Righteous Brothers, which employed Phil Spector's Wall of Sound technique.

HOTEL CALIFORNIA

Eagles

1977

Originally titled "Mexican Reggae," the instrumental demo submitted to the Eagles by Don Felder caught the attention of Don Henley, who thought that he might be able to pen some lyrics for the song that eventually became "Hotel California." As Felder recalled: "Don Henley and Glenn [Frey] wrote most of the words. All of us kind of drove into L.A. at night. Nobody was from California, and if you drive into L.A. at night. . .you can just see this glow on the horizon of lights, and the images that start running through your head of Hollywood and all the dreams that you have, and so it was kind of about that. . .what we started writing the song about."

The concept was Frey's; he wanted the feel to be one you'd experience in a cinema. "Every time he walks through a door there's a new version of reality," Frey told music journalist and director Cameron Crowe. "We wanted to write the song just like it was a movie." He later told Bob Costas: "We decided to create something strange, just to see if we could do it." Henley took that and ran, using the concept as the driving force behind his writing. His muse? The Beverly Hills Hotel, as he told Crowe. "We were enamored with hotels," Henley said. "Hotels were a big part of our lives. The Beverly Hills Hotel had become something of a focal point—literally and symbolically. I've always been interested in architecture and the language of architecture, and, at that time, I was particularly keen on the Mission Style of early California. I thought there was a certain mystery and romance about it. Then, there are all the great movies and plays in which hotels figure prominently, not only as a structure, but as a dramatic device. Films such as *Grand Hotel*, *The Night Porter*, and even *Psycho*—motels count, too. There are plays like Neil Simon's *Plaza Suite* and *California Suite*, which Glenn and I went to see while writing the song. We saw it as homework or research. We were looking for things that would stimulate us and give us ideas. Sometimes it was just driving around. We would still take trips out to the desert. At one point, Glenn and I rented a little red house up in Idlewild—way up in the San Bernardino Mountains. We'd drive out there sometimes just to clear our heads, sleep on the floor in sleeping bags. We didn't have any furniture. We were just on the quest."

The song's meaning has been the source of much debate since its release in 1977, despite Henley's insistence that it isn't as nuanced as the lyrics might indicate. "On just about every album we made, there was some kind of commentary on the music business, and on American culture in general," Henley said in the documentary *History of the Eagles*. "The hotel itself could be taken as a metaphor not only for the mythmaking of Southern California, but for the mythmaking that is the American Dream, because it is a fine line between the American Dream, and the American nightmare."

THE MESSAGE

Grandmaster Flash and the Furious Five

-

1982

Often regarded as the first hip-hop record to be driven by a social narrative, "The Message" remains an iconic piece of the genre's history. "Our group, Flash and the Furious Five, we didn't want to do 'The Message' because we were used to doing party raps, boasting about how good we are and all that," Melle Mel said in a 1992 interview. "When the record company brought the record to us to do, we didn't actually want to do it. I was the only one that, like, I just caved in. I said, 'Listen, if this is the record we're going to do, then I'll just do it and it's no big thing. I didn't think it would be pivotal either way, I just thought it was going to be another record."

He continued: "We used to hang out in this club called Disco Fever up in the Bronx. They took the record and tested it on a record shop on 125th Street. You know, just letting it play. Then they tested it in the club where we hung out and people really liked it. That was coming right behind 'Planet Rock,' which was a big, big record back then. When they played 'The Message' in the club and the people liked it, I was kinda shocked. I didn't think that coming from 'Planet Rock' to something serious. . .I thought there'd be a lapse in the level of the crowd, the intensity of the crowd, but there wasn't. That's when I knew that the record was going to be more than I thought it was going to be."

WHEN DOVES CRY

Prince

-

1984

Prince wrote "When Doves Cry" for inclusion in his semi-autobiographical movie *Purple Rain*. The song appears in a scene where he is mourning a lost love while expressing fear that he might one day end up like his abusive father. According to a DVD edition of the film, Prince had composed two songs for the scene, having been asked by the director to write something that matched its theme.

Prince played all of the instruments on the song, which noticeably doesn't include any bass. He removed it at the last minute, as he felt that the song was a touch too conventional with it included. He battled with the decision, telling *Bass Player* magazine that "Sometimes your brain kind of splits in two—your ego tells you one thing, and the rest of you says something else. You have to go with what you know is right."

"Sometimes your brain kind of splits in two—your ego tells you one thing, and the rest of you says something else. You have to go with what you know is right."

The song topped the charts for five weeks in the U.S., and was the top-selling single of 1984, according to *Billboard* magazine. Interestingly enough, the song is the only one with a bird included in the title to reach No. 1 in the Hot 100; "Disco Duck" by Rick Dees & His Cast of Idiots claimed the spot in 1976, but doesn't count due to the fact that a duck does not refer to a specific species of bird. The song reappeared on the charts following Prince's death in 2016, rising to No. 8 in the *Billboard* Hot 100.

MR. BRIGHTSIDE

The Killers

-

2004

In a 2012 discussion with *NME*, the Killers' front man Brandon Flowers dove into the history of the song "Mr. Brightside," saying, "We must've written it around the end of 2001. Dave [Keuning] and I were writing a ton of songs at the time, trying to figure out what it was that made us tick. I remember us going into the Virgin Megastore to buy (The Strokes') *Is This It* on the day it came out and, when we put it on in the car, that record just sounded so perfect. I got so depressed after that, we threw away everything and the only song that made the cut and remained was 'Mr. Brightside.' It came from this cassette of ideas that Dave gave me, and one of them was the 'Mr. Brightside' riff. I was able to slap a chorus and some lyrics onto it, and I knew I liked it. But it wasn't until we first tried it out with a drummer that I knew it was special. We went to the guy's house and showed him the song, and I got the goose bumps after that. Lyrically, it's about an old girlfriend of mine. All the emotions in the song are real. When

I was writing the lyrics, my wounds from it were still fresh. I am Mr. Brightside! But I think that's the reason the song has persisted—because it's real. People pick up on those things. And that goes all the way down to the production; we recorded it in a couple of hours, but it just sounds right, you know?"

Flowers had previously elaborated on his experience with an unfaithful significant other, telling *Q Magazine* in 2009 that "I was asleep and I knew something was wrong. I have these instincts. I went to the Crown and Anchor and my girlfriend was there with another guy."

PAUL REVERE

Beastie Boys

-

1986

"I wrote that sitting on the steps of St. Marks Sounds record store on Eighth Street," said Beastie Boys member Adrock while talking about their groundbreaking hit, "Paul Revere."

"We actually went to the recording studio and we were actually going to record with Run-D.M.C one night. We were waiting outside up on twenty-something street, and. . .we're waiting there and all of a sudden we see Run from Run-D.M.C running down the block at us, screaming something. We didn't know. He kept screaming louder and louder. . . .We were like, 'What're you talking about?' And he was like, 'That's the song!' And that was it, that was the whole song."

After the death of Adam Yauch in 2012, Mike Diamond praised Yauch's idea to play the beats from a Roland 808 drum machine backwards on the song. "Run from Run-D.M.C. was there, and he was like, 'Man, this is crazy.' But Yauch recorded this beat, bounced it to another tape, flipped it around—this is pre-digital sampling—and bounced it back to the multi-track tape," Diamond said. The reversed beat basically became 'Paul Revere.' Yauch saw this thing we couldn't see—and he killed it."

"[Adam] Yauch saw this thing we couldn't see—and he killed it."

KRYPTONITE

3 Doors Down

2000

"The skippy little drumbeat in the song was just me beating on my desk [during a math class]," Brad Arnold, singer of 3 Doors Down, told *SongFacts* while speaking about "Kryptonite." "It's almost exactly the beat we played to, just kind of drumming, just skipping along with it."

It's unlikely that Arnold knew how much he'd get out of that math class at the time, as the song he began working on there would develop into one of the biggest hits of the 2000s. "Thank God for the little dude that sat in front of me, that dude deserves credit on the album!" he said. "I was so bad in math. *So* bad. But my teacher knew I was not good, not paying attention, but he just kind of let me go. I believe I wrote the lyrics to some other songs in that same class. I wrote probably about half of that *Better Life* album sitting in that math class."

Alerted to the fact that the song's meaningful words are "exceptionally deep for 15 [years old]," Arnold responded by saying: "But you know what? That's something that's always stuck with me: every 15-year-old has those questions in their head. They might not know quite how to say it, or they might not feel like it's acceptable to say something. And the biggest thing that I've had as an artist is to be able to say something, and after I say it, it's okay. After an artist says it, if a rock star says it, okay, it's fine. That really boils down to why music inspires pop culture so much: because artists push the envelope. They go out on a limb to say something else. But it also comes with responsibility, you gotta watch what you say, because kids listen. And I try to watch what I say, too."

Arnold denies the commonly held belief that the song contains a reference to Pink Floyd's *The Dark Side of the Moon*. "It wasn't," he said. "That is just a happenstance line. That song is so little about Superman. It's just really about that question. That's just something that everybody can identify with. And it's got that line in there, and all it was, was Superman—I'm not sure which part Superman it was, it might have been the first one—and they're talking about something going to the dark side. . .he's fighting these people in space, it's like they're going around to the dark side of the moon. And I was like, '*What*?!' And it was after I wrote that song. That was *weird*."

WHITER SHADE OF PALE

Procol Harum

-

1967

"We were really excited about it and liked it a lot," Keith Reid, Procol Harum lyricist, told *SongFacts*. "And when we were rehearsing and routine-ing our first dozen songs or so, it was one that sounded really good. But there were a few others that we liked I would say equally—we have a song on our first album called 'Salad Days (Are Here Again)' that was a strong contender. At our first session, we cut four tracks, and 'Whiter Shade of Pale' was the one that recorded best. In those days it wasn't just a question of how good is your song. It was how good of a recording can you make? Because it was essentially live recording, and if you didn't have a great sound engineer or the studio wasn't so good, you might not get a very good-sounding record. And for some reason everything at our first studio session came out sounding really good."

The quality of their recording may not have been as reliant on chance as Reid let on; they had Olympic Sound Studios in London to record in and Denny Cordell to help them do it. Cordell also produced music for Joe Cocker, The Moody Blues, and Leon Russell, among others.

Reid dove into the inspiration behind "Whiter Shade of Pale" in a 2008 interview for *Uncut* magazine, when he said: "I used to go and see a lot of French films in the Academy in Oxford Street (London). *Pierrot Le Fou* made a strong impression on me, and *Last Year at Marienbad*. I was also very taken with surrealism, Magritte and Dali. You can draw a line between the narrative fractures and mood of those French films and 'A Whiter Shade Of Pale.' I'd been listening to music since I was 10, from '56 to '66—The Beatles, Dylan, Stax, Ray Charles. The period of 'A Whiter Shade Of Pale' was the culmination of that 10 years of listening. But my main influence was Dylan. I could see how he did it, how he played with words. I'd met Pete Townshend through Guy Stevens (A&R man and Procol Harum's original manager), and he'd put my name forward when Cream were looking for a lyricist. Then Guy put me and [co-writer Gary Brooker] together. I was writing all the time. 'A Whiter Shade Of Pale' was just another bunch of lyrics. I had the phrase. . .that was the start, and I knew it was a song. It's like a jigsaw where you've got one piece, then you make up all the others to fit in. I was trying to conjure a mood as much as tell a straightforward, girl-leaves-boy story. With the ceiling flying away and room humming harder, I wanted to paint an image of a scene. I wasn't trying to be mysterious with those images, I wasn't trying to be evocative. I suppose it seems like a decadent scene I'm describing. But I was too young to have experienced any decadence, then, I might have been smoking when I conceived it, but not when I wrote it. It was influenced by books, not drugs."

THRILLER

Michael Jackson

1982

"When we started 'Thriller,' the first day at Westlake, we were all there and Quincy [Jones] walked in followed by me and Michael [Jackson] and Rod Temperton and some of the other people," Bruce Swedien, the song's engineer, said. "Quincy turned to us and he said, 'Ok guys, we're here to save the recording industry.' Now that's a pretty big responsibility—but he meant it. And that's why those albums, and especially 'Thriller,' sound so incredible. The basic thing is, everybody who was involved gave 150 percent. . . .Quincy's like a director of a movie and I'm like a director of photography, and it's Quincy's job to cast. Quincy can find the people and he gives us the inspiration to do what we do."

Written by Temperton and Jones, the song's working titles included "Give Me Some Starlight" and "Starlight Sun." "Originally, when I did my 'Thriller' demo, I called it 'Starlight,' Temperton recalled. "Quincy said to me, 'You managed to come up with a title for the last album, see what you can do for this album.' I said, 'Oh great,' so I went back to the hotel, wrote two or three hundred titles, and came up with the title 'Midnight Man'. The next morning, I woke up, and I just said this word. . . .Something in my head just said, this is the title. You could visualize it on the top of the Billboard charts. You could see the merchandising for this one word, how it jumped off the page as 'Thriller.'"

Among Jackson's most memorable songs, it inspired perhaps the most memorable music video ever. John Landis, director of *An American Werewolf in London*, was even brought on to direct. Their first hurdle was a sizeable one, as CBS Records refused to pay for the video. Their response? Sell the rights to *The Making of 'Thriller'* (which Landis nicknamed "The Making of Filler") to MTV and Showtime for $250,000 each, setting their budget at half-a-million dollars. The result was the introduction of the mini-movie concept to music videos, the start of a group dance scene trend in music videos, and the first-ever music video to be included in the Library of Congress. Despite its massive success, Jackson took heat from his fellow Jehovah's Witnesses for helping to create and star in a video featuring evil creatures. The disclaimer at the beginning of the video, which reads "Due to my strong personal convictions, I wish to stress that this film in no way endorses a belief in the occult" was a product of his faith.

Peggy Lipton, then the wife of Rod Temperton, suggested he reach out to Vincent Price to star on his song; Temperton knew he wanted a speaking section at the end of his song and he knew that it had to be the voice of somebody involved with the horror genre. Price was so "fabulous" that even what didn't make the cut was great, including a section that mentions evil keeping one from dancing to the song's undeniable groove.

THE TIMES THEY ARE A-CHANGIN'

Bob Dylan

-

1964

"This was definitely a song with a purpose," Bob Dylan, discussing his classic "The Times They Are a-Changin'," told Cameron Crowe in a 1985 interview. "It was influenced of course by the Irish and Scottish ballads. . .'Come All Ye Bold Highway Men,' 'Come All Ye Tender Hearted Maidens.' I wanted to write a big song, with short concise verses that piled up on each other in a hypnotic way. The Civil Rights Movement and the folk music movement were pretty close for a while and allied together at that time."

That time was October 1963, a period of intense change. The Civil Rights Movement was in full force, photos of Buddhist monk Thích Quảng Đức burning himself alive in protest of Buddhist oppression by the South Vietnamese government made the rounds in the U.S. months earlier, and U.S. forces were beginning to increase their presence in Vietnam. Nothing was more emblematic of the times, however, than President John Kennedy being assassinated in Dallas,

"I know I had no understanding of anything. Something had just gone haywire in the country and they were applauding the song. And I couldn't understand why they were clapping, or why I wrote the song. I couldn't understand anything. For me, it was just insane."

Texas, just one month after Dylan had recorded the song. Set to perform a concert the following night, he recalled "I thought, 'Wow, how can I open with that song? I'll get rocks thrown at me.' But I had to sing it, my whole concert takes off from there. I know I had no understanding of anything. Something had just gone haywire in the country and they were applauding the song. And I couldn't understand why they were clapping, or why I wrote the song. I couldn't understand anything. For me, it was just insane."

FOR WHAT IT'S WORTH

Buffalo Springfield

1967

As he recalls in *Neil Young: Long May You Run: The Illustrated History*, Buffalo Springfield front man Stephen Stills, when talking about his instant classic "For What It's Worth," said: "I had had something kicking around in my head. I wanted to write something about the kids that were on the line over in Southeast Asia that didn't have anything to do with the device of this mission, which was unraveling before our eyes. Then we came down to Sunset from my place on Topanga with a guy —I can't remember his name—and there's a funeral for a bar, one of the favorite spots for high school and UCLA kids to go and dance and listen to music. [Officials] decided to call out the official riot police because there's three thousand kids sort of standing out in the street; there's no looting, there's no nothing. It's everybody having a hang to close this bar. A whole company of black and white LAPD in full Macedonian battle array in shields and helmets and all that, and they're lined up across the street, and I just went 'Whoa! Why are they doing this?' There was no reason for it. I went back to Topanga, and that other song turned into 'For What It's Worth,' and it took as long to write as it took me to settle on the changes and write the lyrics down. It all came as a piece, and it took about fifteen minutes."

The name of the song came to Stills when he offered it to record executive Ahmet Ertegun, saying, "I have this song here, for what it's worth, if you want it."

JAILHOUSE ROCK

Elvis Presley

1957

Though the song was released three years before the film, "Jailhouse Rock" was written by songwriting duo Jerry Leiber and Mike Stoller as part of its score.

"We flew in to New York from LA, where were living at that time, and we had a hotel suite," Stoller recalled to *Mojo* in 2009. "We had a piano put in, in case the muse struck us, and Jean

Aberbach. . .handed us a script for a movie. We threw it in the corner with the tourist magazines that you get in hotels. We were having a ball in New York, going to the theatre, going to jazz clubs to hear Miles Davis and Thelonious Monk, doing a lot of drinking. On a Saturday morning—we'd been there about a week—Jean knocked on the door and said, in a very Viennese accent, 'Vell boys, you vill haf my songs for the movie.' Jerry said, 'Don't worry Jean, you'll have them.' Jean said, 'I know.' And he pushed a big chair in front of the door and sat down and said, 'I'm going to take a nap and I'm not leaving until you have my songs.' So we wrote four songs in about five hours and then were free to go out." Among those four songs was "Jailhouse Rock," which became a hit when the film by the same name, starring Presley, came out in 1960.

CHANDELIER

Sia

-

2014

Sia spent much of her time after the 2010 release of *We Are Born* writing songs for the likes of Eminem, Beyoncé, and Katy Perry. That process was still going on in 2014, though, for once, it ended with her at the mic, performing the massive hit "Chandelier."

"I usually think, 'Oh this would work for Rihanna, or this would be a good one for Bey or Katy," Sia said. "But this time I was like, 'Uh oh I think I just wrote a full-blown pop song for myself by accident!' My friend Jesse Shatkin and I were jamming in the studio—I was playing piano and him on the marimba—and this gem popped out."

WHOLE LOTTA LOVE

Led Zeppelin

1969

As Led Zeppelin bassist John Paul Jones told *Uncut* magazine while discussing "Whole Lotta Love" in 2009: "The backwards echo stuff. A lot of the microphone techniques were just inspired. Using distance-miking. . .and small amplifiers. Everybody thinks we go in the studio with huge walls of amplifiers, but [Jimmy Page] doesn't. He uses a really small amplifier and he just mikes it up really well, so that it fits into a sonic picture."

Zeppelin guitarist Jimmy Page produced this song with audio engineer Eddie Kramer, who explained that one of the first-ever uses of the backwards echo that Jones referenced happened by accident. "At one point there was bleed-through of a previously recorded vocal in the recording of 'Whole Lotta Love,' he recalled. "It was the middle part where Robert [Plant] screams. . . .Since we couldn't re-record at that point, I just threw some echo on it to see how it would sound and Jimmy said 'Great! Just leave it.'"

Page decided to record the drums in the big room at Olympic Sound Studios in London so that they could lay a strong foundation for the track. The room had 28-foot-high ceilings, allowing him to set microphones up at distances that wouldn't be available to him in a normal studio. "For the song to work as this panoramic audio experience, I needed Bonzo [John Bonham, Zeppelin drummer] to really stand out, so that every stick stroke sounded clear and you could really feel them," Page told *The Wall Street Journal*. "If the drums were recorded just right, we could lay in everything else."

Everything else included lyrics that were very similar to those from Muddy Waters' "You Need Love" from 1962. The Small Faces recorded a cover of the song called "You Need Loving," which caught the attention of Page and Plant, according to Small Faces vocalist Steve Marriott. "He sang it the same, phrased it the same, even the stops at the end were the same," said Marriott of Plant. Zeppelin eventually settled a lawsuit with the song's original writer, Willie Dixon, for an undisclosed amount of money and a writer's credit on "Whole Lotta Love." Said Plant on the incident: "Page's riff was Page's riff. It was there before anything else. I just thought, 'Well, what am I going to sing?' That was it, a nick. Now happily paid for. At the time, there was a lot of conversation about what to do. It was decided that it was so far away in time and influence that. . .well, you only get caught when you're successful. That's the game."

MR. TAMBOURINE MAN

Bob Dylan

1965

Written in the liner notes in Dylan's Biograph box set is the following: "'Mr. Tambourine Man,' I think, was inspired by Bruce Langhorne. Bruce was playing guitar with me on a bunch of the early records. On one session, [producer] Tom Wilson had asked him to play tambourine. And he had this gigantic tambourine. It was like, really big. It was as big as a wagon-wheel. He was playing, and this vision of him playing this tambourine just stuck in my mind. He was one of those characters. . .he was like that. I don't know if I've ever told him that."

Langhorne passed away in April 2017 at age 78, having lived a life worthy of the highest regards in terms of music. "If you had Bruce playing with you, that's all you would need to do just about anything," Dylan wrote in *Chronicles: Volume One*. On top of playing on and inspiring Dylan's hit "Mr. Tambourine Man," Langhorne was also involved in Dylan's "Outlaw Blues," "Corrina, Corrina," "Mixed Up Confusion," "Maggie's Farm," and "Subterranean Homesick Blues."

The song inspired a cover version by The Byrds, who experienced at least as much success with the tune as Dylan had; both are included in *Rolling Stone*'s list of 500 best songs ever, and both have received Grammy Hall of Fame Awards.

YOU REALLY GOT ME

The Kinks

-

1964

"I wanted it to be a jazz-type tune, because that's what I liked at the time," said Ray Davies, The Kinks' vocalist and writer of "You Really Got Me." "It's written originally around a sax line . . .Dave [Davies, The Kinks' guitarist] ended up playing the sax line in fuzz guitar and it took the song a step further."

The song started on a piano in Davies' household in March 1964. "I hadn't been writing songs very long at all," he said. "It was one of the first five I ever came up with." Rock photographer Allen Ballard, remembering the house where Davies composed the song, said: "It was quite a small, pokey, Victorian Terrace, a bit scruffy, and in the hallway they had an upright piano. Ray sat down and plonked out, 'Der-der, der, Der-der!' He said, 'What do you reckon to this?' It meant nothing to me at the time, but it ended up as 'You Really Got Me.'"

"I was playing a gig at a club in Piccadilly and there was a young girl in the audience who I really liked. . . .I wrote 'You Really Got Me' for her, even though I never met her."

In a 2016 interview with *Q Magazine*, Davies spoke about the girl who inspired the song, saying "I was playing a gig at a club in Piccadilly and there was a young girl in the audience who I really liked. She had beautiful lips. Thin, but not skinny. A bit similar to Françoise Hardy. Not long hair, but down to about there (points to shoulders). Long enough to put your hands through. . . .long enough to hold. I wrote 'You Really Got Me' for her, even though I never met her."

EVERY BREATH YOU TAKE

The Police

-

1983

Skewered by the media and condemned by the public for his affair with his wife's best friend, Sting retreated to the Caribbean to escape the spotlight. As he recalled in a 1993 interview with *The Independent*, "I woke up in the middle of the night with that line in my head, sat down at the piano and had written it in half an hour. The tune itself is generic, an aggregate of hundreds of others, but the words are interesting. It sounds like a comforting love song. I didn't realize at the time how sinister it is. I think I was thinking of Big Brother, surveillance and control."

Sting presented "Every Breath You Take" to the rest of his band mates when they got together to work on the *Synchronicity* album. Andy Summers recalls the interaction in a 2000 interview with *Revolver* magazine, saying, "This was a difficult one to get, because Sting wrote a very good song, but there was no guitar on it. He had this Hammond organ thing that sounded like Billy Preston. It certainly didn't sound like

The Police, with that big, rolling synthesizer part. We spent about six weeks recording just the snare drums and the bass. It was a simple, classic chord sequence, but we couldn't agree how to do it. I'd been making an album with Robert Fripp, and I was kind of experimenting with playing Bartok violin duets and had worked up a new riff. When Sting said 'Go and make it your own,' I went and stuck that lick on it, and immediately we knew we had something special."

The simplicity upon which "Every Breath You Take" is based is elaborated on in a piece by *Sound On Sound*, written by Richard Buskin in 2004, with contributions from album engineer and co-producer Hugh Padgham. Buskin writes, "Sting introduced 'Every Breath You Take' by way of a simple demo, consisting of himself singing over a Hammond organ part that would subsequently be replaced by Andy Summers's guitar (keyboards were never the strong suit of this band). The demo had been recorded in a small eight-track suite at North London's Utopia Studios and, according to Padgham, provided a solid delineation of the song in terms of the main riff, the vocal melody and the already-completed lyrics."

"Like most of the other songs, the actual recording started out with loads of takes of the backing track, because [drummer Stewart Copeland] usually screwed up," Padgham asserts. "It was hot, there was no air conditioning where he was playing and he'd be really sweaty, so sometimes the sticks would fly out of his hands when it all got very exciting. In fact, I even gaffered the sticks to his hands and the headphones onto his head to keep them in place. So, that was part of the problem, and then there was the fact that Sting wanted to keep 'Every Breath You Take' really simple, meaning that we'd have to go for another take if Stewart played a fill that he didn't like, and then cobble the whole thing together. Remember, this was in the days before Pro Tools, when we'd have to use a razor blade, and even though it was Sting who'd generally be involved in those decisions, it would still be hard to keep his interest. He's not one to show patience or any interest in studio techniques."

Sting's disregard for the opinions of his band mates particularly irked Copeland, who would frequently engage in both verbal and physical fights with Sting during recording sessions. In the interview with *Revolver* magazine, Copeland stated, "In my humble opinion, this is Sting's best song with the worst arrangement. I think Sting could have had any other group do this song and it would have been better than our version—except for Andy's brilliant guitar part. Basically, there's an utter lack of groove. It's a totally wasted opportunity for our band. Even though we made gazillions off of it, and it's the biggest hit we ever had."

Buskin did an excellent job of breaking that tension down in his book, writing, "'Every Breath You Take' brought to a head the tension between Sting and Copeland." "Sting wanted Stewart to just play a very straight rhythm with no fills or anything," Padgham recalls, "and that was the complete antithesis of what Stewart was about. Stewart would say, 'I want to f*cking put my drum part on it!' and Sting would say, 'I don't want you to put your f*cking drum part on it! I want you to put what I want you to put on it!' and it would go on like that. It was really difficult. I remember calling my manager, Dennis [Muirhead], and telling him 'I can't handle this,' and I also remember quite clearly working full-on for 10 days in Montserrat and having nothing on tape that was playable." The band's manager, Miles Copeland, was duly sent for, and a meeting was convened by the swimming pool next to the studio in order to determine whether or not the sessions should continue. "That album was actually one meeting away from not happening," Padgham confirms. Fortunately, it did happen, both at AIR Montserrat for the backing tracks and Studio Morin Heights in Quebec for the overdubs and mix, and the result was a classic blend of sophisticated sounds and skillful songwriting that included the aforementioned 'Every Breath' track, a haunting, hypnotic testament to lost love and obsessive domination. Tensions aside, Sting has gone on to express surprise and concern at the way fans consume the song. He has stated on BBC Radio 2 that he thinks the song "is very, very sinister and ugly and people have actually misinterpreted it as being a gentle little love song, when it's quite the opposite."

RING OF FIRE

Johnny Cash

-

1963

Some speculate that June Carter Cash found the phrase that inspired the song's title underlined in one of her uncle's books of poetry. Others, namely Johnny Cash's first wife Vivian Liberto, contend that Carter Cash played no part in the writing of the song and that Cash only gave her a co-writer credit because she needed the money. In her book, *I Walked the Line: My Life with Johnny*, Liberto writes, "To this day, it confounds me to hear the elaborate details June told of writing that song for Johnny. She didn't write that song any more than I did. The truth is, Johnny wrote that song, while pilled up and drunk, about a certain private female body part. All those years of her claiming she wrote it herself, and she probably never knew what the song was really about."

Musician Curly Lewis, who toured with Cash, backs up this claim, saying that he was there when Cash wrote it himself. "Johnny and Merle Kilgore and I were fishing in Casitas, Calif., and that's when 'Ring of Fire' was created," he said. "After it got pretty well settled, Johnny told Merle Kilgore that this is gonna be one big song. He said, 'I'm going to be going through a divorce, and I don't want it tied up in my divorce, so put June's name down as the writer.'"

What's even more shocking are Curly's claims that the devout Cash used "ring of fire" as a double entendre for June's genitalia. "Well, use your imagination," Curly testified on tape. "We got a female part involved. [The] vagina is the ring of fire."

All that said, authorship for the song is still credited, whether legitimate or otherwise, to June Carter Cash and Merle Kilgore. The song is said to have come to June one night as she drove around aimlessly, trying to make sense of her feelings toward her then-married future husband. Despite Cash's influence on the lyrics, the song was given first to Anita, June's sister. Johnny recorded his own version of the song months later, this time with mariachi-style horns, as he claimed to have had a dream in which the song was accompanied by "Mexican horns."

The single had a genre-defining impact and is among Cash's most notable works. The legacy, however, was put in jeopardy by co-writer Merle Kilgore, who proposed licensing the song for a hemorrhoid cream commercial in 2004. June's heirs, perhaps possessing more cultural awareness than Kilgore, refused to allow the song to be licensed for such a purpose.

MY GIRL

The Temptations

-

1965

Smokey Robinson, in a 2000 interview with NPR, recalls the great impression he made with his boss, Motown founder Berry Gordy. Robinson said, "Berry called me to his office because we had a thing in those days whereas if you got a No. 1 record, then you got a thousand-dollar bonus as the producer of that record. So he called me into his office and he said, 'Hey, man, I want to give you your producer's bonus check.' So I said, 'Wow.' I said, 'For what?' you know? He said, `You got a smash hit.' I said, 'What is it?' He said, '"My Girl" on The Temptations.' He said, 'It's not No. 1 yet, but it's most definitely going there.'"

"My Girl" was the first Temptations song to include David Ruffin on lead vocals. Ruffin first caught the attention of Robinson at a Motor Town Revue show, in which Ruffin had a solo as part of the song "Under the Boardwalk." "David Ruffin, I knew, was like this sleeping giant in this group because he had this—it's sort of like a mellow gruff-sounding voice," Robinson said. "And all I needed was the right song for his voice and I felt like I would have a smash hit record. So I sat down at the piano to write a song for David Ruffin's voice. I wanted to make it something that he could belt out, but yet make it melodic and sweet. We were playing at the Apollo Theater, and every day in between the shows—at the Apollo Theater, you did four or five shows a day, and in between every show, I would take The Temptations down on the stage where there was a piano, and I would work on 'My Girl' with them until they knew it like the back of their hands. And I always let The Temptations make up their own background vocals, because they were always so great at doing their own background vocals. They could all sing so good. So I was just showing David Ruffin how to sing 'My Girl' or the melody and what I thought how he should interpret it, and they would be over standing on the side of the piano making up the background vocals."

BLITZKRIEG BOP

Ramones

-

1976

"Blitzkrieg Bop," the Ramones' debut single that was released in February 1976, was written in response to "Saturday Night" by the Bay City Rollers. "I hate to blow the mystique," Joey Ramone said, "but at the same time we really liked bubblegum music, and we really liked the Bay City Rollers. Their song 'Saturday Night' had a great chant in it, so we wanted a song with a chant in it. . . .'Blitzkrieg Bop' was our 'Saturday Night.'"

The Ramones' career-making chant was stumbled upon one night while drummer Tommy Ramone was walking home. In *Ramones: Soundtrack of Our Lives*, Tommy reveals the origins of the chant, saying: "I came up with the chant walking home from the grocery store carrying a bag of groceries. It was based on. . .the song, 'Walking The Dog' by Rufus Thomas." Tommy wrote most of the song, though bassist Dee Dee Ramone cleverly shifted the title from "Animal Hop" to "Blitzkrieg Bop."

"We really liked bubblegum music, and we really liked the Bay City Rollers. Their song 'Saturday Night' had a great chant in it, so we wanted a song with a chant in it. . . .'Blitzkrieg Bop' was our 'Saturday Night.'"

I STILL HAVEN'T FOUND WHAT I'M LOOKING FOR

U2

-

1987

U2 guitarist The Edge called "I Still Haven't Found What I'm Looking For," "'Eye of the Tiger' played by a reggae band," while bassist Adam Clayton said that it had "a bit of a one-note groove."

"We were listening to some Gospel during *The Joshua Tree* sessions—I remember The Mighty Clouds and the Reverend Cleveland and The Staple Singers," The Edge told *Q Magazine* in 1998. "The original was more loose, almost Jamaican. Bono hit on the melody and I had the title in a notebook. At first, no one took it that seriously because it sounded so unlike anything we'd ever done and it didn't gel until the mix, but when it was finished we all realized that we had something special."

It wasn't until Larry Mullen Jr. found his groove that the band's second No. 1 hit began to take off. As co-producer Daniel Lanois recalled: "It was a very original beat from Larry. We always look for those beats that would qualify as a signature for the song. And that certainly is one of those. It had this tom-tom thing that he does and nobody ever understands. And we just didn't want to let go of that beat, it was so unique."

FORTUNATE SON

Creedence Clearwater Revival

-

1969

Often thought of as being conceived as part of the anti-establishment movement of the 1960s, particularly in regards to the Vietnam War, "Fortunate Son" is one of the more popular songs used to invoke protest against elitism in Western society.

John Fogerty, himself a military veteran, makes clear that the inspiration for the song wasn't singular in his 2015 memoir *Fortunate Son: My Life, My Music*, where he wrote, "'Fortunate Son' wasn't really inspired by any one event. Julie Nixon was dating David Eisenhower. You'd hear about the son of this senator or that congressman who was given a deferment from the military or a choice position in the military. They seemed privileged and whether they liked it or not, these people were symbolic in the sense that they weren't being touched by what their parents were doing. They weren't being affected like the rest of us."

Fogerty shared a more personal explanation for writing the song while on the television show *The Voice*, where he said, "The thoughts behind this song—it was a lot of anger. So it was the Vietnam War going on. . . .Now I was drafted and they're making me fight, and no one has actually defined why. So this was all boiling inside of me and I sat down on the edge of my bed. . . .You know, it took about 20 minutes to write the song."

CRAZY

Gnarls Barkley

2006

"Cee-Lo and I started talking, and I somehow got off on this tangent about how people won't take an artist seriously unless they're insane," Brian Burton, better known as Danger Mouse, told Chuck Klosterman in a 2006 *New York Times* interview. "And we were saying that if we really wanted this album to work, the best move would be to just kill ourselves. That's how audiences think; it's retarded. So we started jokingly discussing ways in which we could make people think we were crazy. We talked about this for hours, and then I went home. But while I was away, Cee-Lo took that conversation and made it into 'Crazy,' which we recorded in one take. That's the whole story. The lyrics are his interpretation of that conversation."

"People won't take an artist seriously unless they're insane."

Downtown's A&R Josh Deutsch, who received the song from Danger Mouse's manager, knew that the song was a hit after his first listen. "In this particular case I have a long history with Danger Mouse's manager who sent me the song," he recalled. "They were looking for an independent label that has the same resources as a major. I heard the record and signed it after one listen. . . .Once in a while you hear a record that is obviously so important on so many levels. The beauty of my position is that it's very direct. If I find something I like there's no bureaucratic process associated with signing it."

The song was a wild success; it became the most downloaded song in U.K. history and was named the "Song of the Decade" by *Rolling Stone.*

YOU CAN'T ALWAYS GET WHAT YOU WANT

Rolling Stones

-

1969

"I liked the way The Beatles did 'Hey Jude,'" Mick Jagger remarked in 1969. "The orchestra was not just to cover everything up—it was something extra. We may do something like that on the next album." As he recalled once "You Can't Always Get What You Want" was released: "'You Can't Always Get What You Want' was something I just played on the acoustic guitar—one of those bedroom songs. It proved to be quite difficult to record because Charlie [Watts, drummer for the Rolling Stones] couldn't play the groove and so Jimmy Miller [producer] had to play the drums. I'd also had this idea of having a choir, probably a gospel choir, on the track, but there wasn't one around at that point. Jack Nitzsche [the arranger], or something, said that we could get the London Bach Choir and we said, 'That will be a laugh.'"

Regarding Charlie Watts and Jimmy Miller, pianist and organist on the song Al Kooper recalled to NPR that Miller attempted to show Watts how to play the drum piece after he was struggling, to which Watts said: "Why don't you play it, then," before leaving.

The identity of the Mr. Jimmy character mentioned in the third verse of the song remains a mystery; the most popular, and most plausible, theory is that it is a reference to Stones producer Jimmy Miller. Another comes from a Minnesota man named Jimmy Hutmaker who claimed to have been at one of their shows in Excelsior, Minnesota during the band's first U.S. tour. He was allegedly standing behind Jagger at a local drug store when he tried to order a Cherry Coke, only to find out that they didn't have any. "Well, you can't always get what you want," Hutmaker told Jagger afterwards. Another man, in a letter sent to *SongFacts* in 2008, claims to have been the inspiration, writing: "I introduced myself as Jim and asked him his name. He said Mick, of course, and we had a bit of small talk about a dealer I knew that was named Mick before he asked me my surname. Now, where I am from they call it your last name and I didn't really know what a surname was. I remembered that when you called someone 'sir' you usually used his first name. So I said James. . . .thinking he wanted to know my proper first name. 'No, no, I mean your family name,' he clarified. I figured he meant the nickname that my family called me and I said, 'Jimmy.' This cracked him up; I suppose by then he thought me a complete idiot. He said 'So you're Mr. Jimmy, huh, that's great.'"

THE BOXER

Simon & Garfunkel

-

1970

"I think I was reading the Bible around that time," Paul Simon recalled. "I think the song was about me: everybody's beating me up, and I'm telling you now I'm going to go away if you don't stop."

"The Boxer" was recorded at several different locations and took 100-plus hours of studio work to get right; despite this, the song's chorus could never get better than the placeholder that was in Simon's first draft. "I didn't have any words! Then people said it was a 'lie' but I didn't really mean that. That it was a lie. But, it's not a failure of songwriting, because people like that and they put enough meaning into it, and the rest of the song has enough power and emotion, I guess, to make it go, so it's all right. But for me, every time I sing that part, I'm a little embarrassed."

As guitarist Fred Carter Jr. recalled, the song's origins can be traced back to New York. "When we started the record in New York with Roy Halee, the engineer, and Paul was playin' his Martin—I think it's a D-18 and he was tuned regular—he didn't have the song totally written lyrically, but he had most of the melody," Carter Jr. told *Fretboard Journal*. "And so all I was hearin' was bits and pieces while he was doin' his fingerpicking . . . .I think he was fingerpicking in an open C. I tried two or three things and then picked up a baby Martin, which was about a third above his guitar, sound-wise. And I turned down the first string to a D, and tuned up the bass string to a G, which made it an open-G tuning, except for the fifth string, which was standard. Did some counter fingerpicking with him, just did a little backward roll, and lucked into a lick. And that turned into that little roll, and we cut it, just Paul and I, two guitars. Then we started to experiment with some other ideas and so forth. At the end of the day, we were still on the song. [Art] Garfunkel was amblin' around the studio, hummin', and havin' input at various times. They were real scientists. They'd get on a part, and it might be there [unfinished] six weeks later."

He continued: "On my guitar, they had me miked with about seven mics. They had a near mic, a distant mic, a neck mic, a mic on the hole. They even miked my breathing. They miked the guitar in back. So Roy Halee was a genius at getting around. The first time we were listenin', they killed the breathing mic. And they had an ambient mic overhead, which picked up the two guitars together, I suppose. And so, I was breathin', I guess, pretty heavy in rhythm. And they wanted to take out that noise, and they took it out and said, 'Naw, we gotta leave that in.' That sounds almost like a rhythm on the record. So they left the breathin' mic on for the mix. I played [Telecaster] on it and a 12-string, three or four guitars on it. I was doing different guitar parts. One was a chord pattern and rhythm pattern. Did the Dobro lick on the regular six-string finger Dobro—not a slide Dobro. I never heard the total record until I heard it on the air. . . .I thought: 'That's the greatest record I heard in my life,' especially after the scrutiny and after all the time they spent on it and breakin' it apart musically and soundwise and all of it. There was some magic in the studio that day, and Roy Halee captured it. Paul and I had a really nice groove."

BROWN EYED GIRL

Van Morrison

-

1967

"Brown Eyed Girl" was recognized in 2011 for having been played on U.S. radio airwaves 10 million times, and it remains the most played and downloaded song of the entire 1960s. The song has aged particularly well, especially when considering what the playback value would have been for a song originally titled "Brown-Skinned Girl."

Van Morrison recalled: "That was just a mistake. It was a kind of Jamaican song. Calypso. It just slipped my mind. . . . After we'd recorded it, I looked at the tape box and didn't even notice that I'd changed the title. I looked at the box where I'd lain it down with my guitar and it said 'Brown Eyed Girl' on the tape box. It's just one of those things that happen."

The song was the result of Morrison's rushed decision to sign a contract with Bang Records after going through a rough patch in the mid-1960s; his band, Them!, broke up and his contract with Decca Records had expired. "Brown Eyed Girl" came during the 22nd take on the first day of a two-recording session in 1967, which was meant to capture four singles that Bang could put out. Though the song came as a result of his signing the contract, his failing to seek legal counsel beforehand has left him without a single cent of royalties to show for the massive hit. Oddly enough, Morrison has never liked the song, as it was much more commercial and poppy than he had ever intended to be. "I mean, I've got about 300 songs that I think are better," he told *Time* magazine.

HALO

Beyoncé

-

2009

"I was playing a pickup game right before a show in Michigan and I tore my Achilles' heel," Ryan Tedder, front man for OneRepublic, told *Billboard*. "It was the most intense pain I ever experienced in my life. I passed out. So I ended up going home for two weeks. My wife forbade me from writing or doing any work whatsoever. Evan Bogart [songwriter] and I were super close friends. He was having his explosion as a songwriter, and I texted him and said, 'My wife's gone for three hours, will you come over? Let's write one song.' Beyoncé had contacted me because of a song on our first album called 'Come Home.' So he came over and I said, 'Dude, Beyoncé wants me to do a song. Let's do a song in three hours.' I had this idea for a patch of this weird choir of angels thing, started playing it and within three hours we had 'Halo.'"

"On [Ryan's] first day back in LA I was going to take over some food and hang out with him," Bogart told *Singersroom*. "When I got there, he was like, 'Dude, we should write. We should write a song,' and I'm like, 'Well, you're not supposed to be writing. You're supposed to be in bed.' Eventually we ended up in his studio and, with him on crutches, we wrote 'Halo' in three hours."

Despite it being written by Tedder and Bogart, the song has, does, and always will belong to Beyoncé, despite claims that it was originally offered to Leona Lewis. "That was never the case," Tedder said. "That song was written for Beyoncé. What happened was that Beyoncé waited long enough to record that song. . .I thought this would be a brilliant first single for Leona, which it would have. . . .What I did was foolishly say to Leona's camp, 'I have it on hold for another A-list artist and I'm pretty sure they'll take it, but if they don't, I just want to know if you like it enough to consider it.' I sent it to them and they flipped on it. They loved it and instantly said they wanted to do it. I was like, 'Wait, wait, wait, no, it's not free yet!'"

Tedder also defended Beyoncé adding herself to the writing credits, telling *The Guardian*: "I can't speak for all of the songs that she does but I'll say this: she does stuff on any given song that, when you go from the demo to the final version, takes it to another level that you never would have thought of as the writer. For instance, on 'Halo,' that bridge on her version is completely different to my original one. Basically, she came in, ditched that, edited it, did her vocal thing on it and now its become one of my favorite parts of the song. The whole melody, she wrote it spontaneously in the studio. So her credit on that song stems from that."

SHOUT (PARTS 1 AND 2)

The Isley Brothers

-

1959

In an interview featured in the Marc Myers book *Anatomy of a Song: The Oral History of 45 Iconic Hits That Changed Rock, R&B and Pop*, Ronald Isley, of The Isley Brothers, details the impromptu origins of "Shout."

"In July 1959, we were booked into the Uptown Theater in Philadelphia as part of a soul revue hosted by local disc jockey Georgie Woods," he said. "There were about fifteen other acts on the bill, like The Flamingos and the Dells. I loved Jackie Wilson then—everyone did. Jackie had a powerful church voice, but it was more than that. He had this easy, natural way of being on stage—taking off his jacket in one move, dancing smoothly, rolling his eyes, and using his entire body to illustrate song lyrics. All of this knocked out the audiences. 'Lonely Teardrops' was a big hit for Jackie in 1958, so I sang it with my brothers during our performances. It became such a strong number for us that the promoters put us on last to close the shows. Which was great, since audiences left the theater thinking of us on their way to record stores, not the other groups. Jackie's 'Lonely Teardrops' had this part at the end where he'd sing. . .and his backup singers would respond in kind. Then Jackie would ad-lib. That was straight out of gospel.

"During one of our performances at the Uptown Theater, I was singing 'Lonely Teardrops' when I saw that everyone in the audience was standing up and really getting into it. The place was packed and the audience was yelling their approval, like at church. The energy level was so strong that I didn't want to end the song yet. I began to ad-lib, the way Jackie did. . .and the band picked right up on it with that galloping beat. The people standing went crazy, and I began to ad-lib more lines. I'd wait a second at the end of each line so my brothers and the audience had a chance to answer me with 'Shout!' That song just took over."

GO YOUR OWN WAY

Fleetwood Mac

1977

"Well, you know, as were all the songs on *Rumors*, they were dialogues to the other person in the band," Fleetwood Mac guitarist Lindsey Buckingham explained. "That was one of the unique things about *Rumors* and about Fleetwood Mac.

We were two couples who were breaking up, we were making rumors, all of these songs were sort of cross dialogues to each other. It was a musical soap opera if you will. 'Go Your Own Way' was filled with anger, it was filled with angst, it was filled with passion, and maybe just a little bit of humor. And irony at the situation, because we needed all of that. In order to get through the making of this album, we needed to compartmentalize all these feelings and get on with what needed to be done in the room in order to fulfill our destiny. That song, I think, pretty much summarizes the range of emotions that existed, but mostly the ones that were uplifting and about what you had to do in order to make that album happen."

"From the second that it was written and recorded, it became the last song in the set. That is a very, very important position for a song."

Stevie Nicks added, "Also think about the fact that 'Go Your Own Way' became the last song in our set. From the very, very beginning. From the second that it was written and recorded, it became the last song in the set. That is a very, very important position for a song."

"You know, the thing was that I wasn't very happy," Nicks added. "I just wasn't happy. I didn't look at it. . .I was looking for some kind of peace because Lindsey and I were in such turmoil. . .I was basically saying the same thing to him that he was saying to me. I was saying it in my over the top poetic thing, and he was saying. . .both of us were screaming desperately at each other in just a different way with different words."

"Even if it's not overly optimistic about the specifics of this particular dynamic, the tone is very optimistic about moving on and about the fact that there is salvation at the end of the road. I think that's the subtext of the song," Buckingham concluded.

STAND BY ME

Ben E. King

-

1961

"Ben E. [King] had the beginnings of a song—both words and music," composer and "Stand By Me" co-writer Mike Stoller said. "He worked on the lyrics together with Jerry [Leiber, lyricist and co-writer], and I added elements to the music, particularly the bass line. To some degree, it's based on a gospel song called 'Lord Stand By Me.' I have a feeling that Jerry and Ben E. were inspired by it. Ben, of course, had a strong background in church music. He's a 50% writer on the song, and Jerry and I are 25% each. . . .When I walked in, Jerry and Ben E. were working on the lyrics to a song. They were at an old oak desk we had in the office. Jerry was sitting behind it, and Benny was sitting on the top. They looked up and said they were writing a song. I said, 'Let me hear it.'. . .Ben began to sing the song a cappella. I went over to the upright piano and found the chord changes behind the melody he was singing. It was in the key of A. Then I created a bass line. Jerry said, 'Man that's it!' We used my bass pattern for a starting point and, later, we used it as the basis for the string arrangement created by Stanley Applebaum."

King's account of the song contradicts Stoller's. The documentary *History of Rock 'n' Roll* notes that King had originally written the song for The Drifters, his former band. They passed and, after recording "Spanish Harlem," King played it for Stoller and Leiber, who expressed interest. The song would go on to make nine appearances in the *Billboard* Hot 100, which includes the original release, a re-release in 1986, and seven covers. The original release charted the highest, topping out at No. 4 in 1961.

THE HOUSE OF THE RISING SUN

The Animals

1964

Though made famous by The Animals, "The House of the Rising Sun" was first recorded by Clarence Ashley and Gwen Foster in September 1966. Then titled "Rising Sun Blues," the song was apparently taught to Ashley by his grandfather, Enoch. Roy Acuff, Georgia Turner, Bert Martin, Daw Henson, Woody Guthrie, Libby Holman, and Josh White had all recorded versions of the song before Lead Belly recorded two versions, the second of which was dubbed "House of the Rising Sun." Since then, Glenn Yarbrough, Pete Seeger, Andy Griffith, Miriam Makeba, Joan Baez, Nina Simone, Tim Hardin, Bob Dylan, and Dave Van Ronk have all gone on to record their own version of the song.

"I had learned it sometime in the 1950s, from a recording by Hally Wood, the Texas singer and collector, who had got it from an Alan Lomax field recording by a Kentucky woman named Georgia Turner," Van Ronk said. "I put a different spin on it by altering the chords and using a bass line that descended in half steps—a common enough progression in jazz, but unusual among folksingers."

Further departure from convention was the goal for The Animals, who performed the song as a way to separate themselves from the conventional rock bands of the day. They debuted their version while on tour with Chuck Berry and, after an overwhelming audience reaction, recorded it in London in between tour stops. The song was recorded in one take and, according to producer Mickie Most, took just 15 minutes to make.

PEGGY SUE

Buddy Holly

-

1958

"I had a girlfriend at the time named Peggy Sue, so I talked [Buddy Holly] into changing it to 'Peggy Sue,' and then we finished it off with a different feel," Crickets drummer Jerry Allison told NPR. The song was originally titled "Cindy Lou," named for Buddy Holly's niece Cindy.

The brownie points that Allison scored as a result of the name change worked for a time; Allison and Peggy Sue Gerron were married for 11 years.

Holly was given a writing credit at the insistence of Allison following his death in 1959. Writing credits originally went to just Allison and producer Norman Petty, both of whom were responsible for the percussion on the song.

BORN TO BE WILD

Steppenwolf

-

1968

Canadian rock musician and songwriter Mars Bonfire, real name Dennis Edmonton, offered Steppenwolf the gift of a timeless classic when he provided the band the rights to his song "Born to be Wild." Bonfire was a member of the band The Sparrows, which eventually evolved into Steppenwolf; his brother, a drummer, stayed after Bonfire left. Yet the familial connection that remained proved to hold little weight for Mars, who offered his then-ballad to other bands before giving it to Steppenwolf.

The song eventually made its way into the right hands, as the band sped up the song's tempo and, as put by *AllMusic*'s Hal Horowitz, turned it into "a roaring anthem of turbo-charged riff rock."

MAGGIE MAY

Rod Stewart

-

1971

Released as the B-side on his "Reason to Believe," the label's expectations for the song were about as underwhelming as the experience that Rod Stewart drew inspiration from while writing "Maggie May."

"At 16, I went to the Bealieu Jazz Festival in the New Forest," Stewart wrote in his memoir. "I'd snuck in with some mates via an overflow sewage pipe. And there on a secluded patch of grass, I lost my not-remotely-prized virginity with an older (and larger) woman who'd come on to me very strongly in the beer tent. How much older, I can't tell you—but old enough to be highly disappointed by the brevity of the experience." The label originally rejected the song for inclusion on his album, as it lacked a melody; it wasn't until Stewart reminded them that the album was due and that they had run out of time that the label ceded. The song caught on after WOKY in Milwaukee began playing the song as a single on the radio, leading other stations to do so as well. The song became one of Stewart's most identifiable hits, and a staple at his major live performances. He even had a particular way of introducing it so as to take advantage of its being a play on words, saying "This is 'Maggie May'—sometimes she did, sometimes she didn't."

"How much older, I can't tell you—but old enough to be highly disappointed by the brevity of the experience."

That play on words might be the reason he chose that name in the first place, as it didn't belong to his "acquaintance" at the music festival. The title of the song was actually borrowed from a Liverpool folk song about a Lime Street prostitute.

IN THE MIDNIGHT HOUR

Wilson Pickett

1965

Said "In the Midnight Hour" co-writer Steve Cropper: "[co-writer Wilson Pickett] says he wrote the song but, you know, I listened to some old church stuff he sang on and he was singing...

and I said, 'I'm gonna see my girl in the midnight hour,' what about that?'" Cropper was a session guitarist at Stax Studios in Memphis, where Atlantic Records president Jerry Wexler brought Wilson Pickett to record.

Aside from allegedly developing the song's concept, Cropper also helped write the guitar part. "I say in my shows that playing the guitar is real simple, you just follow the dots—the dots on the neck on every guitar are in the same place," Cropper told *Uncut* in a 2015 interview. "That's how I came up with the intro for this. They go, 'It couldn't be that simple,' then all of them go home and get their guitars and go, 'Wow, it is!'"

Pickett changed the rhythm of the song so that it was easier to dance to after the first recording left those involved unsatisfied. The craze at the time was a dance known as "The Jerk," which involved an emphasized "two-beat." Obviously, Pickett's change was a good one, as the song eventually reached No. 1 on *Billboard*'s R&B Chart.

PURPLE RAIN

Prince and The Revolution

-

1984

"I've still got it [the demo cassette]—with the whole instrumental track and a little bit of Prince singing, 'Can't get over that feeling,' or something," Stevie Nicks told *Mojo* magazine in 2013. "I told him, 'Prince, I've listened to this a hundred times but I wouldn't know where to start. It's a movie, it's epic.'" In fact, the song "Purple Rain" was written for the film by the same name, in which Prince plays the song as a means to successfully follow up a rival band. The film was a point of obsession for him; as former band mate Lisa Coleman put it to *Spin*, "You know how he is—it wasn't about coming out with the next record. The next record had to be a whole environment."

Prince's former manager Bob Cavallo recalled that the idea for the movie had been brewing for some time, saying: "We managed Prince in '78, '79, something like that, until '89, the ten really good years, as far as I'm concerned. I call [partner Steve Fargnoli] and he's on the road with Prince: 'Steve, there's about a year left on our deal, mention to Prince that we'd like to re-up.' A day or so later I get a response: 'He'll only sign with us if he gets a major motion picture. It has to be with a studio—not with some drug dealer or jeweler financing. And his name has to be above the title. Then he'd re-sign with us.' He wasn't a giant star yet. I mean, that demand was a little over the top." After much clawing and scratching to find people qualified enough to make a movie, Prince was able to release his film during the summer of 1984. It was a massive success; the film made just over $80 million, more than ten times what it cost to make, and won an Oscar for Best Original Song.

According to Dr. Fink, former keyboardist for The Revolution, the inspiration for "Purple Rain" came from a tour schedule strikingly similar to that of Bob Seger and his band. "During that tour, we kept running into Bob Seger and the Silver Bullet Band," Fink recalled. "After one of the shows, Prince asked me what made Seger so popular. I said, 'Well, he's playing mainstream pop-rock.' Michael Jackson and Prince were breaking ground, but there was still a lot of segregation on mainstream radio. I said, 'Prince, if you were to write something along these lines, it would cross things over for you even further.'" The song cemented Prince as a star and will forever be cited by anybody arguing for Prince's genius; it reached No. 2 in the United States when it was released in 1984, and claimed the No. 4 spot after the artist's death in 2016.

On the meaning of the song, Prince said: "When there's blood in the sky—red and blue [equals] purple. . .purple rain pertains to the end of the world and being with the one you love and letting your faith/god guide you through the purple rain." The song was first recorded at the Minnesota Dance Theatre during a benefit concert. "With Prince, you never knew," David Rivkin, who recorded the performance, said. "I thought we were recording a concert, but I wasn't sure if it was going to be a record, too. I knew they were working on the movie as well. You just had to go in prepared to record whatever it was going to be as well as you could."

ROCK LOBSTER

The B-52's

-

1979

"Rock Lobster" might be better known for who it influenced rather than the influence that led to its conception. In a 2013 *SongFacts* interview, Yoko Ono recalled, "Listening to The B-52s, John [Lennon] said he realized that my time had come. So he could record an album by making me an equal partner and we won't get flack like we used to up to then."

Keith Strickland, guitarist for The B-52's, told *Q Magazine* that Lennon's insight was correct. "Cindy [Wilson] does this scream that was inspired by Yoko Ono," he said. "John heard it at some club in the Bahamas, and the story goes that he calls up Yoko and says, 'Get the axe out—they're ready for us again!' Yoko has said that she and John were listening to us in the weeks before he died."

As for the song itself? Front man Fred Schneider explained its genesis in a video that he did for People for the Ethical Treatment of Animals, saying that he was at an Atlanta disco where images of puppies, kittens, and lobsters on a grill were being projected onto the wall. He thought to himself "Rock this, rock that. . .rock lobster," and the song was born. The reason Schneider was narrating the video for the People for the Ethical Treatment of Animals? He stopped eating crustaceans at a young age after watching them be boiled alive. As a result of the experience, he advocated for the humane treatment of animals for the rest of his life.

LUST FOR LIFE

Iggy Pop

-

1977

As Iggy Pop told *Q Magazine* in a 2013 interview, "Once a week the Armed Forces Network [in Berlin] would play *Starsky & Hutch* and that was our little ritual. AFN would broadcast an ID when they came on the air, a representation of a radio tower, and it made a signal sound, 'beep-beep-beep, beep-beep-ba-beep.' And we went, 'A-ha we'll take that!' David [Bowie] grabbed his ukulele, worked out the chords, and away we went." While Bowie based his rhythm off of the Armed Forces Network call signal, the two borrowed the drumbeat for "Lust for Life" from The Supremes' 1966 tune "You Can't Hurry Love."

The song deals with Iggy Pop's heroin addiction and the lifestyle that comes with it. It makes several references to the novel *The Ticket That Exploded* by William S. Burroughs, himself a heroin addict, mentioning Johnny Yen, stripteases, and hypnotizing chickens. Of course, many of those references are omitted by companies that use the song to spread a positive message and connect with a younger audience. Royal Caribbean famously ran an ad campaign for a decade in which no trace of the song's original hedonist intent remained. Pop didn't mind at all, however, saying that he "actually enjoyed Royal Caribbean's usage. And to me, it's just great that it's out there in any form for someone to hear."

FOXY LADY

Jimi Hendrix Experience

1967

"I liked skinny, raw-boned, over-f*cked, underfed-looking guys," Lithofayne Pridgon said. Hendrix's girlfriend in the mid-1960s, the two became inseparable after a few chance encounters. "He used to call every pet we had 'Foxy,'" she said. "He [also] used to like to refer to good-looking girls as foxy. Or if I put on certain things, he'd say, 'Wow, you look foxy in that.'. . .He was always saying, 'This is about you. I wrote this about you.' I just thought it was cute."

Winona Williams, a former model who dated Paul McCartney and David Bowie and is a close friend to Pridgon, insisted that Lithofayne had Hendrix' heart, despite his massive overseas success and desirability. "Jimi would have settled down with Fayne," she said. "I don't see any other woman that he'd have settled down with—but Fayne was not about to settle down. If Fayne had said: 'Look, I want you to leave all of these women alone and we're going to do this,' he would have done it." Of course, Hendrix never publicly commented on the inspiration behind his "Foxy Lady;" his biographer believes that the song was inspired by Roger Daltrey's future wife, Heather Taylor, while Hendrix isn't as forthcoming as the lyrics suggest he is. Still, his insistence on

"If Fayne had said: 'Look, I want you to leave all of these women alone and we're going to do this,' he would have done it."

seeking Pridgon out whenever he was in New York certainly doesn't hurt her claim.

I'M WAITING FOR THE MAN

The Velvet Underground

-

1967

"Everything about that song holds true, except the price." The story is told from the perspective of a New York City man who has travelled up to 125th Street to purchase $26 worth of heroin. Written by Lou Reed in the early '60s while he attended Syracuse University, the song was unsuccessful at first, as it appeared on the commercial failure that was *The Velvet Underground & Nico*. Eventually, both the song and the album came to be revered, thanks to the influence they had on music going forward.

David Bowie saw the song's potential early, as he told *Performing Songwriter* magazine in 2003: "I actually played 'Waiting for the Man' in Britain with my band before the album was even released in America. Talk about one-upsmanship. A friend of mine came over to the States to do some work with Andy Warhol at The Factory, and as he was leaving, Andy said, 'Oh, I just made this album with some people. Maybe you can take it back to England and see if you can get any interest over there.' And it was still the vinyl test pressing. It hadn't got a company or anything at the time. I still have it. There's a white label on it, and it says 'Warhol.' He signed it. My friend gave it to me and he said, 'This is crap. You like weird stuff, so maybe you'll enjoy it.' I played it and it was like 'Ah, this is the future of music!' I was in awe. It was serious and dangerous and I loved it. And I literally went into a band rehearsal the next day, put the album down and said, 'We're going to learn this song. It is unlike anything I've ever heard.' We learned 'Waiting for the Man' right then and there, and we were playing it on stage within a week. I told Lou that, and he loved it. I must have been the first person in the world to cover a Velvet Underground song."

SHOUT

Tears for Fears

-

1984

"A lot of people think that 'Shout' is just another song about primal scream theory, continuing the themes of the first album," Roland Orzabal, co-founder of Tears for Fears, said. "It is actually more concerned with political protest. It came out in 1984 when a lot of people were still worried about the aftermath of the Cold War and it was basically an encouragement to protest."

Among the band's most identifiable songs, "Shout" peaked at No. 1 on the *Billboard* Hot 100 in the summer of 1985 and held the spot for three weeks. The song stood out from other Tears for Fears songs; it employed a powerful sound, guitar and bass solos, and female vocals. The song, as record producer Chris Hughes recalled, was "so simple it should take about five minutes to record." The song would end up taking weeks to finish, though little time had passed before the band knew that they had a hit on their hands. "The song was written in my front room on just a small synthesizer and a drum machine," Orzabal said. "Initially I only had the chorus, which was very repetitive, like a mantra. I played it to Ian Stanley, our keyboardist, and Chris Hughes, the producer. I saw it as a good album track, but they were convinced it would be a hit around the world."

Singer Curt Smith shared the sentiment; when asked in a 2014 interview with *Consequence of Sound* whether he was surprised by the success of the song, he responded "No. It was a weird time, but you're looking at it from the viewpoint of an American, because 'Shout' everywhere else in the world was actually the first single, and to everyone in Europe and to us at the time, we thought that was the obvious single. We actually disagreed with the American company who made 'Everybody [Wants to Rule the World]' the first single. Which is interesting in retrospect, because it was one of those times when the record company was right and we were wrong, because for America, yes, it was a better first single. Everywhere else 'Shout' was actually the first single, so it actually achieved success in other places before it was released in America."

BOHEMIAN RHAPSODY

Queen

-

1975

"That was a great moment, but the biggest thrill for us was actually creating the music in the first place," Brian May, lead guitarist of Queen, told *Q Magazine* while discussing "Bohemian Rhapsody" in 2008. "I remember Freddie [Mercury] coming in with loads of bits of paper from his dad's work, like Post-it notes, and pounding on the piano. He played the piano like most people play the drums. And this song he had was full of gaps where he explained that something operatic would happen here and so on. He'd worked out the harmonies in his head."

According to Mercury's childhood friend Chris Smith, the original iteration of "Bohemian Rhapsody" was called "The Cowboy Song" and contained several lyrics that made the final cut.

"You just knew that you were listening for the first time to a big page in history. Something inside me told me that this was a red-letter day, and it really was."

The recording and production process for the song was intensive; it took three weeks to record and forced Mercury, May, and drummer Roger Taylor to sing upwards of 12 hours a day. The band overdubbed to the point where the tapes used to record, when held up to light, became see-through. "Nobody really knew how it was going to sound as a whole six-minute song until it was put together," producer Roy Thomas

Baker recalled. "I was standing at the back of the control room, and you just knew that you were listening for the first time to a big page in history. Something inside me told me that this was a red-letter day, and it really was." Baker was right, as the song went on to become the U.K.'s third-best selling single of all time.

"Freddie was a very complex person: flippant and funny on the surface, but he concealed insecurities and problems in squaring up with his childhood," May said. "He never explained the lyrics, but I think he put a lot of himself into that song." Mercury was more vague, saying, "I think people should just listen to it, think about it, and then make up their minds as to what it says to them."

LOSING MY RELIGION

R.E.M.

-

1991

"When I listened back to it the next day," recalls R.E.M. guitarist Peter Buck, "there was a bunch of stuff that was really just me learning how to play mandolin, and then there's what 'Losing My Religion' [is], and then a whole bunch more of me learning to play the mandolin."

The song based around Buck's mandolin playing soon evolved into a full group effort. That group effort involved singer Michael Stipe, whose vocal part was recorded in a single take. He had said that the singing was simply about romantic expression, that it was "just a classic obsession pop song." He went on to say that he's "always felt like the best kinds of songs are the ones where anybody can listen to it, put themselves in it and say, 'Yeah, that's me.'"

99 PROBLEMS

Jay-Z

2003

"For me it was like I was being. . .rap can sometimes be provocative," Jay-Z explained. "I was being provocative. I just thought that it was deeply funny that people hear certain words and immediately hear white noise after that. It's almost like, 'I don't hear anything else that he's talking about.' It struck me as deeply funny, so I kind of did it on purpose. . . . The second verse deals with this exchange between people. You have this guy who's in the car and he has drugs on him. He's all the way in the wrong, and he's going on the highway, and here you have this cop, who's on the turnpike. He pulls the car over not because he has drugs in the car, but because the driver is black, which happened a lot if you look at the surveys between '88 and '96. There was a big investigation about that, driving while black. So, this officer pulls the car over, and they have this exchange. Both guys are used to getting their way, so the driver knows he's in the wrong but also knows that he hasn't done anything to get pulled over . . . .This guy knows a bit about the law because he's used to breaking it, so he's protecting himself. He knows that you can't go in my glove compartment without a search warrant and you can't go in my trunk. You can't go in anywhere that your hands can't. . .that you can't see or reach. You can't open a locked glove compartment unless you have the proper search warrant . . . .So it's this conversation between these two people and he's waiting for a K9 unit to come. A K9 unit comes and we're all in trouble. The K9 smells the drugs, the car gets pulled over, we get locked up. But the K9 was on another call, and he couldn't hold us for that long, so we pulled off. And as we're pulling off, about five minutes down the road, we see a car screeching, lights blaring, and we see K9 unit coming up the highway. So, I have 99 problems, but THAT b*tch ain't one."

According to producer Rick Rubin, the idea for the song came from comedian Chris Rock. In an interview he did with *Rolling Stone*, Rubin said, "[Chris] said, 'Ice-T has this song, and maybe there's a way to flip it around and do a new version of that.' And I told Jay Z the idea and he liked it. The Ice-T song is. . .a list of him talking about his girls and what a great pimp he is. And our idea was to use that same hook concept, and instead of it being about the girls that are not his problem, instead of being a bragging song, it's more about the problems. Like, this is about the other side of that story."

DREAM ON

Aerosmith

-

1973

"When I wrote 'Dream On,' I went, 'Where did this come from?'" Steven Tyler told *Rolling Stone.* "I didn't question it. When I read the lyrics back now, for a guy who was stoned, stupid and dribbling, I got something out of there.

The song traces various aspects of the different stages of Tyler's life; he credits laying beneath his father's piano as he played when he was just three years old as the source of the "Dream On" chord progression. "Never in a million years did I think I'd take it to guitar," Tyler told *SongFacts* in an interview. "'Dream On' was written four or five years before the group even started. I wrote it on an upright piano in my parents' living room at Trow-Rico Lodge, in New Hampshire. When I transposed it to guitar Joe [Perry] played the right fingers and Brad [Whitford] played the left hand on guitar. Sitting there working it out on guitar and piano I got a little melodramatic. The song was so good it brought a tear to my eye."

"Nobody sings like that. I was in fear. I didn't know. And of course, the band didn't like it because we were into rocking out and that was a ballad I wrote."

Tyler had been working on pieces of the song for about six years before bringing it to the band, though he was concerned the song's style might be an issue for Perry and Whitford.

"When you listen back to 'Dream On,' and you go, 'Oh my God. That's so weird. I'm a little afraid. We're gonna get thrown out of town,' Tyler told *USA Today*. "That's what I thought. I thought if I sing that (high-pitched climax of 'Dream On'), nobody sings like that. I was in fear. I didn't know. And of course, the band didn't like it because we were into rocking out and that was a ballad I wrote. They'll say they liked it, but it was a big drag to play every night. Some people in the band didn't like playing it."

Tyler's fears, though ultimately inconsequential, weren't ill-founded, as Joe Perry wasn't a fan of the song from the jump. "Back in those days you made your mark playing live," he told *Classic Rock* magazine in 2002. "And to me rock 'n' roll's all about energy and putting on a show. Those were the things that attracted me to rock 'n' roll, but 'Dream On' was a ballad. I didn't really appreciate the musicality of it until later, but I did know it was a great song, so we put it in our set. We also knew that if you played straight rock 'n' roll you didn't get played on the radio and, if you wanted a top 40 hit, the ballad was the way to go. I don't know if we really played it much live, in those days if you only had half an hour to make your mark, you didn't play slow songs. So it wasn't until after it became a single that we really started playing it."

Tyler found reassurance in the musical tastes he indulged while growing up, saying: "Trust me, I listened to Gary Lewis and the Playboys. . . .I came from that era of hearing weird stuff that was dumb when you first heard it but then you couldn't stop singing it. It was very cool. So after writing 'Dream On,' I went 'Oh sh*t.' That's happened a couple of times in my career, where it's like, 'Wow, what is this?' And I've just come to realize that when that happens, that's when the magic has arrived."

WILD THING

The Troggs

-

1966

Chip Taylor was asked to write "Wild Thing" for the The Wild Ones, a New York City house band produced by Gerry Granahan, who sought Taylor's help. "I started just chuggin' away on a couple of chords and within a couple of minutes of getting off the phone I had the chorus and I was kind of likin' it," Taylor recalled. "I didn't really know what I was going to say in between but I was thinking there was something cool and sweaty about this. So I went to the studio. . . .Because it was a sexual-kind-of-feeling song, I didn't want to be embarrassed, I wanted to let myself sing it, so I asked [producer] Ron [Johnson] to turn the lights out when I got there and have my stool ready and have my microphone ready and when I got there, I said, "Put the tape in record and just let it go and let me just keep playin'. . . .And then I stomped on a board, just to give a cool little edge to it and I banged on a tambourine and then Ron was foolin' around. As the track was playing back, he was doing this little thing with his hands, like when you put a blade of grass in there and you get a whistling sound? Only he was able to it without the blade of grass in it. It sounded cool. . . .I listened back and I thought it sounded great. I was a little afraid to play it for people because it was so different than anything I'd done before; it wasn't one of those pretty little country songs. And it was very sexy."

The original version of the song flopped; it wasn't until The Troggs got a hold of it that it skyrocketed in popularity. The song was offered on two different labels, as The Troggs' manager sought out a distribution contract from Atco Records in the U.S. after Fontana Records in England expressed some doubts about the song's release. They eventually ceded and, as a result, "Wild Thing" is the only single to top the *Billboard* Hot 100 chart for two record companies simultaneously.

DANCING QUEEN

ABBA

1976

The quality of ABBA's "Dancing Queen" was immediately apparent—so much so that their first live performance of the song was deemed fit for royalty. They performed it on June 18, 1976 at the Royal Swedish Opera for King Carl XVI Gustaf of Sweden and Silvia Sommerlath, his fiancée, on the night before their wedding, a fitting song choice considering Sommerlath's soon-to-be rank.

Originally titled "Boogaloo," band members Benny Andersson and Björn Ulvaeus, along with manager Stig Anderson, penned the song with George McCrae's "Rock Your Baby" in mind. Dr. John's *Dr. John's Gumbo* was also credited for inspiring the drumming on the song. Upon hearing the song's backing track, singer Anni-Frid Lyngstad allegedly began to cry. "I found the song so beautiful," she said. "It's one of those songs that goes straight to your heart." The sentiment was shared; Anderson called it "one of those songs where you know during the sessions that it's going to be a smash hit," while singer Agnetha Fältskog said "It's often difficult to know what will be a hit. The exception was 'Dancing Queen.' We all knew it was going to be massive." It was; the song reached No. 1 in the United States, Australia, the Netherlands, Belgium, Ireland, Mexico, New Zealand, Norway, South Africa, Spain, Sweden, the United Kingdom, West Germany, and Zimbabwe.

"It's often difficult to know what will be a hit. The exception was 'Dancing Queen.' We all knew it was going to be massive."

FREE FALLIN'

Tom Petty

1989

Talking about how his hit "Free Fallin'" came to be, Tom Petty told *Billboard* magazine: "Jeff Lynne and I were sitting around with the idea of writing a song and I was playing the keyboard and I just happened to hit on that main riff, the intro of the song, and I think Jeff said something like, 'That's a really good riff but there's one chord too many,' so I think I cut it back a chord and then, really just to amuse Jeff, honestly, I just sang that first verse. Then he starts laughing. Honestly, I thought I was just amusing Jeff but then I got to the chorus of the song and he leaned over to me and said the word, 'freefalling.' And I went to sing that and he said, 'No, take your voice up and see how that feels.' So I took my voice up an octave or two, but I couldn't get the whole word in. So I sang 'freeee,' then 'free falling.' And we both knew at that moment that I'd hit on something pretty good. It was that fast. He had to go somewhere, and I wrote the last verse and kind of just polished the rest of the song and when I saw him the next day I played him the song and he was like, 'Wow, you did that last night?' And I was like, 'Yeah.' And he said. 'We've got to go cut this,' and we just took off to Mike Campbell's studio where we knew we could get in and get it done that day. So we went in and made the record that day.

"I don't know [who] the girl in 'Free Fallin'' is. I was having to make this drive every day. The studio was in the valley and I was driving from Beverly Hills to the valley and back every day and on that drive I just used to look at Ventura Boulevard, and just life's great pageant was going on up and down that street. And I tried to grab a little bit of these characters on the road and it was kind of how I saw it. It's pretty true of that time and that era, I remember. . .maybe it's still that way, I don't know. The skateboarders and the shoppers and the young kids in the trendiest possible clothes and the auto-tellers and the drive-through banks. It's a scene, it's a never-ending scene. I thought, you could probably start at one end of this road and by the time you got to the end of it you could purchase everything you could ever need in your life. It was kind of like that.

"With 'Free Fallin'' I was very lucky because it came very quickly and we recorded that song in a day and we went very soon after that, maybe the next day or two, to another studio to mix the tracks—because I like to just finish the song, I don't like songs to sit around not be mixed and all of that—and while they were working on some technical stuff in the mix room Jeff and I took our guitars into a little vocal booth they had off to the side and we wrote 'I Won't Back Down' while they were mixing 'Free Fallin''. So we came out of that saying, 'We think we've got another one,' and we went back and did that one in the next day or two."

HEY YA!

OutKast

-

2003

"'Hey Ya!' is pretty much about the state of relationships in the 2000s," OutKast member Andre 3000 explained. "It's about some people who stay together in relationships because of tradition, because somebody told them, 'You guys are supposed to stay together.' But you pretty much end up being unhappy for the rest of your life. . . .So 'Hey Ya!' is really about saying, 'F*ck it. Live life, you know?'"

The rapper drew some inspiration for the song from his *The Love Below*, a screenplay concept in which the protagonist falls in and out of love. As he explained to the *Huffington Post*: "There was never a screenplay but I did envision a story about a guy that went to Paris and each song represented a different woman. The concept started off as songs, then I reached out to a buddy to talk about filming it. We were green and didn't realize how long it would take to get it done. At the time, shooting a movie wasn't done on digital cameras. It took time to shoot and a lot of money to finance. Musically, there was one vehicle (the record company) and you released full albums. Those realities affected the original plan."

Originally titled "Thank God for Mom and Dad," Andre started writing the song during OutKast's *Stankonia* tour, three years before it was released on the album *Speakerboxxx/The Love Below*. Certain aspects of the song were inspired by bands like the Ramones and The Smiths—"I was heavy into that—this was my 'bad' version of that because I didn't know how to do it," he said—while others went straight from Andre's head to the track. "I've never seen him write anything down, lyrically," John Frye, a session recorder, told *MTV News*. "What he likes to do is drive around and live it and think about it. And he comes in and says, 'Ready.' I can't remember him ever coming in to do vocals unprepared." Andre was the only vocalist on the track, save the female voice shouting in the background. That was the voice of one studio employee that was then made to sound like many. Hers is a voice that has been heard by many, as "Hey Ya!" was the most downloaded song in iTunes' first year of service. It was also the first song to hit the one million paid downloads mark, as pointed out by the *Huffington Post*.

HELLS BELLS

AC/DC

-

1980

The second single on AC/DC's album *Back in Black*, "Hells Bells" was among the first tracks written by vocalist Brian Johnson. "I was just sitting on my bed one night," Johnson told *Classic Rock*, "and these bedrooms were just breeze-block cells with a bed and a table with a light on it and a toilet. That was it.

I was sitting there wondering how good it had been. Cause we were doing it so quick, Mutt [Robert Lange, producer] would never let me listen to what I'd done because we had to get the guys in straight away. There was no luxury of sitting around thinking, nothing like that. Then Mutt came in and said: 'Are you all right?' He was a wonderful man; he knew the pressure I was feeling. I thought: 'Phew!' I'd already written three songs and it was day after day. I'm going: 'I'm f*cking running out of ideas here. . . .'"

Johnson was right to feel pressure, he was tasked with taking over the lead vocalist spot after the death of Bon Scott, who passed away on February 19, 1980 after a night of intense drinking. His death came less than a year after the band released *Highway to Hell* and less than half a year before releasing *Back in Black*, which was written and recorded in Scott's honor.

Johnson continued: "Mutt says: 'Tonight we're gonna do "Hells Bells," Brian.' I'm thinking: 'Hmm. . ."Hells Bells," right.' I'd just done 'Back in Black', so I thought: 'Can it get any moodier?' And then, right at that moment, there was a tropical thunderstorm the likes of which I'd never seen before. Mutt said: 'Listen. . .thunder!' And I said: 'That's rolling thunder, that's what they call it in England.' He says: 'Rolling thunder—write that down.' And this is true—it went 'boom!' The f*cking rain came down in torrents, you couldn't hear yourself. . . .I was gone. The song was ready that night. I hadn't even heard the track cause they were busy doing it. It was whacked down in the greatest haste."

STAYIN' ALIVE

Bee Gees

-

1977

"People crying out for help," Barry Gibb said. "Desperate songs. Those are the ones that become giants. The minute you capture that on record, it's gold. 'Stayin' Alive' is the epitome of that. Everybody struggles against the world, fighting all the bullsh*t and things that can drag you down. And it really is a victory just to survive. But when you climb back on top and win bigger than ever before, well that's something everybody reacts to."

As Robin Gibb put it, "The subject matter of 'Stayin' Alive' is actually quite a serious one; it's about survival in the streets of New York, and the lyrics actually say that." The song was written at the request of Robert Stigwood, a film producer and the Bee Gees' manager, for a film based in New York that explored the Disco Era. The film was the 1977 hit *Saturday Night Fever*, during which John Travolta walks through the streets of New York City to the tune of "Stayin' Alive."

Dennis Bryon, the band's drummer, lost his mother during the recording process and had to take a leave of absence, resulting in the band scrambling to find a replacement. As they were recording in France for tax purposes, qualified replacements were almost non-existent, which led to them trying to utilize a drum machine on the track. They eventually took pieces from the drum track on their hit "Night Fever," arranged it into a loop, and played it on "Stayin' Alive." "Barry and I listened carefully to find a bar that felt really good," producer Albhy Galuten recalled. "Everyone knows that it's more about feel than accuracy in drum tracks. We chose a bar that felt so good that we ended up using that same loop on 'Stayin' Alive,' and 'More Than a Woman,' and then again on Barbra Streisand's song 'Woman in Love.' To make the loop, we copied the drums onto one-quarter-inch tape. Karl spliced the tape and jury-rigged it so that it was going over a mic stand and around a plastic reel. At first, we were doing it just as a temporary measure. As we started to lay tracks down to it, we found that it felt really great—very insistent but not machinelike. It had a human feel. By the time we had overdubbed all the parts to the songs and Dennis came back, there was no way we could get rid of the loop."

> **"Desperate songs. Those are the ones that become giants. The minute you capture that on record, it's gold."**

Despite Stigwood's attempts, the Bee Gees refused to change the name from "Stayin' Alive" to something their manager felt was more appropriate for the movie. Including "Saturday" in the title was out of the question, as too many songs featured the word at the time. They also refused to include the word "night," as their album already included the song "Night Fever."

FREE BIRD

Lynyrd Skynyrd

1973

You'd think the lyrics for a song as epic as "Free Bird" would take a while to write. But Lynyrd Skynyrd guitarist Gary Rossington insists that that wasn't the case.

"Allen [Collins] had the chords for the beginning, pretty part for two full years and we kept asking Ronnie [Van Zant] to write something and he kept telling us to forget it; he said there were too many chords so he couldn't find a melody," Rossington said. "He thought that he had to change with every chord. Then one day we were at rehearsal and Allen started playing those chords again, and Ronnie said, 'Those are pretty. Play them again.' He said, 'I got it,' and wrote the lyrics in three or four minutes—the whole damned thing!"

REHAB

Amy Winehouse

-

2007

In a 2011 interview with BBC Radio's Zane Lowe, "Rehab" producer Mark Ronson told the story of how the song started out, which was later confirmed by singer Amy Winehouse's father, Mitch. Ronson said: "I was walking down the street with Amy. We were in New York and we'd been working together for about a week and we were walking to some store. She wanted to buy a present for her boyfriend and she was telling me about a specific time in her life that was. . . I feel bad, like, talking about a friend like this, but I think I've told this story enough times. . .but she hit, like, a certain low and her dad came over to try and talk some sense into her." Winehouse's father recommended she go to rehab, which she dismissed. Ronson continued, "And the first thing I was like, 'Ding ding ding ding ding.' Like, I mean I'm supposed to be like, 'How was that for you?' and all I'm like is, 'We've got to go back to the studio.'"

"I mean I'm supposed to be like, 'How was that for you?' and all I'm like is, 'We've got to go back to the studio.'"

According to Mitch Winehouse's memoir, *Amy, My Daughter*, Winehouse penned the lyrics in just three hours. Her mentions of "Ray" and "Mr. Hathaway" in the song's lyrics are references to Ray Charles and Donny Hathaway, two soul musicians who helped inspire the sound that Winehouse and Ronson were going for.

SWEET CHILD O' MINE

Guns N' Roses

-

1988

"I was f*cking around with this stupid little riff," Slash recalled. "Axl [Rose] said, 'Hold the f*cking phones! That's amazing!'" Rose already had most of the lyrics for "Sweet Child O' Mine," based on a poem he had written for then-girlfriend Erin Everly. Taking his cue from Slash's riff, he decided to deliver them in a fashion similar to that of Lynyrd Skynyrd. "I'm from Indiana, where Lynyrd Skynyrd are considered God to the point that you ended up saying, 'I hate this f*cking band!'" Rose said. "And yet for 'Sweet Child'. . .I went out and got some old Skynyrd tapes to make sure that we'd got that heartfelt feeling."

Though "writing and rehearsing it to make it a complete song was like pulling teeth" according to Slash, the song fell quickly into place thanks to producer Mike Clink, who instituted a "No drugs in the studio" policy for the band. "We partied really hard," Slash said, "but when we were in the studio, we were pretty much together. There was no doping and all that stuff."

Once *Appetite for Destruction*, the album on which "Sweet Child O' Mine" was featured, was completed, it was sent along to producers Michael Barbiero and Steve Thompson for mixing. "'Sweet Child O' Mine' sounded like a hit to all of us," Barbiero said. "So much so that I remember Axl asking me when we were finished if I thought the album would actually sell. I told him that, despite the fact that it was nothing like what was on the radio, I thought it would go gold. I was only off by 20 million records." The song would reach the No. 1 spot on the *Billboard* Hot 100 chart and achieve platinum status in both the U.S. and the U.K., and double platinum status in Italy.

FIGHT THE POWER

Public Enemy

-

1989

"I wanted it to be defiant, I wanted it to be angry, I wanted it to be very rhythmic. I thought right away of Public Enemy," Spike Lee said, recalling how he knew exactly what he wanted for his 1989 film *Do the Right Thing*, which explored the racial tension in Brooklyn, New York. "I wanted this song to be an anthem that could express what young black America was feeling at this time. Around this time, New York City under Mayor Ed Koch was racially polarized, and I wanted this song to be in the film."

The inspiration for the song came to Chuck D while flying over Italy during Public Enemy's Run's House tour with Run-D.M.C. "I wanted to have sorta like the same theme as the original 'Fight the Power' by The Isley Brothers and fill it in with some kind of modernist views of what our surroundings were at that particular time." Among the modernist elements of the track were the many samples that it included, some of which are deployed at the same time. In a 1990 interview with *Keyboard* magazine, Chuck D laid out the creative process, saying: "We approach every record like it was a painting. Sometimes, on the sound sheet, we have to have a separate sheet just to list the samples for each track. We used about 150, maybe 200 samples on *Fear of a Black Planet.* 'Fight the Power' has, like, 17 samples in the first ten seconds. For example, there's three different drum loops that make one big drum loop: One is a standard Funkadelic thing, another is a Sly [Stone] thing, and I think the third one is The Jacksons. Then we took some sounds from a beat box. The opening lick is the end of a Trouble Funk record, processed with doubling and reverb. And the chorus is music going backwards."

The song wasn't without controversy, despite bassist Brian Hardgroove clarifying that the song was anti-abuse of power, not anti-law enforcement. The flames of controversy were flamed when Professor Griff, one of the group's members, told *The Washington Times* that Jewish people are responsible for "The majority of wickedness that goes on across the globe." The article was published in May 1989, after which Chuck D fired Professor Griff; Lee's film was set to come out two months later and the group wanted to avoid the firestorm that would follow in the wake of his comments. The group got back together a year later.

LOSER

Beck

-

1994

"I don't think I would have been able to go in and do 'Loser' in a six-hour shot without having been somewhat prepared," Beck told *Elle* magazine. "It was accidental, but it was something I'd been working on for a long time."

Part of that preparation was living as a homeless musician in New York City, where his financial woes became such that he had to move back home to Los Angeles in 1991. He started playing coffeehouses in between jobs, where his particular style of performing caught the ear of Tom Rothrock, co-owner of an independent record label. "I'd be banging away on a Son House tune and the whole audience would be talking, so maybe out of desperation or boredom, or the audience's boredom, I'd make up these ridiculous songs just to see if people were listening. 'Loser' was an extension of that." Rothrock introduced Beck to record producer Karl Stephenson, with whom he ended up creating the final version of the song. Beck, who tried to channel his inner Chuck D of Public Enemy when rapping the vocals, said of the chorus "When [Stephenson] played it back, I thought, 'Man, I'm the worst rapper in the world, I'm just a loser.'"

COME TOGETHER

The Beatles

1969

"The thing was created in the studio," John Lennon, talking about "Come Together," recalled in an interview with *Playboy*. "It's gobbledygook; 'Come Together' was an expression that [Timothy] Leary had come up with for his attempt at being president or whatever he wanted to be, and he asked me to write a campaign song. I tried and tried, but I couldn't come up with one. But I came up with this, 'Come Together,' which would've been no good to him—you couldn't have a campaign song like that, right?" Leary was running for governor of California in the 1970 election against Ronald Reagan, a campaign that was cut short at the end of 1969 after Leary was charged with possession of marijuana. The song was penned by Lennon as a thank you to Leary after he contributed to the chorus of "Give Peace a Chance."

"The Learys wanted me to write them a campaign song, and their slogan was come together," Lennon told *Rolling Stone*. Leary was given an incomplete demo, which he distributed to a few California radio stations, but never received a complete track. "I never got around to it, and I ended up writing 'Come Together' instead," Lennon recalled.

The original version of the song was speedier, which Paul McCartney addressed in *The Beatles Anthology*. "I said, 'Let's slow it down with a swampy bass-and-drums vibe.' I came up with a bass line, and it all flowed from there." He also commented on not being a featured vocalist in a 1970 interview with *The Evening Standard*, saying: "Even on Abbey Road we don't do harmonies like we used to. I think it's sad. On 'Come Together' I would have liked to sing harmony with John, and I think he would have liked me to, but I was too embarrassed to ask him, and I don't work to the best of my abilities in that situation."

The song, which hit No. 1 in the U.S. and No. 4 in the U.K., bore striking similarities to Chuck Berry's "You Can't Catch Me." A lawsuit was brought on by Morris Levy, who owned the rights to the song, in 1973; the result was an out-of-court settlement that ordered Lennon to record covers of three other songs owned by Levy.

ROCKIN' IN THE FREE WORLD

Neil Young

1989

"Rockin' in the Free World" has been adopted by many as a patriotic anthem, despite its scathing indictment of the America's political climate in the late-1980s. As *Thrasher* pointed out, some of the lyrics are taken verbatim from President George H.W. Bush. Neil Young coupled Bush's phrases with a few of his own, in an effort to emphasize the emptiness in Bush's promises.

In *Shakey: Neil Young's Biography* by Jimmy McDonough, "Rockin' in the Free World" was inspired by newspaper photos of mourners for the Ayatollah Khomeini burning American flags in the streets. "Whatever we do, we shouldn't go near the Mideast," Frank Sampedro, a guitarist, told Young while on tour. "It's probably better we just keep on rockin' in the free world." With Sampedro's blessing, Young decided to write a song around that concept. Though most accounts are consistent in that Sampedro comes up with the line, some differ when it comes to what inspired it. This is worth noting on account of the fact that Ayatollah Khomeini died after the song was first performed live. Regardless, it's likely that some form of intense overseas protest started the conversation.

...BABY ONE MORE TIME

Britney Spears

-

1998

"I had been in studio for about six months listening and recording material, but I hadn't really heard a hit yet," said Britney Spears, in an interview with *Billboard*. "When I started working with Max Martin in Sweden, he played the demo for 'Baby One More Time' for me, and I knew from the start it [was one] of those songs you want to hear again and again. It just felt really right. I went into the studio and did my own thing with it, trying to give it a little more attitude than the demo. In 10 days, I never even saw Sweden. We were so busy."

Martin, a music producer, first showed Spears the song as she began recording her debut album in 1998, having just had a full album ordered by Jive Records president Clive Calder a month after submitting a demo to the record label. Spears recalled not doing well on the first day of recording, saying that she was "just too nervous." She went on to say that she "went out that night and had some fun. The next day I was completely relaxed and nailed it. You gotta be relaxed singing 'Baby One More Time.'" The song was originally recorded for the Backstreet Boys and TLC, but both bands rejected it. Spears, on the other hand, fell in love with the song; she claims that she knew it would be a hit, and executives at Jive said the song was a "smash."

SORRY

Justin Bieber

-

2015

"We were in a session, and we were asked to go write with (writer/producer) Blood Diamonds late one night," said Julia Michaels, co-writer of Justin Bieber's hit "Sorry." "So we went to this session. Sometimes you hear a track, and you instantly know what you want to do on it. For some reason, the word "sorry" popped out of my head—we were in a (vocal) booth and Justin Tranter and I just hashed it out from there. Then we sent [the demo] in, and Chelsea Avery, who works with [Bieber's manager Scooter Braun], loved the song and sent it to Justin Bieber. [Bieber] loved the song and he changed a couple things to make it feel more like him, because it's his song he wanted to make it feel specific to him. It was crazy. . .we wrote the song in about 40 minutes. We finished it and said, 'Oh that's really fun, let's go to dinner,' and three weeks later (after Bieber recorded and released it), the song was everywhere!"

Bieber had hesitations about the song; though he really liked it, he thought that it might be a little bit too safe. Both Blood and Skrillex, who worked with Bieber on *Purpose*, disagreed. Said Blood, "From the perspective of the producer, I find the muffled vocal chops to represent the people or situations in which Justin or the listener could be apologetic towards. The vocal manipulations make an ambiguous sound and a moment later Justin replies. I love that narrative. Justin's vocal delivery and the triumphant key of the song gave the narrative a warm color. I am most excited by music that allows the beat to tell a story as much as the vocal and in 'Sorry,' the beat is saying moving forward, and apologizing, can be exciting and fun." Bieber eventually came around, saying that "the more [he] listened to it the more [he] fell in love with it. The melodies are really catchy and some people would misinterpret

"I am most excited by music that allows the beat to tell a story as much as the vocal and in 'Sorry,' the beat is saying moving forward, and apologizing."

that for being safe. . .but it's like The Beatles 'Let It Be,' simple melodies but it's so effective. Music right now is missing those effective real songs."

WALK ON THE WILD SIDE

Lou Reed

-

1972

Perhaps inspired by the struggle with his own sexuality, Lou Reed's "Walk on the Wild Side" was inspired by the "superstars" at Andy Warhol's The Factory. The song deals with cross-dressing prostitutes living in New York City. "Candy" was based on a transgender woman named Candy Darling, "Little Joe" was a reference to Joe Dallesandro, an actor who claimed that the song's lyrics were based on his Flesh character and not himself. "Sugar Plum Fairy" was based on a Joe Campbell character by the same name in the 1965 film *My Hustler*, and "Jackie" was based on Jackie Curtis, another actor in the Warhol scene. Then there was "Holly," who was based on the transgender actress Holly Woodlawn. She ran away from home and hitchhiked from Miami Beach to New York City to escape constant bullying from other teenagers.

"In New York I was living on the street," Woodlawn told *The Guardian*. "Then I met Jackie Curtis and Candy Darling, and they'd watch Marlene Dietrich and Greta Garbo movies at 1 a.m. There was this club called Max's Kansas City. Jackie and Candy had just done this movie called *Flesh*, and they said, 'You have to meet Andy [Warhol]. He's gonna make you a superstar.' I didn't want to be a superstar. My wig looked like yak hair. One day Jackie put on a show and I was in the chorus. I saw this bag of glitter and a jar of Vaseline, and smeared myself with it and got this boyfriend to throw the glitter on me. [Director] Paul Morrissey said, 'I don't know who she is but she's a star.' Next thing Paul's calling me up to star in a movie called *Trash*, and the rest is history. One day a friend called me and said, 'Turn on the radio!' They were playing 'Walk on the Wild Side.' The funny thing is that, while I knew the Velvet Underground's music, I'd never met Lou Reed. I called him up and said, 'How do you know this stuff about me?' He said, 'Holly, you have the biggest mouth in town.' We met and we've been friends ever since."

Reed referred to "Walk on the Wild Side" as being an "outright gay song," noting that the lyrics were "carefully worded so the straights can miss out on the implications and enjoy them without being offended." It worked—the song wasn't censored by a number of prominent radio stations despite overt references to sexual acts.

PAPER PLANES

M.I.A.

-

2007

M.I.A. explored the genesis of "Paper Planes" in an interview with *Fader* magazine, saying: "I worked on it with Wesley [Pentz, aka Diplo]. I think 'Paper Planes' is Wes' idea, and Dave [Taylor, aka M.I.A.'s collaborator Switch] worked on it. We worked on it in London to get the sound of it right. But the idea was Wes', with the Clash 'Straight to Hell' sample.

Speaking about the unique vocals on the song, M.I.A. didn't see what all the fuss was about. "That's how I sing. Most the time when I go into the studio to sing, I get really bored. If I'm going to sing then I'm going to have to sing a bit weird. But with that one I just woke up and just sang the whole song in one go. It was in the morning and I wasn't thinking too much. I hadn't brushed my teeth."

The song, which features samples of a gun reloading and a cash register ringing, is a reflection of visa troubles M.I.A was having at the time. "[The samples were] a joke. I was having this stupid visa problem and I didn't know what it was, aside from them thinking that I might to fly a plane into the Trade Center—which is the only reason that they would put me through this. I actually recorded that in Brooklyn, in Bed-Stuy. I was thinking about living there, waking up every morning—it's such an African neighborhood. . . .People don't really feel like immigrants or refugees contribute to culture in any way. That they're just leeches that suck from whatever."

ROCKET MAN

Elton John

-

1972

In a video posted to Elton John's YouTube channel, he and songwriter Bernie Taupin discussed the origins of "Rocket Man." John started, saying, "'Rocket Man' was our first-ever No. 1 record, I think. It was on the *Honky Château* record, and it was a pretty easy song to write the melody to, because it's a song about space. So it's quite a spacious song."

Taupin then chimed in: "Yeah. Actually, the interesting thing about 'Rocket Man' is that people identify it, unfortunately, with David Bowie's 'Space Oddity.' It actually wasn't inspired by that at all. It was inspired by a story by Ray Bradbury, from his book of science fiction short stories called *The Illustrated Man*. In that book there's a story called 'The Rocket Man', which was about how astronauts in the future would become an everyday job. So I kind of took that idea and ran with it."

John, referencing the many misconceptions about the song, then said: "No one ever knew that."

JUMP

Van Halen

-

1983

"I just happened to be very much into playing keyboards at the time," legendary guitarist Eddie Van Halen recalled in the television special *Song to Soul.* "So, because I was playing so much piano and keyboard, somehow a keyboard song came through me. Where it came from? Some experience. I don't remember if it was getting my ass kicked down the street, or a girlfriend breaking up with me, or a bad hot dog or what. We're all filters, you know? Or sponges. You soak stuff up, you squeeze it out, (and) whatever comes out, well. . .it was 'Jump,' that time."

Ever modest, Van Halen had just laid the foundation for the band's only chart-topping hit, though the concept was initially rejected by the rest of the group. Wrote Richard Crousse in his book *Who Wrote The Book Of Love?*: "Guitarist Eddie Van Halen had written the track two years previously only to have it spurned by the band. 'We don't need this sh*t,' was reportedly the reaction of one band member. At the goading of producer Ted Templeton and Warner Brothers, the heavy-metal band was persuaded to resurrect the lilting synthesizer riff."

"Jump" marked the beginning of the end for that iteration of Van Halen, as David Lee Roth couldn't condone the stylistic shift, even just for one song. That said, Warner Brothers had set a January 1, 1984 release date, and the band needed songs for their album *1984*. Roth played the recording in his 1951 Mercury Lowrider over and over again, letting his mind wander until he found some sort of lyrical inspiration. "Sprawled in the tufted leather backseat of the vintage car, Roth let his mind drift to a television newscast he'd seen the night before," Crousse wrote. "Live coverage showed a man perched on the ledge of a skyscraper, threatening to jump. Imagining himself in the crowd outside the skyscraper, Roth wondered what their reaction would be. Using [a roadie] as a sounding board, Roth leaned over the front seat, asking the roadie what he thought of the lyrics."

"He's probably the most responsible for how it came out," Roth told *Musician*. Though Roth eventually rejoined Van Halen, the success of "Jump" wasn't enough to justify the use of a synthesizer, leading him to leave the band.

ALL THE YOUNG DUDES

Mott the Hoople

1972

Widely regarded as an anthem for glam rock, "All the Young Dudes" was written by David Bowie for the band Mott the Hoople after he heard that they were breaking up due to a lack of commercial success. Bowie was so intent on getting this song to the band that he penned the lyrics while sitting on the floor in front of the band's lead singer, Ian Hunter. Bowie claims that the song, which hit the No. 3 spot in the U.K. Singles Chart, is often misinterpreted; Lou Reed once said "It's a Gay Anthem! A rallying call to the young dudes to come out in the streets and show that they were beautiful and gay and proud of it."

As it turns out, the song was never intended to be an anthem, but a message of the apocalypse. "The time is five years to go before the end of the earth. It has been announced that the world will end because of lack of natural resources. Ziggy [Stardust] is in a position where all the kids have access to things that they thought they wanted. The older people have lost all touch with reality and the kids are left on their own to plunder anything. Ziggy was in a rock and roll band and the kids no longer want rock and roll. There's no electricity to play it. Ziggy's adviser tells him to collect news and sing it, 'cause there is no news. So Ziggy does this and there is terrible news. 'All the Young Dudes' is a song about this news. It is no hymn to the youth as people thought. It is completely the opposite," Bowie told author William Burroughs in an interview with *Rolling Stone.* Oddly enough, "All the Young Dudes" was only written because Mott the Hoople rejected Bowie's first song, "Suffragette City."

"It is no hymn to the youth as people thought. It is completely the opposite."

JESUS WALKS

Kanye West

-

2004

"Kanye and I grew up together," Che Smith, the co-writer of Kanye West's "Jesus Walks," told *The Guardian* newspaper in a 2006 interview. "I found a gospel song by a choir of reformed drug addicts in New York. Even though I'm not a Christian it moved me and the beat was kinda like a rap groove. We jacked the whole song but it came to life when Kanye added the army sounds and made it like God's soldiers. Then the writing began. If you make the verses about Jesus it takes away the power of the chorus, so the verses were the sinner speaking. We got the [n-word] sound from a Curtis Mayfield song.

"When we write together we'll listen to a beat and I'll come up with a line and he'll flip it around into something else, then I'll add more lines and before you know it we got a song. Kanye will remember each way we flipped it; he has an ability to memorize. I look at it like this: that was not my record and not Kanye's record; that was a record from the creator to his creations. I'm grateful."

SEVEN NATION ARMY

The White Stripes

-

2003

"I thought if I ever got to write the next James Bond theme, that would be the riff for it," Jack White once said about his famous riff that plays through most of his "Seven Nation Army." He came up with it while warming up his guitar for a show in Melbourne, Australia.

"There's an employee here at Third Man [Records] named Ben Swank," White recalled, "and he was with us on tour in Australia when I wrote that song at soundcheck. I was playing it for Meg [White] and he was walking by and I said, 'Swank, check this riff out.' And he said, 'It's OK.'"

The song deals with a person finding out that his friends are gossiping about him behind his back. "He feels so bad he has to leave town, but you get so lonely you come back," he said. "The song's about gossip. It's about me, Meg, and the people we're dating." Though Jack and Meg White divorced in 2000, they continued to be prevalent figures in each other's lives as a result of The White Stripes' success.

Jack White would eventually get to play on a James Bond theme, teaming with Alicia Keys on the song "Another Way to Die" for the 2008 film *Quantum of Solace*.

STAN

Eminem ft. Dido

-

2000

When asked about his hit "Stan," Eminem said, "Basically it's just about crazy fan mail that I get from people. It's about a kid who is really sick and takes everything that I say literally. Like, if I say 'I wanna slit my wrist,' he'll slit his wrist. It's like, he's crazy for real and I'm not. Everything I say, he can relate to. . . it's kind of like a message to the fans to let them know that everything that I say is not meant to be taken literally. Just most of the things that I say."

"It's like, for people to look up to me like this is really crazy for me. I go through things in my head every day, like 'What is going on?'"

He continued, "Yeah, I get crazy letters like that. That's what I'm saying, you know? All of this is crazy to me, I never knew that I'd have all of this. It's all a little bit much for me to even imagine. It's like, for people to look up to me like this is really crazy for me. I go through things in my head every day, like 'What is going on?'"

SHE'S NOT THERE

The Zombies

-

1964

"The idea was that we'd record the Gershwins' 'Summertime' as our first single," Rod Argent, The Zombies' keyboardist said while discussing "She's Not There." "But a couple of weeks before we were due to go in our producer Ken Jones said: 'You should really try and write something for the session.' I had only ever written one song before." The session came as a result of the band winning a talent contest at their college.

"She's Not There" started as a single verse that Argent played for Jones following a 1964 performance at St. Albans Market Hall. Seeing potential in the verse, Jones encouraged Argent to keep writing so that they could record it at their studio session set to happen several weeks later. Argent found inspiration in one of the track names listed on a John Lee Hooker album. The song, "No One Told Me," lent its name to the opening line of "She's Not There." "If you play that John Lee Hooker song you'll hear 'No one told me, it was just a feeling I had inside' but there's nothing in the melody or the chords that's the same," Argent recalled. "It was just the way that little phrase just tripped off the tongue. I'd always thought of the verse of 'She's Not There' to be mainly [A minor] to D. But what I'd done, quite unconsciously, was write this little modal sequence incorporating those chord changes. There was an additional harmonic influence in that song. In the second section it goes from D to D minor and the bass is on the thirds, [F sharp] and F, a little device I'd first heard in 'Sealed with a Kiss' and it really attracted me, that chord change with bass notes not on the roots. And I'm sure I was showing off in the solo as much as I could!"

The song reached No. 12 in the U.K. singles chart and No. 2 on the *Billboard* Hot 100, making it The Zombies' biggest hit. The song received a huge boost while appearing on the television show *Juke Box Jury*, where guest panelist George Harrison gave it a good review. The song was also the first hit song in the U.K. to feature an electric piano as a lead instrument. As for the song's final composition, Argent said "Words have to sit, they have to sort of combine seamlessly with the way the melody is being sung. I know I was very concerned with the lyrics on 'She's Not There' but in the sense that they had to really complement the melody. They had to stand on their own, and had to have their own rhythm and, in that last section I was using the words with different stresses at different times to propel it along towards the final chord. So lyrics have always been very important to me in that way, but not necessarily in a sense of having to explain something concrete. They're an important part of the jigsaw, because I think bad lyrics can screw up a song."

ROCK THE CASBAH

The Clash

-

1982

When asked in an interview about his involvement with "Rock the Casbah," The Clash drummer Topper Headon responded, "I had been working on the idea on the piano for quite a while. By the time we came to record *Combat Rock*, which is the album that it was on, we were kind of on our last legs anyway. We hadn't been getting on too well. I turned up at the appointed time at the studio, which was midday, and Mick [Jones] and Paul [Simonon] were late, Joe [Strummer] was late, and I thought 'All right, here's a chance to get the piano track down.' I put the piano track down, and. . .sorry, no I didn't. I put the drum track down first, thinking that they would turn up and I could say, 'Let's work on this as an idea.' They still weren't there, so I decided also, I had already put the piano on top of the drums, so I put the bass down, because I can play the bass in D and I can play the piano in D. They still didn't show up, so I put some percussion on. By the time Joe, Paul, and Mick had gotten there, I said, 'I'd like to play this idea.' And they listened to it and went, 'Well that's great, we don't have to do anything. I said, 'Wait a minute, I've only done half of it, there're supposed to be like four verses and two choruses and an intro.' So they said, 'Well, we can splice the tape.' In those days, we had that two-inch tape. We spliced it and made the backing track twice as long. Joe then went into the toilet, and within about 15 or 20 minutes came out with the words. Then, because Mick hadn't been involved up till now, he went into the studio and put his wristwatch on it, much to my annoyance. He had to be in on that track."

WATERFALLS

TLC

-

1994

Jarett E. Nolan famously pointed out that TLC's "Waterfalls" was the first song to ever reach No. 1 on the *Billboard* Hot 100 while also referencing AIDS in one of its verses.

Fitting, considering that one of the co-writers, Lisa "Left Eye" Lopes, was huge on HIV-AIDS awareness; when performing, she would often wear Trojan sunglasses and attach condoms to her clothing. The broader intention of the song was to encourage individuals to consider the consequences of their actions and the long-term effects they can have on your life. The song highlights the dangers of dealing drugs for money and having casual, irresponsible sex for pleasure.

WISH YOU WERE HERE

Pink Floyd

-

1975

"Although 'Shine On You Crazy Diamond' is specifically about Syd [Barrett]," David Gilmour said in the documentary *Pink Floyd: The Story of Wish You Were Here*, "and 'Wish You Were Here' has a broader remit, I can't sing it without thinking about Syd." Their former front man had suffered a complete mental breakdown; his addiction to psychedelic drugs and schizophrenic behavior resulted in his becoming increasingly distant. Barrett left the band in 1968, having been unable to contribute anything of value to Pink Floyd after the album *A Saucerful of Secrets*, and, according to Roger Waters, spent his final recording session with the band playing a trick on them. He presented the song "Have You Got It Yet" to the group and, as they were playing it, would make meaningless changes to its arrangement, all the while singing "Have you got it yet?" Waters called it "a real act of mad genius."

Absence and detachment are prominent themes in "Wish You Were Here," as the band had grown disconnected from one another in the wake of the massive success that was *The Dark Side of the Moon*. They rarely recorded together, having lost the camaraderie they had when their music was more cult and less commercial. Barrett's decline into madness made matters worse. The disconnect would never really heal, and Waters eventually left the band after years of fighting with

Gilmour. But the loss of their friend was enough to bring the two together for "Wish You Were Here," as Gilmour had the riff and helped Waters, who wrote the lyrics, come up with the chorus.

WE WILL ROCK YOU

Queen

1977

"We did an encore and then went off," said Queen guitarist Brian May, referring to a show at Birmingham's Bingley Hall during the band's 1977 British Tour. "And instead of just keeping clapping, they sang 'You'll Never Walk Alone' to us, and we were just completely knocked out and taken aback—it was quite an emotional experience really, and I think these chant things are in some way connected to that. . . .I went to bed thinking, 'What could you ask them to do?' They're all squeezed in there, but they can clap their hands, they can stamp their feet, and they can sing. In the morning I woke up and had the idea in my head for 'We Will Rock You.'" The idea, as May put it, was to "create a song that the audience could participate in."

SPIRIT IN THE SKY

Norman Greenbaum

-

1970

"I thought, 'Yeah, I could do that,' knowing nothing about gospel music," said Norman Greenbaum, speaking about his reaction to watching Porter Wagoner sing a gospel song on television. "So I sat down and wrote my own gospel song. It came easy. I wrote the words in 15 minutes." The result was "Spirit in the Sky," a song that sold two million copies from 1969 to 1970 and is rated No. 333 on *Rolling Stone*'s list of "The 500 Greatest Songs of All Time."

Greenbaum, a man of Jewish faith and a former goat farmer, got his start with Dr. West's Medicine Show and Junk Band, a psychedelic jug band, before earning a solo contract with producer Erik Jacobsen. Though Greenbaum is widely considered to be a one-hit wonder, his is a lasting one, and he stated: "It sounds as fresh today as when it was recorded. I've gotten letters from funeral directors telling me that it's their second-most-requested song to play at memorial services, next to 'Danny Boy.'"

BILLIE JEAN

Michael Jackson

-

1983

"Billie Jean is kind of anonymous," Michael Jackson explained. "It represents a lot of girls. They used to call them groupies in the '60s. They would hang around backstage doors, and any band that would come to town they would have a relationship with, and I think I wrote this out of experience with my brothers when I was little. There were a lot of Billie Jeans out there. Every girl claimed that their son was related to one of my brothers."

In his autobiography, *Moonwalk*, Jackson gets detailed about realizing that the song could resonate with people. "A musician knows hit material," he wrote. "It has to feel right. Everything has to feel in place. It fulfills you and it makes you feel good. You know it when you hear it. That's how I felt about 'Billie Jean.' I knew it was going to be big while I was writing it. I was really absorbed in that song. One day during a break in a recording session I was riding down the Ventura Freeway with Nelson Hayes, who was working with me at the time. 'Billie Jean' was going around in my head and that's all

"We were getting off the freeway when a kid on a motorcycle pulls up to us and says, 'Your car's on fire.'. . .If the car had exploded, we could have been killed. But I was so absorbed by this tune floating in my head that I didn't even focus on the awful possibilities until later."

I was thinking about. We were getting off the freeway when a kid on a motorcycle pulls up to us and says, 'Your car's on fire.' Suddenly we noticed the smoke and pulled over and the whole bottom of the Rolls-Royce was on fire. That kid probably saved our lives. If the car had exploded, we could have been killed. But I was so absorbed by this tune floating in my head that I didn't even focus on the awful possibilities until later."

Fitting that the story appeared in an autobiography titled *Moonwalk*, as Jackson debuted the famous dance move while performing "Billie Jean" on a television show called *Motown 25: Yesterday, Today, Forever.* Don't be surprised that the song moved Jackson so much. As he told producer Quincy Jones during an argument over the song's intro, "But that's the jelly! That's what makes me want to dance."

BABA O'RILEY

The Who

1971

"There is this moment of standing there just listening to this music and looking out to the audience and just thinking, 'I f--king did that. I wrote that," Pete Townshend told *Rolling Stone*. "I just hope that on my deathbed I don't embarrass myself by asking someone, 'Can you pass me my guitar? And will you run the backing tape of 'Baba O'Riley'? I just want to do it one more time.'" Townshend originally penned "Baba O'Riley" for *Lifehouse*, a follow-up to The Who's *Tommy*. The setting was England, a polluted wasteland hosting a concert, an event that helped inspire the phrase "Teenage Wasteland."

Said Townshend: "A self-sufficient drop-out family group farming in a remote part of Scotland decide to return South to investigate rumors of a subversive concert event that promises to shake and wake up apathetic, fearful British society. Ray is married to Sally, they hope to link up with their daughter Mary who has run away from home to attend the concert. They travel through the scarred wasteland of middle England in a motor caravan, running an air conditioner they hope will protect them from pollution. There are regular people, but they're the scum off the surface; there's a few farmers there, that's where the thing from 'Baba O'Riley' comes in. It's mainly young people who are either farmer's kids whose parents can't afford to buy them [expensive] suits; then there's just scum, like these two geezers who ride around in a battered-up old Cadillac limousine and they play old Who records on the tape deck. . .I call them Track fans."

"I could feel in the audience was—I won't say religious—but there was certainly a spiritual component to what people wanted their music to contain."

The project was squashed and the songs salvaged, with "Baba O'Riley" one of eight to make it on to the band's 1971 *Who's Next*. The album would go on to be the most successful thing the band put out in their decades-long run, thanks in large part to the opening track. Townshend talked to *Billboard* magazine 40 years after the song was released and said: "the music there was about living in the present and losing yourself in the moment. Now that has changed. Boomers kind of hang on to that as a memory. When I go back and listen to those songs, The Who songs in particular of the late '60s and early '70s, there was an aspiration in my writing to attune to the fact that what I could feel in the audience was—I won't say religious—but there was certainly a spiritual component to what people wanted their music to contain. There's definitely a higher call for the music now which is almost religious. U2, for example, are hugely successful with songs about inner longing for freedom, ideas. . . .What we fear is that in actual fact we have wasted an opportunity. I think I speak for my audience when I say that, I hope I do."

SEMI-CHARMED LIFE

Third Eye Blind

1997

"It's a song about always wanting something," Stephan Jenkins, Third Eye Blind's lead singer, told *Reverb*. "It's about never being satisfied, and reaching backwards to things that you've lost and towards things that you can never get. I think everybody has some identification with that. The story line between the people, the demise of this relationship, is just an extreme example of that condition. I think that's what makes people really relate to 'Semi-Charmed Life.'"

In an interview with *SongFacts*, Jenkins said, "A fan recently tweeted me—I have a lot of exchanges with fans on Twitter. It seems to be a manageable level of exchange. They said, 'I listen to that song because for one moment it's summer and everything is perfect.' I was like, 'Huh?' The song was always about falling apart, so it makes sense that perfection is the moment right before gravity comes back in."

Jenkins has also said that the song was meant to provide a San Franciscan perspective to the narrative provided in Lou Reed's "Walk on the Wild Side," from which the band borrowed the "doot doot doot" part for their 1997 hit.

WATCHING THE DETECTIVES

Elvis Costello

1977

Born Declan McManus in 1954, Elvis Costello approached music with an aggression that would have been easily dismissed had it not been backed by an unflappable confidence. That confidence, or "arrogance," as the English musician puts it, had him drawing inspiration from what he felt was an underwhelming record from The Clash.

"I wrote it when I heard the first Clash record," Costello said of his "Watching the Detectives." "I sort of locked myself in the flat that we were living in and listened to their record over and over again through headphones. It was the new thing, and I wanted to know what this thing was about. Reggae was part of my teenage years, as party music. But this was the more radical, political reggae. By the end of it, I thought, with the arrogance of youth, 'Well, I can do better than this.' So I just wrote the whole song. There was that reggae part of it going on and, also, I had grown up on all the American detective shows. All that music, some of it by Bernard Herrman, some of it by Neil Hefti. In the piano part, I had the idea of having these parts [*sings jittery counterpoint lines*]. That's kind of like Herrman. We were trying to do these orchestral things but all we could afford was a piano. That's the charm of the record, is that it has this incredibly tough rhythm section and then it's got these things that came from other places. There's a noir thing going through a lot of the songs in my catalog. This is just the first one."

Costello has called the song his favorite from the first five years of his career.

TEARS IN HEAVEN

Eric Clapton

-

1991

Eric Clapton sought peace in his music, trying to come to grips with a tragedy that left him isolated for a time. As he told *ABC News* in an interview, "I almost subconsciously used music for myself as a healing agent, and lo and behold, it worked.... I have got a great deal of happiness and a great deal of healing from music." The grief was born out of the loss of his 4-year-old son Conor, who fell out of the 53rd-floor window of a New York City apartment in 1991. This came just seven months after the loss of his friend Stevie Ray Vaughan, who was killed in a helicopter accident along with Clapton's manager and two of his roadies. After a period of inactivity, Clapton began working on a movie called *Rush*, where he partnered with songwriter Will Jennings.

As Jennings recalled in an interview with *SongFacts*: "Eric and I were engaged to write a song for a movie called *Rush*. We wrote a song called 'Help Me Up' for the end of the movie... then Eric saw another place in the movie for a song and he said to me, 'I want to write a song about my boy.' Eric had the first verse of the song written, which, to me, is all the song, but he wanted me to write the rest of the verse lines and the release, even though I told him that it was so personal he should write everything himself. He told me that he had admired the work I did with Steve Winwood and finally there was nothing else but to do as he requested, despite the sensitivity of the subject. This is a song so personal and so sad that it is unique in my experience of writing songs."

Clapton stopped playing the song in 2004, saying that he no longer felt the loss to the degree that he did when he wrote the song. He did bring it back for his 50th anniversary world tour in 2013.

SWEET DREAMS (ARE MADE OF THIS)

Eurythmics

1983

"I can't think of any other couple that did what we did—to break up and then start a band," Eurythmics' Dave Stewart told *The Guardian* in a 2016 interview. "Sonny and Cher did it the other way around: They were famous, then they broke up. What we went through was insane." Stewart is referring to his partnership with musician Annie Lennox, with whom he had an extensive, decade-spanning relationship. "I know every tiny molecule of Annie," he claimed.

They met in 1976 and became romantically involved shortly thereafter, bonding over music to the point where they eventually formed a band called The Catch with musician Peet Coombes. The Catch would become The Tourists, who went on to enjoy a decent level of success before breaking up in 1980. Oddly enough, the breakup would mark the end of the romantic partnership between Stewart and Lennox, and enabled them to form a new musical group called Eurythmics. "When we broke up as a couple for some strange reason it was like we were always going to be together, no matter what," Stewart says in his book, titled *The Dave Stewart Songbook*. "We couldn't really break that spell so we just carried on making music. This causes many problems, yet through all of this we ended up writing a lot of great songs, some were about 'our' relationship and some were about our relationship with the world around us. Whatever we wrote always had a dark side and a light side and in a way I describe it as 'realistic music,' full of the ups and downs of real relationships and life itself."

The duo was broke when they formed Eurythmics and were forced to take out a loan from the bank in order to purchase equipment, which included a drum machine and an eight-track recorder. Those, along with Lennox' keyboard and Stewart's synthesizer, were enough to lay the foundation for their defining hit "Sweet Dreams (Are Made Of This)." Lennox came up with the title, while Stewart had the idea to create a bit of a break in the middle of the song. "I suggested there had to be another bit, and that bit should be positive," Stewart told *SongFacts*. "So in the middle we added these chord changes rising upwards. . . .To us it was a major breakthrough. It just goes from beginning to end and the whole song is a chorus, there is not one note that is not

"The whole song is a chorus, there is not one note that is not a hook."

a hook." The song was very well received, reaching No. 2 on the U.K. Singles Chart and No. 1 on the U.S. *Billboard* Hot 100. It was also the band's first single released in the United States.

The hit is more than a song for Lennox, who believes it approaches the level of mantra. "It contains an overview of human existence. Whatever it is that makes you tick, that is what it is," she told Malcolm Bragg on *The South Bank Show*.

WHITE ROOM

Cream

-

1968

Cream owes a fair portion of their success to Pete Brown, a poet friend of bass player Jack Bruce. It was his room that inspired the band's hit "White Room," and it was his writing that made the hit possible in the first place. In an interview with *SongFacts*, Brown said, "It was a meandering thing about a relationship that I was in and how I was at the time. It was a kind of watershed period really. It was a time before I stopped being a relative barman and became a songwriter, because I was a professional poet, you know. I was doing poetry readings and making a living from that. It wasn't a very good living, and then I got asked to work by [drummer Ginger Baker] and Jack with them and then started to make a kind of living. And there was this kind of transitional period where I lived in this actual white room and was trying to come to terms with various things that were going on. It's a place where I stopped, I gave up all drugs and alcohol at that time in 1967 as a result of being in the white room, so it was a kind of watershed period. That song's like a kind of weird little movie: it changes perspectives all the time. That's why it's probably lasted—it's got a kind of mystery to it."

FAKE PLASTIC TREES

Radiohead

-

1995

"I was given a brief from the record company to deliver a follow-up to 'Creep' for the American market," producer John Leckie told *Blender*. "But Radiohead don't think in terms of making hit singles, and they were disowning 'Creep.'" The 1993 single was a worldwide hit; as singer Thom Yorke put it: "[Fans] used to come for the first U.S. tour and f*ck off after we played 'Creep' mid-set. I wish they never turned up in the first place!"

All the same, the band wasn't done making music, and they were never going to depart from a creative process that had always been true to who they were.

Yorke claims that "Fake Plastic Trees" was conceived as the result of a "drunken evening and, well, a breakdown of sorts." He sat on the melody that he had "no idea what to do with" until Leckie decided to utilize a cellist and violinist for a few of the tracks that they were recording, as they were already going to be in studio to play on the track "(Nice Dream)." "So the night before the string players arrived," Leckie said, "Thom went into the studio—under duress, really—and recorded a take of 'Fake Plastic Trees.'"

"That was one of the worst days for me. I spent the first five or six hours at the studio just throwing a wobbly."

"That was one of the worst days for me," Yorke elaborated. "I spent the first five or six hours at the studio just throwing a wobbly. I shouted at everyone, and then John Leckie sent everybody else away. He sat me down, and I did a guide vocal on 'Fake Plastic Trees.'" Guitarist Jonny Greenwood claimed that Yorke "burst into tears" after the third take, while engineer Nigel Godrich described the session as "deeply moving."

Yorke got the title for the song from Canary Wharf, an area of east London littered with artificial plants.

BITTER SWEET SYMPHONY

The Verve

1997

"This was certainly the most successful track I've done," said Martin "Youth" Glover, a producer on "Bitter Sweet Symphony."

"I think [Verve lead singer Richard Ashcroft] had actually cut a version with John Leckie but, by the time I came on board, he didn't want to do the song. I persuaded him to have a go at cutting a version but at first he wasn't really into it. It was only once we'd put strings on it that he started getting excited. Then, towards the end, Richard wanted to chuck all the album away and start again. What was my reaction? Horror. Sheer horror. All I could say was, 'I really think you should reconsider.'"

The 1997 hit started with The Staple Singers, whose 1961 "The Last Time" inspired the Rolling Stones' 1965 hit of the same name. That would go on to inspire a symphonic version of the Stones' song by the Andrew Oldham Orchestra, the main theme of which was sampled by The Verve for "Bitter Sweet Symphony."

Upon its release the song generated a ton of attention, particularly from major companies; Nike, Budweiser, and Coca-Cola all expressed interest. Members of The Verve were staunchly opposed to their work appearing in commercials, but their purist stance did nothing to quell accusations of plagiarism.

Though the details regarding the band's forfeit of the song's publishing rights are murky, the crux of the situation was that Allen Klein, former Rolling Stones manager, had the leverage to demand 100% of the royalties made by the song. According to his book, *Allen Klein: The Man Who Bailed Out the Beatles, Made the Stones, and Transformed Rock & Roll*, Ashcroft was given $1,000 when he signed over his rights to the song. When asked about what transpired by *Q Magazine*, Keith Richards replied, "I'm out of whack here, this is serious lawyer sh*t. If The Verve can write a better song, they can keep the money." Oldham wasn't so charitable, telling *Uncut* magazine: "As for Richard Ashcroft, well, I don't know how an artist can be severely damaged by that experience. Songwriters have learned to call songs their children, and he thinks he wrote something. He didn't. I hope he's got over it. It takes a while."

"He thinks he wrote something. He didn't. I hope he's got over it. It takes a while."

Ashcroft did write the song's lyrics and had a hand in much of its instrumentation. As a result of the alleged plagiarism, however, he had to share composer credit with Mick Jagger and Richards. Ashcroft, less than thrilled with this result, said that it was "The best song Jagger and Richards have written in 20 years."

TINY DANCER

Elton John

1971

Liberty Records placed an advertisement in the *New Musical Express* hoping to find competent songwriters to add to its staff. It's doubtful that the realistic intent was to provide the vehicle by which one of the most impactful duos in the history of music would be formed, yet that's exactly what happened when the ad piqued the interest of both Elton John and Bernie Taupin. The two met in 1967 and have worked together on 30 albums since.

Coming up with a list of five Elton John hits that Taupin didn't contribute lyrics to would be a tough task, as he has writing credits on songs such as "Daniel," "The B*tch Is Back," "Goodbye Yellow Brick Road," "Levon," and many more. Most notable among those songs is "Tiny Dancer," which went platinum in the United States despite having never been released as a single (the song's lack of a hook kept it out of singles consideration in the lead up to the release of *Madman Across the Water*). In an interview with *Rolling Stone*, Taupin shared what inspired his lyrics, saying "We came to California in the fall of 1970 and it seemed like sunshine just radiated from the populace. I guess I was trying to capture the spirit of that time, encapsulated by the women we met, especially at the clothes stores and restaurants and bars all up and down the Sunset Strip. They were these free spirits, sexy, all hip-huggers and lacy blouses, very ethereal the way they moved. They were just so different from what I'd been used to in England. They had this thing about embroidering your clothes. They wanted to sew patches on your jeans. They mothered you and slept with you. It was the perfect Oedipal complex."

Taupin's explanation to *Rolling Stone* flies in the face of the commonly held belief that his first wife, Maxine Feibelmann, inspired him to write the song. Although she may have been on Taupin's mind as he penned a line or two, it appears as though she fueled her husband's dedication to the song more than provided the inspiration for it.

ROCK AROUND THE CLOCK

Bill Haley & His Comets

-

1954

Recorded as part of a three-hour studio session, the bulk of which was spent laying down the track "Thirteen Women (and Only One Man in Town), Bill Haley & His Comets were only able to get two takes down before their time in the studio ran out. That proved to be long enough for a studio engineer, as they had produced enough audible material to be spliced together and included as a B-side to "Thirteen Women." The record experienced moderate success until Glenn Ford came along and chose "Rock Around the Clock" to play over the opening credits to the film *Blackboard Jungle*.

One million copies were sold the following March. "We were travelling on the New York thruway from Buffalo to Boston to do a television show," Marshall Lytle, bassist for the Comets, recalled. "I turned the radio on and 'Rock Around the Clock' was playing. This was a new Cadillac that Bill had just bought. It had one of those Selectrix dials where you just push the bar and it goes to the next station. I pushed the bar and it was playing again on another radio station. I pushed the bar again and it was playing again. At one given moment, it was playing five times on the dial. Within five minutes, I must've heard it a dozen times. I said: 'This is a monster hit.' When you hear a song that many times on that many different radio stations, you know damn well that it was a monster hit."

EYE OF THE TIGER

Survivor

-

1982

"We knew it was something special because we saw that movie in its rough form," Jim Peterik, co-writer of "Eye of the Tiger," told *The Tennessean*. "We wrote this for the movie. I got home one day, and there's my big, old answering machine. I hit 'Play' and I hear, 'Hey, yo, Jim that's a nice answering machine you got there. Give me a call. It's Sylvester Stallone.' I go, 'Yeah, right.' I play it back again (and say), 'Karen, does this sound like Stallone, or is that just Sal, my roadie?' 'No, that's him.' So I call him up, and he answers, 'Yo.' I go, 'Is this Sylvester Stallone? This is Jim Peterik.' He says, 'Yeah, call me Sly.' Suddenly, I'm calling him 'Sly'—a kid from Berwyn, Illinois! I was already this huge fan of Stallone anyway, me and my wife. He says, 'I've got this new movie called 'Rocky III,' and I don't want to use that 'Gonna Fly Now' song. It's a good song, but I want something for the kids. Something with a pulse. Can you help me out?' I go, 'Uh, is the Pope Catholic?'"

He continued: "The pressure was on, and the next day I rented a big Betamax Pro (an early video cassette player) and the FedEx came. [Co-writer Frankie Sullivan] came over, and we see this montage that we're supposed to write to. Mr. T rising up, and Stallone getting kind of soft, doing commercials. I had my Les Paul around my neck, and I just caught that vibe. I just started going (plays chugging guitar intro). And then the punches were being thrown, and I just went (plays power chords). It was like electricity in that room, but we couldn't get any further because we didn't know the story. But we had this amazing intro. The next day he sent us the whole movie, and that's when we really got the story. We were very inspired by this story, and Burgess Meredith, the trainer, going 'Rocky, you're losing the eye of the tiger.' I go, 'Bingo. There's our hook.' We went into the studio and demoed it. Stallone absolutely flipped. But he said, 'You got a little lazy on me. You didn't write me a third verse.' Busted. So we went back to the drawing board. . .and that demo version was the one that went in the film. That's how tight the schedule was. That's the demo."

(DON'T FEAR) THE REAPER

Blue Öyster Cult

-

1976

"'Guys, this is it!' Engineer Shelly Yakus announced at the end of the first take. 'The legendary once-in-a-lifetime groove!'" That passage, from *Mojo* magazine, describes the creation of Blue Öyster Cult's hit "(Don't Fear) the Reaper." The song, which featured a distinctive guitar riff and use of the cowbell, was the band's most successful piece of work; it was named Song of the Year in 1976 by *Rolling Stone*, and remained on the *Billboard* Hot 100 for 20 weeks.

The song was intended to speak to the inevitability of death and encourage the listener not to fear that which cannot be changed, though the song was interpreted by many to be about a fearlessness in regards to suicide. In a 1995 *College Music Journal* interview, songwriter Buck Dharma explained: "I felt that I had just achieved some kind of resonance with the psychology of people when I came up with that, I was actually kind of appalled when I first realized that some people were seeing it as an advertisement for suicide or something that was not my intention at all." His intention was to convey that people should, "not to be afraid of it (as opposed to actively bring it about). It's basically a love song where the love transcends the actual physical existence of the partners," Dharma elaborated in Issue 72 of *Performing Songwriter*. "I was thinking about my own mortality. I wrote the guitar riff, the first two lines of lyric sprung into my head, then the rest of it came as I formed a story about a love affair that transcends death. I was thinking about my wife, and that maybe we'd get together after I was gone."

"I formed a story about a love affair that transcends death. I was thinking about my wife, and that maybe we'd get together after I was gone."

"(Don't Fear) the Reaper" was introduced to a new audience in 2000, when *Saturday Night Live* ran a skit in which a producer (played by Christopher Walken) continued to call for "More Cowbell" during a studio recording of the song. The producer's name in the skit was Bruce Dickinson, who is a musical producer, though not the one on "(Don't Fear) The Reaper." The actual producer who called for the cowbell was

David Lucas, who told the *Just My Show* podcast that the song "needed some momentum." His answer? "More Cowbell!"

ENTER SANDMAN

Metallica

-

1991

Production efforts on Metallica songs usually required sewing pieces together, as the band often recorded each element of the song separately. "Enter Sandman" marked a departure from that, as producer Bob Rock suggested recording together rather than separately.

The song was born out a guitar riff that lead guitarist Kirk Hammett came up with. "It was very specific," he recalled on the radio show *Toucher and Rich*. "I have a very specific memory. It was about two or three o'clock in the morning. I had just been listening to *Louder Than Love*, the Soundgarden album. It was when Soundgarden [were] still somewhat underground and [were] on an independent label. I just love that album; it's a great Soundgarden album. And I heard that album, I was inspired, I picked up my guitar and out came that riff." As he later told *Rolling Stone*, "When Lars heard the riff, he said, 'That's really great. But repeat the first part four times.' It was that suggestion that made it even more hooky."

The song was among the first conceived for their *Metallica* album, but was the last to get lyrics. Part of the holdup was due to Hetfield's fear that the song sounded too commercial, a worry that he mitigated by writing lyrics that involved destroying "the perfect family" by means of a crib death. Rock, in his first time working with the band, convinced Hetfield to change the lyrics to make the song a touch friendlier for an audience, a request which Hetfield obliged. "I wanted more of the mental thing where this kid gets manipulated by what adults say," Hetfield said, speaking to *Uncut* about his rewritten lyrics. "And you know when you wake up with that sh*t in your eye? That's supposedly been put in there by the sandman to make you dream. So the guy in the song tells the little kid that and he kinda freaks. He can't sleep after that and it works the opposite way. Instead of a soothing thing, the tables turned."

UMBRELLA

Rihanna ft. Jay-Z

2007

"At first I was thinking about God," "Umbrella" songwriter Terius Nash told *Blender*. "Like, God would say, 'I've got you under my umbrella. I'll protect you.'"

The track started with Christopher Stewart playing hi-hat sounds on the Mac application GarageBand and, just several hours later, ended with all of the lyrics and chords composed. "I came in the house, and my wife was like, 'What's that look on your face?' Nash said of the night he arrived home after recording the demo. "So we get into the car to go to the movies, and as she's listening to the record she starts crying. She said, 'Boy, you done did it now! Now who's gonna sing this?'"

The song would go on to launch Rihanna, then just 19 years old, into the highest echelon of superstardom; it was one of the most played songs on the radio in the 2000s, despite having been released in 2007. The intent originally, however, was for the song to resurrect a one-time A-lister whose career was flatlining as a result of a personal meltdown. "Britney [Spears] was starting work on her new album, and her personal life was a little out of control," Nash recalled. "We thought, 'Let's save our friend; let's give her a record.'" Unbeknownst to Spears, her management company turned the track down on account of her album, *Blackout*, having a full track list. Nash and Stewart, who co-wrote the song, decided to shop the record around instead.

"When the demo first started playing, I was like, 'This is interesting, this is weird.'" Rihanna said. "But the song kept getting better. I listened to it over and over. I said, 'I need this record. I want to record it tomorrow.'" A break in communication almost prevented that from ever happening; as Rihanna was listening to the demo, Stewart was pitching it to an associate of Mary J. Blige, going as far as promising her the song if she wanted it. "My heart stopped in my chest," Rihanna recalled. "I knew we were never going to get

'Umbrella.' Who wouldn't want Mary J. to sing their record?" After much convincing—"I made the producers an offer they couldn't refuse," chairman of Island Def Jam Records Antonio Reid said—Rihanna was selected to carry the track.

IN BLOOM

Nirvana

1991

"When we first started playing that, it sounded like a Bad Brains song," bassist Krist Novoselic recalled in an interview with *Rolling Stone*, while talking about "In Bloom."

"But then Kurt went home and he hammered it. He kept working on it. Then he called me on the phone and said, 'Listen to this song.' He started singing it on the phone. You could hear the guitar. It was the 'In Bloom' of *Nevermind*, more of a pop thing. We were listening to things like the Smithereens then, and The Beatles. We had one tape we listened to in the van—this was before we recorded *Bleach*. On one side was the Smithereens. And on the other side was this heavy-metal band, Celtic Frost. That tape was always getting played, turned over and over again. I think back now and go, 'Yeah, maybe that was an influence.'"

Kurt Cobain claimed that the song was an attack on the ignorant, as he had grown up around those with views less inclusive than his own. "For ages I thought I might be homosexual, because I didn't like the cheerleader type of girl or want to hang out with the jock boys," Cobain told *Melody Maker* in a 1992 interview. "I chose to live the life of a recluse. I didn't hang out with anyone else because I couldn't handle their stupidity."

THE BOYS OF SUMMER

Don Henley

-

1984

As is so often the case, Interscope Records and Beats Electronics co-founder Jimmy Iovine had a hand in producing a bit of musical greatness. No soundboard was necessary for "The Boys of Summer," however, as Mike Campbell had already written the song for Tom Petty and the Heartbreakers. All that was required was a phone call, as Don Henley was looking for some music and Petty had just turned down the piece over concerns that it wouldn't fit with his album's flow. Iovine made the connection, Henley penned the lyrics, and "The Boys of Summer" was born.

Henley draws on dissatisfaction from the past to generate a lot of his lyrical material; "The Boys of Summer" was no different, as Henley said in a 1987 interview with *Rolling Stone* magazine. Asked if the '60s were a more exciting age than the '70s, Henley responds: "I'm also not convinced we really accomplished all that much. Kennedy was president and everybody thought it was Camelot, but look at what we did. We raised all that hell in the Sixties, and then what did we come up with in the Seventies? Nixon and Reagan. The country reverted right back into the hands it was in before. I don't think we changed a damn thing, frankly. That's what the last verse of 'The Boys of Summer' was about. I think our intentions were good, but the *way* we went about it was ridiculous. We thought we could change things by protesting and making firebombs and growing our hair long and wearing funny clothes. But we didn't follow through. After all our marching and shouting and screaming didn't work, we withdrew and became yuppies and got into the Me Decade."

"I don't think we changed a damn thing, frankly. That's what the last verse of 'The Boys of Summer' was about. I think our intentions were good, but the way we went about it was ridiculous."

PIANO MAN

Billy Joel

1973

"I did this gig for six months, and people would go up to me and go, 'You're too good for this place. What're you doing here? I can get you a regular deal,' because everybody in Hollywood was an entrepreneur. 'I can get you a deal, I can hook you up with a producer.' Everybody in Los Angeles is a producer. I don't really know what a producer is. I thought that it was somebody who produces, but produces what? In Hollywood they produce producing, you know. . .they would say 'What're you doing here, man, what're you doing here?' I would go, 'Oh, no, I love it here. I hate the music business, I want to be here.' I was lying through my teeth, but I really didn't want to deal with another shyster. So, it was a true story. And I thought, as I was playing in this gig, I said 'I gotta write a song about this. Nobody's gonna believe this, I gotta write a song about this.' So, that's where the idea came from."

AMERICAN IDIOT

Green Day

-

2004

"It's about the confusion of where we're at right now," Green Day front man Billy Joe Armstrong told *Spin* magazine in a 2004 interview. "My education was punk rock—what the Dead Kennedys said, what Operation Ivy said. It was attacking America, but it was American at the same time." The idea to politicize their rock opera *American Idiot* came in a fit of rage brought on by a Lynyrd Skynyrd song, as Armstrong recalled to *Q Magazine* in 2009: "It was like, 'I'm proud to be a redneck' and I was like, 'Oh my God, why would you be proud of something like that? This is exactly what I'm against.'"

The lyrics of the song were inspired by Armstrong's views on mainstream media. "They had all these Geraldo [Rivera]-like journalists in the tanks with the soldiers, getting the play-by-play," Armstrong recalled. He believed that coverage, specifically in regards to the Iraq War, was becoming irresponsibly commercialized.

"It was kind of a conscious effort to have a lack of conscience. For the first time, we separated from our pasts, from how we were supposed to behave as Green Day."

The idea to make a rock opera in the first place came in the form of a remedy; the group felt as though rock was getting stale, and a departure from their traditional music might bring some needed inspiration. "Rock's become such a conservative business," Armstrong told *Spin*. "You have a bunch of songs, put out a single, do your video, hope you get played on the radio, go on tour. People like OutKast are kicking rock's a**, because there's so much ambition."

Part of the band's exhaustion with the status quo came as a result of having the master tapes for their near-complete 2002 album stolen from Studio 880 in Oakland. When producer Rob Cavallo had asked them "Did you really kill yourselves to make [the lost record]?" the band responded with a unanimous "No."

The band claims The Who's "A Quick One, While He's Away," provided the inspiration necessary for "Jesus of Surburbia," the song that established the record as a rock opera. "You can listen to it like you'd listen to a song like 'My Generation,' Armstrong said. "That's what we were trying to do—you can listen to this record like you would one of our short-attention-span records."

Once they had the concepts and written products in place, the band began their recording sessions, which often had to be scheduled to accommodate hangovers. As bassist Mike Dirnt put it, "sh*t got kinda weird." Armstrong told *Spin* magazine that "It was kind of a conscious effort to have a lack of conscience. For the first time, we separated from our pasts, from how we were supposed to behave as Green Day. For the first time, we fully accepted the fact that we're rock stars. Not to sound arrogant, but it was like, 'Hey, you're only on this earth once, so you might as well enjoy it.'"

THE WORLD IS YOURS

Nas

1994

"I met Nas through Large Professor because he was from Queens," Pete Rock, the famed hip-hop producer, told *Complex*. "When I was hanging out in Queens, he would take me all over meeting different people and different rappers. Once I met Nas, he brought Nas up to my house, and we were going through music, and I played him 'The World Is Yours' beat. It wasn't nothing at the time, it was just a beat that he heard that he liked. But it was a great piano riff, and he wanted to make the song. He had the idea of me singing in the chorus on it. He told me, 'I want you to sing it.' I told him, 'Nah, I'm not singing, I'm not a singer.' But he made me do it, and it came out the way it is now.

"Large knew that he had a jewel [in Nas]. And once I started working with him, he just had me on board. I was already convinced [of his talents] after that. The album started coming together when we started hearing each other's work. Once I heard 'One Love' I was like, 'Wow, this is dope.' And [DJ Premier] said when he heard 'The World Is Yours,' he went back and made 'Represent.' We were all kind of in competition with the music for a great rapper. No one will ever stop talking about *Illmatic*."

CREEP
Radiohead

-

1993

"Creep," written by singer Thom Yorke while attending England's Exeter University, was first played during an impromptu bit in what was an otherwise by-the-book rehearsal. The song was introduced to producers Sean Slade and Paul Q. Kolderie as the band's "Scott Walker song," and it wasn't until the band assured them that the song belonged to them that Kolderie suggested releasing it as their first single. The move forced Yorke to create an edited version of the song for radio play.

Speaking about the song in 1993, Yorke said, "I have a real problem being a man in the '90s. . . .Any man with any sensitivity or conscience toward the opposite sex would have a problem. To actually assert yourself in a masculine way without looking like you're in a hard rock band is a very difficult thing to do. . . .It comes back to the music we write, which is not effeminate, but it's not brutal in its arrogance. It is one of the things I'm always trying: To assert a sexual persona and on the other hand trying desperately to negate it." He's also said that the song is about feeling inadequate in the eyes of the person you love, saying, "There's beautiful people and then there's the rest of us."

"It is one of the things I'm always trying: To assert a sexual persona and on the other hand trying desperately to negate it."

Radiohead credited "The Air I Breathe" songwriters Albert Hammond and Mike Hazlewood as co-writers, as the chord progression of "Creep" is the same as The Hollies' 1972 hit.

I WANNA BE YOUR DOG

The Stooges

-

1969

"Have you ever seen like a really good looking girl, really nicely dressed, and she's walking down the street with her dog, right?" Iggy Pop asked Howard Stern in a 1990 interview. "And like her dog is. . .intimate with her body, and she likes him and everything. Basically, it's the idea of I want to unite with your body. I don't wanna talk about literature with you or judge you as a person. I wanna dog you."

The track, which features a single repeated piano note and a three-chord riff, helped establish Pop as a punk presence going into the '70s, as the 1969 hit was The Stooges' first of that caliber. The energy that Pop puts into the performance of the song is such that, as he told *Classic Rock Revisited*, he still stage dives while playing it live. "Because it is our oldest, and most very, very memorable number, I do it," he said. "I also do it on that song because I push so hard on the first two verses that I can't think of anything to do by the time the guitar solo comes around. When the guitar solo comes, I tend to do a stage dive to go with the solo."

PINK HOUSES

John Mellencamp

-

1983

"I was driving through Indianapolis on Interstate 65 and I saw a black man holding either a cat or a dog," John Mellencamp told *Rolling Stone* in a 2013 interview. "He was sitting on his front lawn in front of a pink house in one of those sh*tty, cheap lawn chairs. I thought, 'Wow, is this what life can lead to? Watching the f*ckin' cars go by on the interstate?' Then I imagined he wasn't isolated, but he was happy. So I went with that positive route when I wrote this song."

Mellencamp, himself a native of rural Indiana, was a staunch defender of the working class. That mentality often shone through in his songs, as "Pink Houses" served as a scathing critique on the American way of the early '80s.

"This one has been misconstrued over the years because of the chorus—it sounds very rah-rah," Mellencamp continued. "But it's really an anti-American song. The American Dream had pretty much proven itself as not working anymore. It was another way for me to sneak something in."

Twenty-one years after the song was released as part of the 1983 album *Uh-Huh*, Mellencamp is still unhappy with the last verse that he wrote for the song. He said as much at a 2014 press conference: "Now when I hear that song, all I can think is: 'Why didn't I do a better job on that last verse?' If I had written it today, the last verse would've had more meaning."

I SHOT THE SHERIFF

Bob Marley & The Wailers

-

1973

On his "I Shot the Sheriff," Bob Marley once said, "I want to say 'I shot the police' but the government would have made a fuss. . . ." His decision to instead reference a smaller enforcement institution resulted in one of the more iconic lines ever, one that held its meaning between both iterations. "It's the same idea," Marley said, "justice."

The song, first released on The Wailers' 1973 album *Burnin'*, experienced modest success before reaching No. 1 on the *Billboard* Hot 100 as a cover performed by Eric Clapton. The song has remained popular since it debuted, a reggae staple that invokes a familiar sense of awareness regardless of when you listen to it. The song did gain a particular amount of attention in 2012, when Marley's ex-girlfriend Esther Anderson claimed that his opposition to her using birth control inspired the song.

SURRENDER

Cheap Trick

-

1978

"I used to hear my friends saying they thought their parents were strange," Cheap Trick lead guitarist and songwriter Rick Nielsen told *Blender* magazine while discussing "Surrender." "The first thing I got was the opening line of the chorus. It just rolled off in one sitting. Those opening lines. . . That's the advice to the lovelorn, and obviously inspired by the old Shirelles' hit ['Mama Said.'] It's a good way to start a song, if you can make it go with a chord progression."

Make it go they did, as Nielsen had to "go back and put myself in the head of a 14-year-old" to inspire what is arguably Cheap Trick's best-known song.

WELCOME TO THE JUNGLE

Guns N' Roses

-

1987

Appetite for Destruction was the best-selling debut album in the history of U.S. music. Its defining track, "Welcome to the Jungle," was born in the basement of Slash's mother's house, where Axl Rose was living in 1985. As Slash recalls: "I had this riff, and I remember playing it for Axl on an acoustic guitar. I said: check this out."

It was Slash's riff that they went on to develop, but it was Axl who came up with the title and lyrics. "If you lived in Los Angeles, and lived in the trenches, so to speak, you could relate to it," Slash said. "And knowing Axl, I could relate to exactly where it was coming from." While Slash felt the song spoke to his life in L.A., it was actually Seattle that inspired the song. "It's a big city, but at the same time, it's a small city compared to L.A. and the things that you're gonna learn," he said. "It seemed a lot more rural up there. I just wrote how it looked to me. If someone comes to town and they want to find something, they can find whatever they want."

LAST NITE

The Strokes

-

2001

"The Strokes took 'American Girl' [for 'Last Nite'], there was an interview that took place with them where they actually admitted it," Tom Petty told *Rolling Stone* in a 2006 interview. "That made me laugh out loud. I was like, 'OK, good for you.' It doesn't bother me."

The accusation is an apt one, as The Strokes' Julian Casablancas once told producer Gordon Raphael that he wanted "Last Nite" to sound "like a band from the past that took a time-trip into the future." The accusation is also fitting in that the song's structure and opening riff really do resemble Petty's hit.

I WANT TO KNOW WHAT LOVE IS

Foreigner

-

1984

"Part of my dream at the beginning was to be on Atlantic Records, because of the heritage: all the R&B stars of the '50s, people like Ray Charles and Aretha Franklin," Foreigner guitarist Mick Jones explained to *SongFacts*. "It meant so much to me and my growing up in music. So it meant a lot to have Ahmet Ertegun, who had been a part of that magical era and a person who I respected and looked up to, come into the studio. I took him aside and I said, 'I have a song to play you, Ahmet.' I took him into the studio, and we just sat there in two chairs, and I put the song on. Halfway through I looked over and indeed, there were tears coming out of his eyes. I thought, 'Whoa, this is a major moment for me. I've been able to impress this man who has heard some of the best, and produced some of the best music in the world. And here he is, and I've reached him emotionally.' By the end of the song we were both in tears.

Wonderful moments like that, they're just very meaningful."

The song was "I Want to Know What Love Is," which was penned by Jones alone. "I always worked late at night, when everybody left and the phone stopped ringing," Jones said. "'I Want to Know What Love Is' came up at three in the morning sometime in 1984. I don't know where it came from. I consider it a gift that was sent through me. I think there was something bigger than me behind it. I'd say it was probably written entirely by a higher force. . .The song was an expression of my tempestuous private life over the three years before. I'd been through a divorce, and met someone else who I was going to marry. There'd been turmoil in the band through the huge pressure of selling millions of albums, and me and [vocalist Lou Gramm] were entering a cold-war situation. I'd just come back to England from New York and was happy to be in touch with my roots. So it was an emotional time that stirred up a lot of things."

"I don't know where it came from. I consider it a gift that was sent through me. I think there was something bigger than me behind it."

Gramm wasn't as quick to take to the song as his band mates. Co-writer of much of the group's work, Gramm felt as though the song strayed too far from the rock style that the band was known for. Said Jones to *Billboard* magazine, "If you look at our whole history, each album had a couple of ballads on it. I think that Lou aired his opinion about it at the time, and that's what led to people jumping on it as a reason for our differences. But I can never really think that having a worldwide No. 1 song would be detrimental to a band." It wasn't; the song continues to impress despite having been released in 1984, thanks in large part to its inclusion in a number of popular films.

The lasting success the song has experienced did nothing to take away from the joy that its immediate success brought. Jones, for one, felt as though his work was more than validated after its release. "It was No. 1 worldwide," Jones said, "and I doubt there are many people who haven't heard it. It was played on the radio all around the world. And I started getting letters from people who weren't necessarily fans but had found comfort in that song at times of suffering and sadness. Everybody took their own meaning from it. And that's all you can hope for as a writer."

I WANT IT THAT WAY

Backstreet Boys

-

1999

Max Martin's Swedish heritage is the likeliest culprit for the Backstreet Boys' smash hit "I Want It That Way" containing lyrics that, according to the song's co-writer Andreas Carlsson, "made absolutely no sense in combination with the chorus." Carlsson is referring to the song's second verse, which features Martin working in English, his second language. "Ultimately, the song doesn't really make sense," Backstreet's Kevin Richardson told *LA Weekly*. "His English has gotten much better, but at the time..."

WHITE RABBIT

Jefferson Airplane

-

1967

The birth of a child added Grace Slick to Jefferson Airplane, as she replaced Signe Toly Anderson when she left the band to tend to her newborn. "I liked Grace's singing because we wanted a good, aggressive singer for the band," Jack Casady, Jefferson Airplane's bassist, said. "She had a unique timbre and sound to her voice; Signe [Anderson], who was our first singer, came out of a folk background and had a contralto voice with smooth harmonies. What I like about Grace was the fact she stood right at the end of the stage and made good contact with the audience. [Guitarist Paul Kantner] had put the vocal sound together for the first year of Jefferson Airplane, where it had the smoothness of his influences in folk music. I liked the individual sound to Grace's voice, so I asked her to be in the band. This was the girl. Also, her attitude was very different. She didn't have a submissive attitude at all, which is what we wanted. We wanted an equal in the band, someone you could work off, someone with fire in their eyes."

With Slick came two songs which she had worked on with her previous band, The Great Society. Among them was "White Rabbit," a song meant to point out the hypocrisy shown by parents that read drug-fueled stories to their children at a young age. "In all those children's stories, you take some kind of chemical and have a great adventure," Slick told writer Mark Paytress. "*Alice in Wonderland* is blatant. Eat me! She gets literally high, too big for the room. Drink me! The caterpillar is sitting on a psychedelic mushroom smoking opium!" Ironically enough, Slick allegedly wrote the song during the tail end of an acid trip during which she listened to *Sketches of Spain* by Miles Davis for a day straight.

I LOVE ROCK 'N' ROLL

Arrows

1975

In an interview with *SongFacts*, the Arrows lead singer Alan Merrill explored the genesis of "I Love Rock 'N' Roll."

"That was a knee-jerk response to the Rolling Stones' 'It's Only Rock 'N' Roll,'" Merrill explained. "I remember watching it on *Top of the Pops*. I'd met Mick Jagger socially a few times, and I knew he was hanging around with Prince Rupert Lowenstein and people like that—jet-setters. I almost felt like 'It's Only Rock and Roll' was an apology to those jet-set princes and princesses that he was hanging around with —the aristocracy, you know. That was my interpretation as a young man: Okay, I love rock and roll. And then, where do you go with that?"

He continued: "I had the chorus, which to me sounded like a hit. And I thought, 'I'll do something really unusual. I'll write it that this is a song separate from the verse.' So the actual chorus is something that's coming out of a jukebox, and the two kids in the disco who are flirting are hearing this song that's a hit. It felt like the Twilight Zone. I was so sure 'I Love Rock and Roll' was gonna be a hit for the Arrows that I thought, 'Well, when we have a hit with it, it's gonna be a hit within a hit.' A fictional hit coming out of the chorus with the kids singing it as their favorite [verse of the song]. So when it actually became a huge hit for Joan Jett, my Twilight Zone concept came true. And I don't think too many people get that about the song, you know? They just like the melody, and it's catchy. But it was actually a pretty clever stroke, one that I'm proud of."

"I was so sure 'I Love Rock and Roll' was gonna be a hit for the Arrows that I thought, 'Well, when we have a hit with it, it's gonna be a hit within a hit.'"

Though the song originally failed to catch on as a result of being released during an English newspaper strike, it caught on after the Arrows performed it live on the U.K. television show *Pop 45*. The performance landed them their own TV show, called *The Arrows Show*, where Joan Jett first heard the tune. Her first version of it came in 1979, when she recorded it with Steve Jones and Paul Cook of The Sex Pistols. "I did a very early version with them, it was great working with them, and no, there was no sense of trepidation on my part, despite the fact that everyone was telling me they were the most notorious band on the planet," Jett told *Uncut* in 2010. She would re-record it in 1981 with her band, the Blackhearts; in 1982, the song topped the *Billboard* Hot 100 for seven straight weeks and was inducted into the Grammy Hall of Fame in 2016.

TIME TO PRETEND

MGMT

-

2008

"When we started writing we didn't know that [Flaming Lips producer Dave Fridmann] was going to produce us," Ben Goldwasser told *Crossfire*. "I mean, we had randomly put him on this list of dream producers who we would like to work with and we ended up talking to him on the phone and we hit it off really well. We love his production work. I mean, we didn't want to work with him because we wanted to sound like the Flaming Lips, it was more that we felt like he understood us on a personal level and he really got our music. We were pretty sure after talking to him that he would make it the album we wanted it to be."

Fridmann was the producer on the group's hit album *Oracular Spectacular*, the lead single from which was "Time to Pretend." Originally included on their *Time to Pretend* EP in 2005, the song was re-recorded and included on their 2007 album, as was "Kids."

In a story that's as strange as the band's sound, MGMT once described the inspiration for the song as coming from their pet praying mantis, Kuivila. "We wrote 'Time to Pretend' our senior year of college, and the music was inspired by a praying mantis we had in our house," they said. "She laid eggs and it died, and we laid the egg case on this kinda model pirate ship on the mantle piece, and the eggs hatched and all these baby praying mantises were climbing up the rigging of the ship, and it was pretty crazy ... uhm so the music was inspired by our praying mantis that liked to dance to The Clash and the lyrics are just about us imagining being rock stars. . .and yeah, fantasy rock star life." The pet's namesake was their Experimental Music professor, according to band member Andrew VanWyngarden.

IGNITION/REMIX

R. Kelly

2003

GQ describes the discovery of "Ignition (Remix)" as "bizarre and counter-logical," while R. Kelly admits that it's "a**-backwards."

The foundation for the remix was laid five years before he created "Ignition." During the interview, Kelly said that he had written the song's first lines five years prior and had put it on the shelf because he didn't think enough of it to turn it into a track. When asked how Kelly could have written a remix to a song before writing the song to be remixed in the first place, he responds by saying "You tell me."

"Ignition" was recorded in 2002 and was to be included on Kelly's *Loveland* album. The album leaked, after which he decided to turn *Loveland* into *Chocolate Factory*, an album complete with new songs and a few remixes to the former. Kelly created "Ignition/Remix" in part because the studio liked the part at the end of "Ignition," which he would include as the intro to the remixed version. Despite it being called a remix, the two versions of the song bear very little resemblance to one another, fitting for an artist as mysterious as Mr. Kelly.

EVERLONG

Foo Fighters

1997

"I remember coming up with the riff while we were recording 'Monkey Wrench,'" Foo Fighters front man Dave Grohl recalled. "We were sitting in the studio, in Washington, in a studio north of Seattle called Bear Creek. The song is in a drop D tune and, in between takes, I was fooling around and found that chord.

I was doing it and I thought 'Oh that just sounds like Sonic Youth. That chord's a little Sonic Youth-y, schizophrenia sort of vibe.' Then I was really into [it] and I formed it into a song song. I didn't really put it together until we had finished with that recording session. We were on this Christmas break and," Grohl said, before Pat Smear, Foo Fighters guitarist, chimed in, "Yeah, I remember we jammed on that. You had the verse happening. It didn't sound great, and then he [Grohl] just came back one day like, 'Hey, check this out.'"

Foo Fighters drummer Taylor Hawkins added "You know, the funny thing about 'Everlong'. . .people consider it to be our biggest hit, and people consider that album kind of our seminal record to a certain degree, but at the time it wasn't that big of a hit. 'Everlong' wasn't a huge hit at first. It's something that took. . .you know, Dave did an acoustic version later. . .and that got played more than the rock version at first. That song took years to build up the kind of steam that has now become the great 'Everlong.'"

BUDDY HOLLY

Weezer

-

1994

"Buddy Holly," released on what would have been the namesake's 58th birthday, wouldn't have made it on to Weezer's *Blue Album* had it not been for Ric Ocasek. The album's producer,

Ocasek had to convince lead singer Rivers Cuomo that the song had merit and wasn't too "cheesy" for the album. "I remember at one point he was hesitant to do 'Buddy Holly' and I was like, 'Rivers, we can talk about it,'" Ric is quoted as saying in the book *River's Edge: The Weezer Story*. "'Do it anyway, and if you don't like it when it's done, we won't use it. But I think you should try. You did write it and it is a great song.'"

Weezer bassist Matt Sharp remembers Ocasek's belief taking a similar shape, saying "Ric said we'd be stupid to leave it off the album. We'd come into the studio in the morning and find little pieces of paper with doodles on them: WE WANT BUDDY HOLLY."

The song, which is about a man defending a platonic female friend, eventually made it on to the album, for which Cuomo was eventually glad; the song reached #2 on *Billboard*'s Modern Rock chart and it's now one of Cuomo's favorite songs to perform.

WAKE ME UP

Avicii

-

2013

In an interview with the *Daily Star*, Avicii said: "I had a demo with Mac Davis singing, the guy who wrote some songs that were covered by Elvis Presley, but I needed another singer to do the parts. At the same time I was tipped off about doing another track with Aloe Blacc, and I started working on that track. When I was with Mike Einziger from Incubus, we came up with the chord progression and the melody for 'Wake Me Up!' but [with] no real lyrics. None of us [could] sing and we really needed to get that demo down and the only person I knew that lived in LA was Aloe, so I called him and he was free. Lyrics come really easy to him so the two of us wrote them in a couple of hours and we finished the track."

"The lyrics started on the plane trip home after IWC's annual Gala event in Geneva," Blacc told *Rolling Stone*. "When I wrote the lyrics I felt like I was making a strong statement but I never imagined that they would touch so many people. In the studio, Mike sat next to me with his guitar and started strumming chords. I sang to him the chorus that I thought would work but was not sure about the second half. . . .Mike thought it was perfect. With that, I started to get the sense that we had something big on our hands."

DECEMBER, 1963 (OH, WHAT A NIGHT)

The Four Seasons

-

1975

As Bob Gaudio told the *Sun Sentinel*, the song was supposed to be set 30 years earlier. "This was all about my courtship with my wife," he said. "She and I wrote it. I had this piano lick I kept playing over and over. It was originally about the repeal of Prohibition in 1933. She stayed up late one night and came back with this. Much better, don't you think?"

Despite the title, "December, 1963 (Oh, What a Night)" wasn't released until December 1975 on the album *Who Loves You*. The song reached the No.1 spot in the U.S., the final Frankie Valli and the Four Seasons song to do so. It also provided the band with a first, as it was their only track to top the charts in the U.K. The song set in 1963 continues to see significant popularity in the 21st century; it's been featured in shows such as *Sherlock* and *Family Guy* and is a staple in college bars across the country.

IT WAS A GOOD DAY

Ice Cube

-

1992

"It's a fictional song," Ice Cube said in an interview with *Moviefone*. "It's basically my interpretation of what a great day would be. Do you know what I'm saying? So, you know, it's a little of this and a little of that. I don't think you can pinpoint the day."

While the day depicted may not have been clear, the song's intent was: show that despite all that was going on, Cube was still enjoying the heights he had reached. "The inspiration was my life at the time. . .I was at the top of the rap game. It was the summer of '92 and I was in a hotel room, really in a state of euphoria. I had all the money I had dreamed of. I was in a good frame of mind. And I remember thinking, 'Okay, there's been the riots, people know I will deal with that. That's a given. But I rap all this gangsta stuff—what about all the good days I had?'" Cube is referencing the Rodney King riots, which started after videotape circulated of white LAPD officers beating King as he lay on the ground. The riots resulted in the deaths of 63 people and the injuries of 2,383 others.

I GOTTA FEELING

The Black Eyed Peas

2009

"It's dedicated to all the party people out there in the world that want to go out and party," will.i.am told *Marie Claire*. "Mostly every song on The Black Eyed Peas' record is painting a picture of our party life. It was a conscious decision to make this type of record. Times are really hard for a lot of people and you want to give them escape and you want to make them feel good about life, especially at these low points."

The Black Eyed Peas front man is likely referencing the 2008 economic collapse, as their "I Gotta Feeling" was released in June the following year. The song replaced the band's "Boom Boom Pow" at the top of the *Billboard* Hot 100, making them just the ninth group in history to succeed themselves at No. 1. Every member of the group received writing credits on the song, as did French producers Frederick Riesterer and David Guetta. Guetta, in an interview with *Blogcritics Magazine*, said: "Will, at the time, was embracing the electronic music from Europe. Other artists have taken sounds from us and incorporated it a little bit. But what I respect a lot about him and the band is that he fully immersed himself in the culture. He called me, and he was like, 'Okay. I love that sound and I want to experiment with it a bit.' So I sent him some tracks, and he selected a few. Then, I went to Los Angeles and we worked together. When the song started coming together, I got a crazy feeling and I was screaming: 'This is huge, this is a monster, this is crazy.' Will came up with a hook of a hook! It has such a positive vibe. And I think a lot of success with the song is because of that really positive message, especially at the time when things are difficult for everybody."

SEPTEMBER

Earth, Wind & Fire

-

1971

Allee Willis remembers her first experience with the band Earth, Wind & Fire not solely because it saw her co-write a hit, but also because her outlook was forever altered. "Their stuff was very much based on Eastern philosophies, an incredibly positive outlook on life; the lyrical content of their songs was not typical of what would have been in soul music at that time," Willis told *SongFacts*. "So when I left the studio that first day, Maurice [White] gave me the name of a book, it was called *The Greatest Salesman in the World*, and he sent me to the Bodhi Tree, which is a very spiritual bookstore here in LA. I got that and a bunch of other books that the saleswoman said was the philosophy. And what went from being a very simple experience turned into, for me, an incredibly complex experience. Because I dove into these books. And even the way they were written, the language they were written in, I kind of didn't understand anything. But Maurice told me right from the jump he thought I was a very spiritual person, and I was put here to communicate. And I thought, if Maurice was saying that to me, I need to hang with this. I was pouring through these books for a couple of months. Lyrics started being 25-30 pages long as I'm trying to figure all this stuff out. Reading all that stuff changed me forever. He lead me to a path I've stayed on."

"I absolutely could not deal with lyrics that were nonsensical, or lines that weren't complete sentences. And I'm exceedingly happy that I lost that attitude."

Referring to the specific date in the song's first line, Willis recalls asking, "'Why the 21st?' Because I'm someone who likes to tie up all the ends very neatly, so if I'm saying the 21st, I want to know during the song what's the significance. But he always told me there was no real significance. So whether that's true or not I can't say. But as far as I know, it's just something that sang really well. And I would say the main lesson I learned from Earth, Wind & Fire, especially Maurice White, was never let a lyric get in the way of a groove. Ultimately it's the feel that is the most important, and someone will feel what you're saying if those words fit in there right. I do remember us experimenting with other dates, but 21st just sang phonetically fantastic."

The experience was more of the same for the song's chorus, of which she says "I absolutely could not deal with lyrics that were nonsensical, or lines that weren't complete sentences. And I'm exceedingly happy that I lost that attitude. I went, 'You cannot leave bada-ya in the chorus, that has to mean something.'

Maurice said, 'No, that feels great. That's what people are going to remember. We're leaving it.' We did try other stuff, and it always sounded clunky—thank God."

The song was a hit, reaching No. 3 on the U.K. singles chart, No. 8 on the *Billboard* Hot 100 and No. 1 on the U.S. R&B chart. Willis, though she may have preferred the lyrics to be backed up by something slightly more substantive, knew from the onset that the song was destined for success. "'September' was fantastic and thrilling, and they had started the intro of it by the time I had walked into the studio to meet everyone," she said. "Just as I opened the door and I heard that little guitar intro, I thought, 'Oh God, please let this be what they want to work with me on.' Because it was so obviously a hit."

MAD WORLD

Tears for Fears

-

1983

Roland Orzabal, co-founder of Tears for Fears, recalled writing "Mad World" in a 2013 essay for *The Guardian*. He began: "Mad World hasn't dated because it's expressive of a period I call the teenage menopause, where your hormones are going crazy as you're leaving childhood. Your fingers are on the cliff and you're about to drop off, but somehow you cling on.

"I wrote it when I was 19, on the dole in Bath. We're known as a synthesizer group, but back then I just had an acoustic guitar. I've not told many people this, but I was listening to Radio 1 on this tinny radio and Duran Duran's 'Girls on Film' came on. I just thought: 'I'm going to have a crack at something like that.' I did and ended up with 'Mad World.' It sounded pretty awful on guitar, though, with just me singing. However, we were fortunate enough to be given an opportunity by a guy called Ian Stanley to go to his very big house and muck about on his synthesizer. Ian became our keyboard player and he had a drum machine, too. All we needed was someone who knew how to work it. Eventually, we made the first demo of 'Mad World' still with me singing. But I didn't like it. So I said to Curt [Smith, singer]: 'Look, you sing it.' And suddenly it sounded fabulous.

"Just before that, we'd been in this mod band called Graduate, but Gary Numan had shocked us out of all that. He was getting No. 1s wearing black eyeliner, and there we were doing knees-ups to Madness. So we split from the band. I got an asymmetrical hairstyle, Curt got plaits, and we started listening to synthesizer music.

"There was a group around called Dalek I Love You. One of their lyrics went something like 'I believe the world's gone mad' which summed up my feelings of alienation from the rat race. I had suffered from depression in my childhood. My dad had been in the Second World War, had electric shock treatment, suffered from anxiety and was abusive to my mum. I kept a lid on my feelings at school but, when I was 18, dropped out of everything and couldn't even be bothered to get out of bed. I poured all this into the song.

"A guitar teacher we knew introduced us to Arthur Janov's psychology book *The Primal Scream*. Mad World's chorus. . .is from Janov's idea that nightmares can be good because they release tension.

"The song was intended as a B-side but Polygram [Entertainment] said it was too good, so it became our third single. I'd come up with this dance for it and used to do it a lot in the studio, so the record company told me I had to do it in the video, since Curt was singing and there was nothing else for me to do. So there I was, stuck by this lake doing my flying wombat impersonation, but it worked."

YOU CAN CALL ME AL

Paul Simon

-

1986

The most identifiable line in Paul Simon's "You Can Call Me Al," came thanks to a mistaken but well-mannered party guest. Legendary French composer Pierre Boulez, a friend of a friend, attended a party hosted by Simon and his then-wife Peggy Harper. Boulez gave his best to Simon upon his departure, saying "Sorry I have to leave, Al, and give my best to Betty." "Ever since then, Peggy would call me Al and I would call her Betty," Simon said. "It became a running joke."

The song's riff was created by guitarist Ray Phiri, of the band Stimela, who jammed with Simon while he was visiting South Africa. Most of "You Can Call Me Al" came out of those sessions, leaving producer Roy Halee quite the task back in New York, as he had to edit together all of the tape that Simon recorded during his visit. "What I came up with was a tape delay feeding the left channel and a different delay feeding the right," Halee recalled. "All of a sudden his vocal receded into the track, at least to some degree, and we could understand the words! Don't ask me why, but it worked, and I couldn't have done that with an echo chamber or EMT 140. In fact, remove that tape delay from 'You Can Call Me Al' and, what with all of the sibilance, pops and other little mouth noises against what was going on in that track, the vocal would be unintelligible."

The song violated the cultural boycott that black leaders had enacted to combat the segregation brought on by apartheid, which had also, up to that point, kept South African music strictly within the confines of the country. "You Can Call Me Al" brought their style to the masses, featuring Phiri, drummer Isaac Mtshali, and bassist Bakithi Kumalo, who also accompanied Simon on his worldwide tour for *Graceland*. "'You Can Call Me Al' is really the story of somebody like me, who goes to Africa with no idea and ends up having an extraordinary spiritual experience," Simon said on the documentary *Under African Skies*.

DAY 'N' NITE

Kid Cudi

-

2009

"My uncle that I lived with passed in 2006," Kid Cudi told *Complex* in a 2009 interview. "We were actually beefing because he forced me out the house when I didn't have another situation set up, so I was bitter. I never apologized for it, and that kills me. That's why I wrote 'Day 'N' Nite.' If he wasn't there to let me stay with him those first few months, there would be no Kid Cudi. It f*cked me up watching him go, but it was like, 'I have to fulfill this destiny now for sure.' Things were moving but they weren't solidified yet. I had 'Day 'N' Nite,' we were just getting started, and I was like, 'This sh*t has got to pop off.' I wasn't taking no for an answer."

"I wasn't really thinking about making a hit record or anything like that, I was just making the song to get my feelings out."

Cudi wrote the song, which he claims started as an idea that he'd "hummed into my Sidekick," from a place of intense emotion. "I was going through a lot of stuff at the time in my life and so I felt like I needed to write those things down just to get them off my chest," he told *The Guardian*. "I wasn't really thinking about making a hit record or anything like that, I was just making the song to get my feelings out."

Cudi told *Complex* that the 1991 single "My Mind Playing Tricks on Me" by the Geto Boys also inspired his hit. "'My

Mind Playing Tricks on Me' is my favorite song in the world," he said. "I love it so much I wanted to make my own version of it. And then 'Day 'N' Nite' came out of it."

ONE DANCE

Drake

-

2016

"It really all started with the Kyla record," Drake, discussing his hit "One Dance," said in an interview with *Radio Ovo Sound*. "I've been personally putting [Kyla's "Do You Mind"] in my own playlist and DJ set for, you know, four or five years now. What really set something off for me was having people in America coming up to me and being like, 'Yo, what was that song you just played?' I'm like, 'Man, people really like that song.' But they don't know it. And so, my brain started working on, like, how can I utilize a bit of this? There's so many good pieces. I introduced the concept to [producer Nineteen85] and was like, 'If we can make a beat. . .I don't want to do a cover, I want to do a whole new song. I just want Kyla to serve as the bridge to the next verse or to the hook.' He was like, 'Ok, ok, cool.' You know, I had the beat for a while and was trying to figure it all out."

WHAT'S UP

4 Non Blondes

-

1993

"For a short time, Linda [Perry] had quit her job and she was living with me in this little 2-bedroom flat in San Francisco," Christa Hillhouse, bassist for 4 Non Blondes, told *SongFacts* while discussing "What's Up." "She wrote the song when she was in a room down the hall. I was in my bedroom having sex, and I stopped because I heard her playing that song. I remember running down the hall and saying, 'Dude, what are you playing? I like that.' We had a lot of rock, thrashy stuff back then, but Linda always would pull her ballads out. I remember being struck by it. She kept looking at me, going, 'Does this sound like something? Am I plagiarizing someone?' I said, 'Finish the song, it's beautiful.' It caught on at our shows right away, people really liked it.

"Any song people are going to try to read deliberate meaning into, but when Linda wrote the song, she was just sitting down the hall," Hillhouse said. "We played guitar all the time, that's all we ever did. We practiced every day. I know people who think about formulas when they write a song or they think about structure—Linda has never lived that way. Linda's pretty organic in that way, she just sits down and starts singing what she's feeling. There is a difference between the songs she wrote then and the songs she writes now. She got to a point now where I think she is thinking about them structurally, but back then, she played acoustic guitar and all the songs she wrote she'd just sit there and here they'd come. A lot of people write like that. I write like that—a song is kind of there already and you're like the speakers. All of the sudden there's a song in my head and I don't know where it came from. I remember when she was writing the verses to 'What's Up,' she knew it so well, she thought she heard it before. I think that's why the song connects with so many people. What she was feeling she was able to translate. If you look at the lyrics, they don't mean anything. It's the way the song makes certain people feel. In Europe, they're not speaking English, but they know every broken-English word, and that song makes them feel something. I knew right when we played it, the song made the whole room feel this thing. It's a connection to humanity. Certain simple songs, that's what they do. There's an honesty there that breaks through that people can relate to. Then of course they played that song to death and a lot of people are really sick of it."

According to Hillhouse, the song would have suffered from intense overproduction had Jimmy Iovine, co-founder of Interscope Records, not voiced his opinion that the demo was better. "It got a little too foofed up in major production land—it softened it up and took something out of it," she said. They re-recorded the song, this time without all of the "fancy equipment" and over-engaged producers.

Though the phrase "What's Up" can't be found anywhere in the song's lyrics, it was used as a means to avoid confusion with Marvin Gaye's 1971 hit "What's Going On."

ZOMBIE

The Cranberries

-

1994

"Zombie" is a song that, as put by lead singer Dolores O'Riordan, speaks to "the Irish fight for independence that seems to last forever."

The song was penned by O'Riordan in memory of Jonathan Ball and Tim Parry, two children who were killed when the Irish Republican Army bombed Warrington, Cheshire, England on March 20, 1993. The attack was one of many since the early 1970s, most of which took place in England or Northern Ireland. The goal that the IRA set out to achieve was to put pressure on the British government to withdraw from Northern Ireland. A terror group both by definition and action, they agreed to disarm in 2005 and to work towards their goals using exclusively peaceful means. Oddly enough, the IRA declared a ceasefire in 1994 just a few weeks after "Zombie" was released, creating a break in what was 25 straight years of conflict.

THIS CHARMING MAN

The Smiths

1983

"I remember writing it, it was in preparation for a John Peel [BBC Radio 1 DJ and producer] single," The Smiths guitarist Johnny Marr told *Guitar Player* in a 1990 interview. "I wrote it the same night as 'Pretty Girls Make Graves' and 'Still Ill.'"

The Peel session was meant to generate buzz around the band and come up with a hit that made up for the track "Hand in Glove," which flopped critically and commercially. It worked, as "This Charming Man" would eventually become the band's highest charting song, reaching the No. 8 spot on the U.K. singles chart when re-released as a single in 1992.

Morrissey, who co-wrote the song with Marr, based it on personal experience. "For years and years I never had a job, or any money," he told *Undress* in a 1984 interview. "Consequently I never had any clothes whatsoever. I found that on those very rare occasions when I did get invited anywhere I would constantly sit down and say, 'Good heavens, I couldn't possibly go to this place tonight because I don't have any clothes, I don't have any shoes.' So I'd miss out on all those foul parties. It was really quite a blessing in disguise." He also meant to ostracize a gay culture that was becoming increasingly normalized in the U.K., a lifestyle which Morrissey has been famously pompous toward.

"I'd miss out on all those foul parties. It was really quite a blessing in disguise."

"People listen to 'This Charming Man' and think no further than what anyone would presume. I hate this angle, and it's surprising that the gay press have harped on more than anyone else. I hate it when people talk to me about sex in a trivial way," Morrissey said.

ARE YOU GONNA GO MY WAY

Lenny Kravitz

-

1993

"We were just jamming in the studio," Lenny Kravitz said while talking about the spontaneous birth of his hit "Are You Gonna Go My Way."

"You know, I was jamming with Craig Ross, who I wrote the song with. It was one of those songs that happened in five minutes. We were jamming. I thought there was something happening. I told Henry to turn the tape machines on, and we played it. And that was it. And then I went and wrote the lyrics on a brown paper bag, I remember at my loft on Broome Street at the time. Went in and sang it the next day. And that was it." Oddly enough, the 1993 single reached No. 2 on the Modern Rock Tracks and No. 1 on the Album Rock Tracks without ever making an appearance on the *Billboard* Hot 100.

OH, PRETTY WOMAN

Roy Orbison

-

1964

Roy Orbison's friend and songwriting partner Bill Dees recalled the part that he played in generating the hit "Oh, Pretty Woman" in a 2008 interview with NPR, saying: "The night we wrote 'Pretty Woman.'. . .[Claudette, Orbison's then-wife] came bopping down the stairs and said, 'Give me some money.' He said, 'What do you need money for?' And she said, 'Well I have to go to the store.' And as she walked away they were whispering and kissing bye. And he came back to the table, and I said, 'Does this sound funny? Pretty woman don't need no money.' He laughed and said, 'There's nothing funny about pretty women.'. . .By the time she got back, we had it written. . . .He turned to me with the guitar lick, and he said, 'I feel like I need to say something while they're playing [that guitar lick]. I said, 'Well, you're always saying 'mercy,' why don't you say mercy?' You know, I said, 'Every time you see a pretty girl you say mercy.'"

"There's a ballad in the midsection of it there: he's very sure of getting the girl when he first sees her, and then he's not so sure, and then he gets desperate, and then he says forget it, and then she comes back," Orbison told *NME* in a 1980 interview. "It's quite complicated, but it's probably in the presentation, or if I'm really singing like I know I can and I'm doing the job that I should be doing, then it could be that the voice quality in parts has a melancholy something."

GOODBYE HORSES

Q Lazzarus

-

1988

William Garvey's "Goodbye Horses," released in 1988 and sung by Q Lazzarus, cemented a darker interpretation than intended when it was featured in the 1991 film *The Silence of the Lambs*. Garvey said as much in 2008, after he had worked on a remix for the movie *Clerks II*.

"As the writer, musician and producer of the song, I wanted to add a bit of light to it," he said, "as it has a rather grisly association with the serial killer in *The Silence of the Lambs*, but really the song is about transcendence over those who see the world as only earthy and finite. The horses represent the five senses from Hindu philosophy (The Bhagavad Gita) and the ability to lift one's perception above these physical limitations and to see beyond this limited Earthly perspective."

"The horses represent the five senses from Hindu philosophy (The Bhagavad Gita) and the ability to lift one's perception above these physical limitations and to see beyond this limited Earthly perspective."

HALLELUJAH

Leonard Cohen

-

1984

Leonard Cohen once told *SongTalk* magazine that "To find that song, that urgent song, takes a lot of versions and a lot of work and a lot of sweat."

He was talking about "Hallelujah," a song which left him in just his underwear, banging his head on the floor during the writing process. He eventually wrote around 80 verses for the song during a single session in the Royalton Hotel in New York.

EVIL WOMAN

Electric Light Orchestra

-

1975

"I wrote this in a matter of minutes," Jeff Lynne told *Rolling Stone*. "The rest of the album [*Face the Music*] was done. I listened to it and thought, 'There's not a good single.' So I sent the band out to a game of football and made up 'Evil Woman' on the spot. The first three chords came right to me. It was the quickest thing I'd ever done. We kept it slick and cool, kind of like an R&B song. It was kind of a posh one for me, with all the big piano solos and the string arrangement. It was inspired by a certain woman, but I can't say who. She's appeared a few times in my songs. Playing concerts in those days wasn't fun. The sound was always bad and we were still playing theaters and town halls, the occasional dance hall. After 'Evil Woman,' we got more gigs, but it didn't change my life all that much. You can't buy a palace or anything after just one hit."

SINCE U BEEN GONE

Kelly Clarkson

2004

Lukasz "Dr. Luke" Gottwald, co-writer and producer of "Since U Been Gone," laid out the inspiration he and Max Martin used for *Billboard* magazine, saying: "That was a conscious move by Max and myself, because we were listening to alternative and indie music and talking about some song—I don't remember what it was. I said, 'Ah, I love this song,' and Max was like, 'If they would just write a damn pop chorus on it!' It was driving him nuts, because that indie song was sort of on six, going to seven, going to eight, the chorus comes. . .and it goes back down to five. It drove him crazy. And when he said that, it was like, light bulb. 'Why don't we do that, but put a big chorus on it?' It worked."

The song was first offered to Pink and Hilary Duff; Pink wasn't interested and Duff had to turn it down on account of her being unable to hit the song's highest notes. Clive Davis, chief creative officer of Sony Music, suggested Kelly Clarkson to Gottwald and Martin. The two were hesitant, as Davis told *Billboard* magazine. "They weren't prepared for the casting idea," he told the magazine. "Max was looking to move on from what he had done with Backstreet Boys, and I really spent time convincing them that an *American Idol* winner could bring all the feeling and passion that was required to the song." The two relented, but Clarkson, who was wrapping up recording for her *Breakaway* album, still needed to be convinced. "It didn't have any lyrics and the melody really wasn't finalized. . .the track was done on a computer, there was no band on it," she said. "My record label was freaking out about it and I was, like, 'Why?'"

She decided to incorporate drums and guitars into the song, as her album had been recorded with a rock-feel to it, and a hit was born. The song went platinum and was a worldwide success, hitting the top 10 in nine countries.

GOOD RIDDANCE (TIME OF YOUR LIFE)

Green Day

-

1997

"I wrote the song about an ex-girlfriend who moved to Ecuador," Green Day lead singer Billy Joe Armstrong recalled. "And I was really bitter at the time."

"Good Riddance (Time of Your Life)" was a significant departure from Green Day's usual sound, so much so that they had to hold the song off of their 1993 album, *Dookie*, because it clashed too much with the rest of the material. In what was dubbed by bassist Mike Dirnt as being the "most punk" thing to do, they released the track on their 1997 album *Nimrod*, a mere seven years after Armstrong had written it. The song was recorded in no more than half an hour, according to producer Rob Cavallo, who worked with Green Day on the album. The song was a hit, though it took the band some time to adjust to playing it live. "That was really the first time we attempted a ballad," Armstrong told *Spin* magazine in 2010. "The first time we ever played that song was during an encore in New Jersey—I had to pound a beer backstage to get up the courage. I knew we were gonna take a tomato to the face."

WHERE IS MY MIND

Pixies

-

1988

A favorite amongst advertisers and film directors alike, the Pixies' "Where Is My Mind" has become one of their lasting hits, despite having not been heralded when it was released. The song was included as the seventh track on their album *Surfer Rosa*, from which they only released one single—"Gigantic" reached No. 93 on the U.K. Singles Chart.

"Where Is My Mind" has been featured in countless advertisements, television shows, and films, most notably in the movie *Fight Club*.

On the inspiration behind the song, Pixies front man and songwriter Black Francis told *Select*: "That came from me snorkeling in the Caribbean and having this very small fish trying to chase me. I don't know why—I don't know too much about fish behavior."

YOU OUGHTA KNOW

Alanis Morissette

1995

The subject of Alanis Morissette's Grammy-winning "You Oughta Know" has long been the center of speculation. The song's lyrics, coupled with her refusing to reveal their inspiration, left listeners desperate for a clearer picture of the singer's broken heart.

Comedian and actor Dave Coulier bore the brunt of the rumors, as he claimed to have dated Morissette in 1992, which puts him in his early 30s and her at 17 or 18 years old. Coulier told the *Calgary Herald* in a 2008 interview that the song was about him, saying: "I said, 'Wow, this girl is angry.' And then I said, 'Oh man, I think it's Alanis.' I listened to the song over and over again, and I said, 'I think I have really hurt this person.' I tried to contact her and I finally got a hold of her. And at the same time, the press was calling and saying, 'You want to comment on this song?' I called her and I said, 'Hi. Uh, what do you want me to say?' And she said, 'You can say whatever you want.' We saw each other and hung out for an entire day. And it was beautiful. It was one of those things where it was kind of like, 'We're good.'"

He backpedaled six years later, however, telling *Buzzfeed*: "I never think about it. I think it's just really funny that's it's become this urban legend, so many years after the fact. . . .You know, it's just funny to be the supposed subject of that song.

First of all, the guy in that song is a real a-hole, so I don't want to be that guy. Secondly, I asked Alanis, 'I'm getting calls by the media and they want to know who this guy is.' And she said, 'Well, you know it could be a bunch of people. But you can say whatever you want.' So one time, I was doing a red carpet somewhere and [the press] just wore me down and everybody wanted to know so I said, 'Yeah, all right, I'm the guy. There I said it.' So then it became a snowball effect of, "OH! So you are the guy!"

The subject of the lyrics aside, Morissette required some reassurance that it was okay to express her emotions honestly. "I thought, this is exactly how I feel, but I don't want to hurt anybody," she said. "[Producer Glen Ballard] just said, 'You have to do this.'" Ballard not only provided Morissette with reassurance, he also provided her with a studio and his production skills on her album *Jagged Little Pill*. Ballard told *Q Magazine* in 1999 that "I was there to say, 'That's really you, that's what it should be and it's beautiful.' When she stood behind that microphone it was obviously coming from such a deep place within her. There are few more intimate moments. I couldn't imagine anything being more precious to her so I had a religious intensity about getting it right."

"I thought, this is exactly how I feel, but I don't want to hurt anybody."

The song features Dave Navarro and Flea of the Red Hot Chili Peppers on the guitar and bass, respectively. Navarro said of the experience "There were no guide tracks, we just had the vocal to work from. . .and we basically jammed until we found something we were both happy with. Alanis was happy too." Flea told *Bass Player* magazine that, "It was very instinctive—I showed up, rocked out, and split. When I first heard the track, it had a different bassist and guitarist on it; I listened to the bass line and thought, 'That's some weak sh*t!' It was no flash and no smash! But the vocal was strong, so I just tried to play something good."

The song was an emotional experience for Morissette, as recording it was a blur. "I wasn't aware of what was coming out of me," she told *Billboard* magazine in 1995. "I'd go in the booth when the ink wasn't even dry and sing. I'd listen the next day and not really remember it."

ELECTRIC FEEL

MGMT

-

2007

"A lot of times when we write songs we have had some kind of influence or a style that we really want to put into our music," Ben Goldwasser, of MGMT, told *Crossfire*. "Like, we'll say let's have that part sound like this and that part sound like that and then we piece it all together. We didn't plan anything, it was more of a song by song thing. We tend to be inspired a lot by artists that switch genres each album. Each song is different. (Anglo-Dutch experimental Rock band) Legendary Pink Dots are like that. When we were writing the album they were a big influence. We literally just wrote whatever came to us. There is a weird combination on the album because it has a couple of older tracks on it which were originally electronic with a more dance-y feel. 'Electric Feel' was one of the first songs we wrote, well the first actual song with lyrics."

Those lyrics, according to lead singer Andrew Van-Wyngarden, are "not about eels," they're about "drugs."

POKER FACE

Lady Gaga

-

2008

Among the best-selling singles of all time, Lady Gaga's "Poker Face" was a sex-fused, gambling-themed song meant to appeal to the men of her past. "I gamble," she told the *Daily Star*, "but I've also dated a lot of guys who are really into sex and booze and gambling, so I wanted to write a record my boyfriends would like too."

Ironically enough, Gaga revealed at Jeffrey Sanker's 20th Annual White Party that the song was born out of her personal experiences with bisexuality; the man whom she is with in the song must read her poker face to understand that she is fantasizing about a woman. Gaga said in a 2009 interview. "It's got an undertone of confusion about love and sex."

Gaga, who developed the song with producer RedOne, revealed another meaning of the song in an interview with *Rolling Stone*, saying: "Obviously, it's my pussy's poker face! I took that line from another song I wrote but never released, called 'Blueberry Kisses.' It was about a girl singing to her boyfriend about how she wants him to go down on her."

REMEDY

The Black Crowes

-

1992

"The essence is, you write songs because that's how you communicate," Chris Robinson of The Black Crowes told Greg Prato of *SongFacts*. The point they wanted to get across in their hit "Remedy" was free livin', as Robinson went on to say that "'Remedy' is a song that essentially is about freedom. We were into the whole idea that the 'war on drugs' was just silly—it was this asinine concept to me and millions of other people. So that song to me is about freedom, plain and simple, just put in a rock & roll framework."

PUMPED UP KICKS

Foster the People

-

2011

"I really didn't have anything to do that day," Mark Foster told *The Columbian*. "I was standing there in the studio, and this thought came in my mind like, 'I'm going to write a song,' which I did all the time. I just kind of built a song from the ground up. . .and then I was like, 'I don't feel like writing. I don't want to write a song.' I was a block away from the beach, and it was a beautiful day. I kind of just wanted to just be lazy and go hang out at the beach or whatever. But I just forced myself to write a song. I was like, 'Nope, I want to write a song.' By that time the next day, the song was finished."

He continued: "I've heard a lot of other artists talk about this as well, like, 'I'm not inspired right now. I've got writer's block. I'm just not really feeling anything.' And I've felt that way, too, just not being inspired and wanting to wait for inspiration to come before I wrote. But I wasn't inspired when I wrote 'Pumped Up Kicks,' and that's what came out. So. . .it just solidified the notion that perspiration is more powerful than inspiration."

Of course, the song's content made it the subject of much controversy post-Newtown tragedy in 2012. Foster, in a statement to CNN, said, "I wrote 'Pumped Up Kicks' when I began to read about the growing trend in teenage mental illness. I wanted to understand the psychology behind it because it was foreign to me. It was terrifying how mental illness among youth had skyrocketed in the last decade. I was scared to see where the pattern was headed if we didn't start changing the way we were bringing up the next generation. I wrote that song three years ago. A lot has changed since then, and a lot has stayed the same. For the past few years I've been an advocate for stricter gun control regulations and have been passionate about reforming our laws so this country would be safer. So my little brothers could go to school and I wouldn't have to worry about them. So people wouldn't have access to weapons that were capable of large-scale destruction i.e.: AR-15's with 30 round magazines. This song was written as a way to create ongoing dialogue for an issue that was being talked about, but when it came to government intervention, was largely being ignored. Now, this topic is finally at the forefront of major discussion and will hopefully lead to some big changes in policy that will prevent these acts of violence from happening in the future. That being said, I respect people's decision to press pause. And if that becomes a catalyst for a bigger conversation that could lead to positive change moving forward, then I absolutely support it."

SOMEBODY THAT I USED TO KNOW

Gotye

-

2011

On how "Somebody That I Used to Know" came to be, Gotye told *Sound on Sound*: "Writing 'Somebody' was a gradual and linear process. I started with the Luiz Bonfá sample, then I found the drums, and after that I started working on the lyric and the melody, and added the wobbly guitar-sample melody. After that, I took a break, and a few weeks later I came back to the session and decided on the chorus chord progression, wrote the chorus melody, and combined that with sounds like the Latin loop and some of the percussion and the flute sounds that further filled the space. At that point I hit a brick wall. I was thinking: 'This is pretty good, how can I get to the end really quickly?' and I was trying to take lazy decisions to finish the song. I considered repeating the chorus, an instrumental bridge, a change in tempo or key, I even considered finishing the song after the first chorus. But nothing felt like it was strong enough. So the third session was all about writing the female part and changing the perspective. The arrangement of 'Somebody' is reflective of me moving towards using sounds that provide me with inspiration for a texture or a platform for an idea, and then through sonic manipulation and coming up with original melodies and harmonic ideas to make it my own. I guess the balance of sounds taken from records and samples I created myself is perhaps 50-50."

After an alleged high-profile female artist canceled the collaboration last minute and Tash Parker, Gotye's girlfriend, didn't have the right sound, he went with Kimbra. "Kimbra has so much she can do with her voice," Gotye told *Tone Deaf*. "On the one hand I feel like she's able to channel all these great jazz vocalists but then with 'Somebody That I Used to Know' what I was really looking for, I just wanted it to be raw and direct. I wanted to hear singing sort of trying to tap into the feeling of it and she did that."

On the inspiration behind the lyrics, Gotye told *Metro Lyrics*: "I mean I've had a few breakups over the years of course, but it's more the memory of different relationships and different points in those relationships that prompted certain images and certain lines that came out in the song. And then those memories were kind of stretched out and embellished and there were elements of fiction added, so it's really a collection of things."

"I mean I've had a few breakups over the years of course, but it's more the memory of different relationships and different points in those relationships that prompted certain images and certain lines."

BAT OUT OF HELL

Meat Loaf

-

1977

Few songwriters have their work so prominently acknowledged as to have their name featured on the cover art for the album to which they've contributed. Then again, few songwriters ever contributed to the extent that Jim Steinman did on Meat Loaf's *Bat Out of Hell.* Steinman met Marvin Lee Aday, also known as Meat Loaf, while the two worked on the 1973 musical *More Than You Deserve.* Collaborations sprung from there, the most notable of which was the titular song of their massive 1977 album.

Steinman wrote the song, along with "All Revved Up with No Place to Go" and "Heaven Can Wait," for the 1977 musical *Neverland.* He and Meat Loaf, who were touring with *National Lampoon* at the time, decided to build an album around those songs. Described by Steinman as the "most extreme crash song of all time," he said "There is something so thrilling to me about that operatic narrative that involves a cataclysmic event, especially one so perfectly in tune with a teenager's world, and rock and roll, as a car or motorcycle crash."

The crash section of the song was written despite the ire of Meat Loaf and producer Todd Rundgren, as both thought that the already written six minutes' worth of material was plenty. "I don't think there's ever been a more violent crash. . .the guy basically has his body opened up and his heart explodes like a bat out of hell," Steinman said.

Extending the song wasn't the only source of debate between Steinman and Rundgren; There was a huge debate over whether to include a motorcycle sound on the track, which Steinman wanted. Rundgren took over and made that point moot. As Meat Loaf recalled in his autobiography *To Hell and Back*: "In fifteen minutes he played the lead solo and then played the harmony guitars at the beginning. I guarantee the whole thing didn't take him more than forty-five minutes, and the song itself is ten minutes long. The most astounding thing I have ever seen in my life." The second point of contention was in regards to whether an all-boys' choir would be included on the track, as Steinman wanted the song to sound like "the film *2001: A Space Odyssey*, they used a choir sounding like it was singing whole clusters of notes." Rundgren triumphed again, as they ended up recording the song without a choir.

It's been speculated that Steinman was inspired by Bruce Springsteen while writing *Bat Out of Hell*. Among those who have speculated this is Rundgren, who told *Mojo* magazine in a 2009 interview: "Jim Steinman still denies that record has anything to do with Springsteen. But I saw it as a spoof. You take all the trademarks—over-long songs, teenage angst, handsome loner—and turn them upside down. So we made these epic songs, full of the silly puns that Steinman loves. If Bruce Springsteen can take it over the top, Meat Loaf can take it five stories higher than that—and at the same time, he's this big, sweaty, unappealing character. Yet we out-Springsteened Springsteen. He's never had a record that sold like *Bat Out of Hell*, and I didn't think that anyone would ever catch on to it. I thought it would be just a cult thing. The royalties from that album enabled me to follow my own path for a long time after that."

ROYALS

Lorde

2013

"I was definitely poking fun at a lot of things that people take to be normal," Ella Marija Lani Yelich-O'Connor, better known as Lorde, said in an interview for VEVO. "I was listening to a lot of hip-hop and I kind of started to realize that to be cool in hip-hop, you have to have that sort of car and drink that sort of vodka and have that sort of watch, and I was like, 'I've literally never seen one of those watches in my entire life.'"

The concept for "Royals" was born out of a photograph taken by Ted Spiegel for the July 1976 edition of *National Geographic*. The picture featured World Series champion and lifelong Kansas City Royal George Brett signing baseballs, with his jersey featured prominently. "I'm really drawn to beautiful words and perfect turns of phrase," she explained. "That really inspires me. I'd been thinking about the concept of the song for a long time, and then I cut this picture out of *National Geographic*, which was a member of a baseball team, the Royals. He was just signing baseballs, but I was like, 'That is so cool.' That word is so beautiful and I was just wondering how I could incorporate it into something."

IRIS

Goo Goo Dolls

1998

"I'll try to talk to the director, if that's possible," John Rzeznik, lead singer of the Goo Goo Dolls, told *SongFacts* while explaining the process of writing for films. "I'll talk to the music supervisor and ask them what kinds of things they want. To me, it's a really great exercise for songwriting because you have to fit what you're doing in a very supporting role. It's not the main thing. You're there to support the vision of the director, and support the story. And enhance whatever part of the movie you're asked to put the music into."

Among his most famous commissioned jobs was the one that produced "Iris," the Goo Goo Dolls' biggest success. The song was written for the 1998 film *City of Angels*, in which Nicolas Cage plays a guardian angel meant to look over and protect humans. "When I wrote it, I was thinking about the situation of the Nicolas Cage character in the movie," Rzeznik said. "This guy is completely willing to give up his own immortality, just to be able to feel something very human. And I think, 'Wow! What an amazing thing it must be like to love someone so much that you give up everything to be with them.' That's a pretty heavy thought."

BLACK HOLE SUN

Soundgarden

1994

While speaking with *Entertainment Weekly* about the origins of "Black Hole Sun," Soundgarden's Chris Cornell recalled, "I had misheard a news anchor, and I thought he said 'black hole sun,' but he said something else. So I was corrected, but after that I thought, 'Well, he didn't say it, but I heard it,' and it created this image in my brain and I thought it would be an amazing song title. It was a thought-provoking phrase, and it became that song. That was a title that came before music, so the music was the inspiration that came from the images created by those words. I didn't think in terms of hits then, and I didn't think tempo-wise or lyrically as being something that could be a hit. Maybe a single at some point late in the release, like an afterthought single. Sometimes when a record has been out for a while, right before the record company decides to stop promoting it, they'll do one last single that's different, like something for the fans or whatever. That's what I thought 'Black Hole Sun' would be. But once we started mixing and mastering it and playing it for friends and the record company, everyone was singling that song out. So it started to occur to us that it might be a single that would have broader appeal. But definitely not lyrically. When I think of hit songs, they have to be somewhat anthemic in the world of rock, and I didn't see 'Black Hole Sun' as being that."

SANTERIA

Sublime

-

1996

"'Santeria,' I wrote the music," Eric Wilson, the bassist for Sublime, told *SongFacts*. "Originally I did it on a four-track on the previous album, *Robbin' the Hood*, and the name of it is 'Lincoln Highway Dub.' It's an instrumental song on that album, and [lead singer Brad Nowell] just put words on it. I couldn't really tell you what inspired 'Santeria' lyrically, but that's how the song came about. It was the music from a four-track, I wrote it in my head, and we re-tracked it and put those lyrics on it. And it went on to be one of our biggest songs."

Considered a signature song from the band's short tenure at the top, "Santeria" offered fans a taste of something they'd never get again, as Sublime front man Nowell died from a heroin overdose two months before the song was released.

COME SAIL AWAY

Styx

-

1977

"I never did a demo," Dennis DeYoung, Styx keyboardist and writer of "Come Sail Away," told *Classic Rock Revisited*. "I just played it and we learned it. We put 'Come Sail Away' together at SIR in Chicago. I had the verses and the chorus and we just did it. I remember the first time I played the song for Tommy [Shaw, Styx guitarist] was in my house. We just put it together in rehearsal. Like all bands, the arrangements of all the songs are collective. The flavor of the band comes from all of the individuals who come together and put their stamp on the song. Rarely, as I told you the story of 'Crystal Ball,' does a song come out like it was written. That was especially true in those days as all you had was a f*cking cassette player; there was no digital recording back then. You didn't have a 16-, 24- or 48-track studio in your house, you just went, 'La, la, la, la, la' into a tape deck and went for it."

He continues: "I think the song 'Come Sail Away' means so much to people because it is a song of a great journey to be someplace else. It is a song of guarded hope that it can be better.

The character in the song says in the very beginning that he wants to set a course for a virgin sea. He doesn't want to be held back; he wants to have all options open to him. It is fraught with peril and he realizes in the second verse that he chased the pot of gold but that he didn't get it. We, Styx, didn't get it either, but that isn't going to stop us from moving forward."

WRECKING BALL

Miley Cyrus

2013

"Originally, the [songwriting session between Dr. Luke and Sacha Skarbek] was booked to write a song for Beyoncé," Skarbek's representative said. "But as the song progressed, the songwriters realized the song would not work for her."

The clarification came after Sacha tweeted "Beyonce song now becoming a Miley Cyrus song?!! Good/bad? I don't know??!!!!" The result was good, as "Wrecking Ball" would become Cyrus' first No. 1 single in the U.S.

The song was written by Sacha Skarbek, Maureen "MoZella" McDonald, Stephan Moccio, Henry Walter, and Lukasz Gottwald, better known as Dr. Luke. The song was inspired by McDonald's recent heartbreak. In an interview with *SongFacts*, Moccio explained: "MoZella was extremely emotional that day. She was very frail because she had broken off her wedding during that week. She almost didn't end up making the session. 'Wrecking Ball' in every way is about MoZella's toxic relationship and then the courage to say, 'I can't go through with this.' So here we are, Sacha and I holding this girl together who was just very emotional, trying to comfort her. We all wanted a strong metaphor as a title and we were just throwing out words. I remember kind of shyly putting up my hand and saying, 'What about 'Wrecking Ball'?' And Sacha went, 'Yeah, 'Wrecking Ball,' that sounds good.' And MoZella kind of ran with that.

TWO PRINCES

Spin Doctors

-

1993

"I loved *The Lord of the Rings* and *The Hobbit* and *Sir Gawain and the Green Knight*," Spin Doctors lead singer Chris Barron told *SongFacts*. "I was really into fantasy fiction and stuff like that. I wrote ['Two Princes'] when I was 19, so I was still coming out of childhood, and as a child I loved wizards and kings and queens and princess and princesses and stuff like that. And I loved Shakespeare—I already was way into Shakespeare. So I gravitated towards that kind of imagery just because I liked books and poems from that period of time."

Barron spent much of his childhood displaced, as his family moved between Australia and Europe before landing in Princeton, New Jersey. His affection for fantasy and his experiences moving from place to place led to him often taking the position of underdog, as is the case in "Two Princes"; Barron plays the role of a young prince trying to win the heart of a woman that he loves despite his being poor.

The 1993 hit rose to No. 7 in the United States, making it the band's best performing song ever. Drummer Aaron Comess attributes much of that success to the song's tempo, which was originally supposed to be much faster. "There are certain songs when you find the right tempo, all of a sudden the lyrics come out, it feels right and I think with 'Two Princes' we really lucked out," Comess told Mikedolbear.com. "It's one of those things, we got in the studio, found a good tempo, we recorded it, everything just really came together. It's very simple, there's not a lot of stuff on it, somehow the sound and feel we got, we just lucked out and found the perfect thing."

Interestingly enough, the song wasn't as well received as its success indicates. While VH1 ranked the song No. 41 on their "100 Greatest Songs of the '90s" list, *Blender* magazine ranked it No. 21 on their "50 Worst Songs Ever."

TODAY

The Smashing Pumpkins

-

1993

"Out of the blue, I heard the opening lick note for note in my head," Billy Corgan claimed. "When I added the opening riff, it completely changed the character of the song. Suddenly, I had a song that was starting out quiet and then got very loud."

"Today," released as the second single off of the album *Siamese Dream*, was a defining hit for the Smashing Pumpkins. Most importantly at the time, the song helped the band re-emerge after their first album, *Gish*, failed to keep them in the spotlight. "The Smashing Pumpkins had put out one album, which was very successful, but as we were promoting our album, the Nirvana album came out, and as everyone knows *Nevermind* was a massive album, and then Pearl Jam came out too at that time, and they were massive," Corgan told Amy Jo Martin on her "Why Not Now?" podcast. "So within a short span of time I went from thinking I was very successful within my given field, to all the rules had changed in my given field. Everything I had built myself up to be and do was no longer as relevant as it needed to be. I went into a very strange depression because I felt like something had been not taken, but the change made me feel kind of inadequate in a way I wasn't prepared for."

The resulting depression came with writer's block, weight gain, and sustained suicidal contemplations. Two bandmates, James Iha and D'arcy Wretzky, had recently broken up while another, drummer Jimmy Chamberlin, was becoming severely addicted to heroin. The situation was such that Corgan finally reached a crossroads; either jump out of a window to his death or make something of his situation. "I woke up one morning, and I kind of stared out the window and thought, 'Okay, well, if you're not going to jump out the window, you better do whatever it is you need to do'," he said. "That morning I wrote, I think it was the song 'Today,' which people would probably be fairly familiar with, it's the ice cream truck video song. It's sort of a wry observation on suicide, but in essence the meditation behind the lyric is that every day is the best day, if you let it be." Corgan liked the song so much that he became a bit of a control freak in the studio, playing both the guitar and bass guitar parts on the track.

"I woke up one morning, and I kind of stared out the window and thought, 'Okay, well, if you're not going to jump out the window, you better do whatever it is you need to do.'"

TOM SAWYER

Rush

-

1981

"'Tom Sawyer' was a collaboration between myself and Pye Dubois, an excellent lyricist who wrote the lyrics for Max Webster," Neil Peart, drummer for Rush, wrote in the

December 1985 edition of the *Rush Backstage Club* newsletter. "His original lyrics were kind of a portrait of a modern-day rebel, a free-spirited individualist striding through the world wide-eyed and purposeful. I added the themes of reconciling the boy and man in myself, and the difference between what people are and what others perceive them to be—namely me, I guess."

"Pye was a little mysterious—kind of a strange fellow!" Alex Lifeson, guitarist for Rush, recalled. "He was very quirky, a bit of a nut, but he did write great lyrics. And around 1980 he sent a poem to Neil with an idea to collaborate on a song. The original draft was called "Louie The Warrior."...Neil took the idea and massaged it, took out some of Pye's lines and added his thing to it."

The song was written and recorded while the band was living at Ronnie Hawkins' farm outside of Toronto. As Lifeson recalled: "It was the coldest I've ever been in my life, that's for sure. We were living in a house beside a lake, and the studio was on the other end of the lake. If we were brave enough, we walked through the woods. It was really beautiful, but it was minus 40 out there! I'm serious!"

Geddy Lee, the band's front man and bassist, called "Tom Sawyer" "the defining piece of music" from Rush in the early '80s. It's been remembered as such; the song was named the 19th greatest hard rock song of all time by VH1 in 2009 and was one of five Rush songs to be inducted into the Canadian Songwriters Hall of Fame in 2010.

GIRLS JUST WANT TO HAVE FUN

Cyndi Lauper

-

1983

As it turns out, Robert Hazard is responsible for writing one of the most recognizable and resounding feminist anthems of all time. The song, which never made it past the demo stage for Hazard, caught the attention of Cyndi Lauper, who recorded a cover version with his blessing.

"The first time I heard it, I understood how I could sing from my point of view and make it a call to solidarity for women," Lauper told *Yahoo! Music*. "In the 1980s, women were still struggling to be seen as equal to men. When the women's movement really started earlier in the '60s and '70s, I felt so empowered and it was thrilling to me. But in 1980s, it seemed that a lot of the hard work by people like Betty Friedan and Gloria Steinem was being forgotten, and women were once again accepting the status quo. We had gotten far—but not far enough—so I sang 'Girls' for all the women around the world to remember our power. . . .I had a different take, obviously. He's a guy; he's not going to write what a woman's going to sing about. I was concerned about how it would be taken, and he said, 'Well, think about what it could mean.' So the parts that were very masculine and didn't pertain to what I wanted to say, I cut out. My idea was to use those Hooters guys [Eric Bazilian and Rob Hyman, who worked on the album] and their reggae feel, and this wonderful new sound of this electronic drum, and use the wonderful new styles that came over from England from groups like The Clash and how they approached their guitars. It was kind of raw. And also [the influence of] Andy Summers [of The Police], who I felt played in a completely different way than what we were listening to, way more blues-oriented. I just felt there was a way to incorporate everything and use a big voice, which I had."

UNDER THE BRIDGE

Red Hot Chili Peppers

-

1992

"I was reaching a demoralizing low, just kind of hanging out on the streets and doing my thing and not much else, sadly to say," Anthony Kiedis, referring to the Red Hot Chili Peppers' "Under the Bridge," told *Rolling Stone* in a 1992 interview.

Producer Rick Rubin found a poem in Kiedis' notebook and insisted on bringing it to the rest of the band. Kiedis initially resisted, citing the fact that the lyrics occupied an emotional place that the Chili Peppers seldom explored in their music, but eventually relented at Rubin's insistence. "I thought it was beautiful," Rubin said. "I said 'We've got to do this.'"

"I ran into some fairly unscrupulous characters involved with miniature Mafioso drug rings, and the hangout for one of these gangs was this particular location under a bridge," Kiedis told *Rolling Stone.* "I ended up going there with this gang member, and the only way that I was allowed to go under this bridge was for him to tell everybody else that I was getting married to his sister. You had to be family to go there. That was one of just hundreds of predicaments that I found myself in, the kind that only drug addiction can bring about. It's not that that one place was more insidious than other places. But that's just one day that sticks very vividly in my memory. Like, how could I let myself get to that point?"

Kiedis had maintained sobriety since August 1, 1988, due in part to the fact that Hillel Slovak, the band's original guitarist and one of Kiedis' closest friends, died of a heroin overdose. That sobriety left Kiedis ostracized and alone; his band mates often left him to smoke weed, and he'd lost his girlfriend, Ione Skye, as a result of his previous drug use. "The loneliness that I was feeling triggered memories of my time with Ione and how I'd had this beautiful angel of a girl who was willing to give me all of her love, and instead of embracing that, I was downtown with f*cking gangsters shooting speedballs under a bridge," Kiedis said. His companion, exclusively for a time, became Los Angeles, a city in which he had lived for 20 years. "It was LA—the hills, the buildings, the people in it as a whole—that seemed to be looking out for me more than any human being. I just started singing this little song to myself. . . .

"I'd had this beautiful angel of a girl who was willing to give me all of her love, and instead of embracing that, I was downtown. . . shooting speedballs."

When I got home that day, I started thinking about my life and how sad it was right now. But no matter how sad or lonely I got, things were a million percent better than they were two years earlier when I was using drugs all the time. There was no comparison. I was reminding myself, 'Okay, things might feel f*cked up right now, but I don't ever want to feel like I did two years ago.' In the end it wasn't like I was writing in any sort of pop-song format. I just started writing about the bridge—and the things that occurred under the bridge."

Guitarist John Frusciante and drummer Chad Smith began to work on chords and a beat which matched the lyrics that Kiedis had composed. "My brain interpreted it as being a really sad song," Frusciante said, "so I thought if the lyrics are really sad like that I should write some chords that are happier." The group of singers at the end of the song is a choir made up of Frusciante's mother and all of her friends. This bit was included at the suggestion of Rubin, who thought that the song could use a grand ending.

Kiedis has never revealed the location of the bridge, though clues unintentionally laid throughout the years indicate that the bridge is likely in MacArthur Park. Others have suggested that the bridge is actually an overpass over Hoover Street or the Belmont Tunnel.

UNDER PRESSURE

Queen & David Bowie

1982

In an article for *The Daily Mirror* written shortly after David Bowie's death, Queen legend Brian May details their collaborating on the hit "Under Pressure."

"David Bowie and we guys from Queen came from the same country, of course. . .and quite close by, in London, at that. But we only hooked up properly because of a coincidence. We all happened to be in a sleepy little town called Montreux in Switzerland at the same time. In the 70s we worked at the small studio there, Mountain Studios, with David Richards, and liked it so much we bought it, and continued to work there until [Freddie Mercury's] passing many years later. David Bowie had actually settled in Switzerland to live, very close by, and since we already knew him a little, he popped in to say hello one day while we were recording. Now time dims the memory a little, but the way I remember it we all very quickly decided that the best way to get to know each other was to play together. So we all bowled down into the studio and picked up our instruments. We had fun kicking around a few fragments of songs we all knew. But then we decided it would be great to create something new, on the spur of the moment. We all brought stuff to the table, and my contribution was a heavy riff in D which was lurking in my head. But what we got excited about was a riff which [Queen bassist John Deacon] began playing, 6 notes the same, then one note a fourth down. Ding-Ding-Ding Diddle Ing-Ding, you might say."

A few hours later, after enjoying a few glasses of wine with lunch, the group returned to the studio to build off what they had started. Once Bowie reminded Deacon of the riff that he had come up with, the group was off and running, letting the music take them where it may.

May continued, "David said something like 'We should just press on instinctively. Something will happen.' And he was right. It did. I put a little tinkling guitar riff on top of John's bass riff (David later was adamant it ought to be played on a 12-string, so I overdubbed that later at some point). And then we all mucked in with ideas to develop a backing track. The track had something that sounded like a verse, then a quiet contemplative bit, which built up ready for a climax. I managed to get my heavy riff in here. I remember saying. . .'Cool—it sounds like The Who!' At which point David frowned a little and said 'It won't sound like The Who by the time we're finished!' Now at this point there is no song. . .no vocal, no words—no title, even—no clue as to what the song will mean—just an instrumental backing track. But it really rocked. Born completely spontaneously, it was fresh as a daisy. Stop there? Go away and write a song for it ? 'No'—says David. He'd been working with a bunch of people who developed a technique for creating the top like by 'democracy' as well as the backing track. The procedure was each of us went into the vocal booth consecutively, without listening to each other, and, listening to the track, vocalized the first things that came into our heads, including any words which came to mind, working with the existing chord structure. At this point Freddie laid down his amazing De Dah Day bits, very unusual, which actually made it to the final mix. The next step was to cut up everybody's bits and make a kind of compilation 'best of' vocal track—which would then be used as the template for the final vocals. It came out pretty strange, but very different. We all went home that night with a rough mix which was provisionally called 'People on Streets,' because these words were part of the rough. The next day we reconvened, and I think I was prepared to try some new ideas out. But David was in there first, and told us he wanted to take the track over, because he knew what he wanted it to be about. So, to cut a long story short, that is what happened. We all backed off and David put down a lyric which now focused on the 'Under Pressure' part of the existing lyric. It was unusual for us all to relinquish control like that but really David was having a genius moment—because that is a very telling lyric. And the rest is history?"

IN THE AIR TONIGHT

Phil Collins

1981

In a 2016 *Rolling Stone* piece, Phil Collins penned a few paragraphs about his hit "In the Air Tonight," which read: "This song has become a stone around my neck, though I do love it. I wrote it after my wife left me. Genesis had done a tour that was far too long. She said to me, 'We won't be together if you do the next tour.' I said, 'I'm a musician. I have to go away and play. Just hold your breath when I'm over there.' Then Genesis toured Japan. When I got back, she said she was leaving and taking the kids. At the time, Genesis had decided to change things up a bit, maybe rattle our cages. The idea was to record separately with these new Roland drum machines we'd been given. I set up a studio in the master bedroom of my house with a Fender Rhodes piano and a drum kit. One day I was working on a piece in D-minor, the saddest [key] of all. I just wrote a sequence, and it sounded nice. I wrote the lyrics spontaneously. I'm not quite sure what the song is about, but there's a lot of anger, a lot of despair and a lot of frustration. Tony Banks [founding member of Genesis] claims I never played him the song, but I don't see why that would be true. But I'm glad he didn't take it, because Genesis would have put their mark on it, and it wouldn't be the piece of music we're talking about now."

The song was originally conceived with extra drums playing

up until the signature drum crash, the inclusion of which was the work of Atlantic Records head Ahmet Ertegun. As Collins recalled: "Ahmet came down to the final mix in the cutting room in New York. . . .The drums don't come in until the end but Ahmet didn't know that at this point, because on the demo the drums hadn't come in at all; it was only drum machine all the way. And he was saying, 'Where's the down beat, where's the backbeat?' I said, 'The drums come in in a minute.' 'Yeah, you know that and I know that, but the kids don't know that; you've got to put the drums on earlier.' So we added some drums to the mix and put it out as a single." The song, which was included on Collins' debut album *Face Value*, peaked at No. 2 on the U.K. Singles Chart and No. 19 on the *Billboard* Hot 100 in the U.S.

SOLSBURY HILL

Peter Gabriel

1977

His first single as a solo artist, Peter Gabriel's "Solsbury Hill" dealt with a good many things; mainly, the song validated Gabriel's ability to make successful music away from his former band, Genesis. "It's about being prepared to lose what you have for what you might get, or what you are for what you might be. It's about letting go," Gabriel said. The song was inspired by an experience atop Solsbury Hill in Somerset, England, which reaches 652 feet at its highest point.

> **"It's about being prepared to lose what you have for what you might get, or what you are for what you might be. It's about letting go."**

It has been speculated that a Bruce Springsteen concert inspired Gabriel to leave Genesis and write "Solsbury Hill," which he addressed in a 2001 interview with *Rolling Stone*: "I'm trying to think, because I think that was written prior. . . I don't know. I saw Bruce's first gig in London, I think at the Odeon House. That blew me away. Second only in my favorite gig list to Otis Redding in 1967. But I don't think it's connected to 'Solsbury Hill'. . .I think that is hogwash. Because when I left Genesis, I just wanted to be out of the music business. I felt like I was just in the machinery. We knew what we were going to be doing in 18 months or two years ahead. I just did not enjoy that."

ALIVE

Pearl Jam

1991

"Everybody writes about it like it's a life-affirmation, thing—I'm really glad about that," Eddie Vedder told Cameron Crowe in a 1993 interview. "It's a great interpretation. But 'Alive' is. . . it's torture. Which is why it's f*cked up for me. Why I should probably learn how to sing another way. It would be easier. It's . . . it's too much. . . . The story of the song is that a mother is with a father and the father dies. It's an intense thing because the son looks just like the father. The son grows up to be the father, the person that she lost. His father's dead, and now this confusion, his mother, his love, how does he love her, how does she love him? In fact, the mother, even though she marries somebody else, there's no one she's ever loved more than the father. You know how it is, first loves and stuff. And the guy dies. How could you ever get him back? But the son. He looks exactly like him. It's uncanny. So she wants him. The son is oblivious to it all. He doesn't know what the f*ck is going on. He's still dealing, he's still growing up. He's still dealing with love, he's still dealing with the death of his father. . . . So what does he do, he goes out killing people—that was [the song] 'Once.' He becomes a serial killer. And 'Footsteps,' the final song of the trilogy, that's when he gets executed. That's what happens. The Green River killer. . . and in San Diego, there was another prostitute killer down there. Somehow I related to that. I think that happens more than we know. It's a modern way of dealing with a bad life. I'm just glad I became a songwriter."

BETTER MAN

Pearl Jam

1994

"Sometimes I think of how far I've come from the teenager sitting on the bed in San Diego writing 'Better Man' and wondering if anyone would ever even hear it," Eddie Vedder told *The Los Angeles Times Calendar* in a 1996 interview. The song was one of Pearl Jam's most successful, reaching the No. 1 spot atop the *Billboard* Mainstream Rock Tracks chart and remaining there for eight weeks—despite not being released as a single.

Vedder originally performed the song with his old band, Bad Radio, but was hesitant to do it with Pearl Jam since it was too poppy. Said producer Brendan O'Brien, "There's a great song we recorded for *Vs.*, 'Better Man,' which ended up on *Vitalogy*. One of the first rehearsals we did they played it and I said 'Man, that song's a hit.' Eddie just went 'Uhhh.' I immediately knew I'd just said the wrong thing. We cut it once for *Vs.*, he wanted to give it away to this Greenpeace benefit record, the idea was that the band was going to play and some other singer was going to sing it. I remember saying to the engineer, Nick [DiDia], 'This is one of their best songs and they're going to give it away! Can't happen!' And we went to record it and I'm not going to say we didn't try very hard, but it didn't end up sounding very good. I may have even sabotaged that version but I won't admit to that. It took us to the next record, recording it two more times, before he became comfortable with it because it was such a blatantly great pop song."

WE BELONG

Pat Benatar

-

1984

Perhaps her most popular song, the origins of "We Belong" had nothing to do with Pat Benatar. Though that isn't entirely unusual, as Benatar seldom wrote any of her popular singles, what is a little bit strange is that the song was later covered by the songwriters themselves, Dan Navarro and David Eric Lowen.

In a 2014 interview with Bart Herbison, Executive Director of the Nashville Songwriters Association International, Navarro dives into the song's genesis, saying: "Eric and I had been in a band together, and it wasn't going well. I had a family business I was helping with in advertising, and my commitment to the band was flagging, so he said, 'You've gotta go.' And he was my best friend. He kicked me out. We didn't talk for six weeks. He had written four songs in his life, and I'd been one of the main writers in this band. . .he calls me one day and says, 'Let's get together and write a song, just for the heck of it.' I did it, because he was my friend. I tried to put aside my anger and my hurt and in 90 minutes, we write 'We Belong.' Almost exactly one year later, it was Top 5, all over the world. One of those things that almost never happens. . . .Except for one thing. I was kind of lamenting an old relationship, and I kind of wanted to get the point across: 'It doesn't matter if you agree, or disagree, if you're here or gone. There are things that are bigger than both of us, and we belong together.' I started with that final line and built everything almost backwards. Then I thought, 'Wouldn't it be fun for us to belong to all of this stuff: the light, the thunder. . . .' So it came from there. I had written this rambling verse. (Eric) goes, 'I don't like the verse. I like this bit, Dan.' He sits down in a corner, writes a first verse, and the first verse was there, whole. And I knew the rest of the song from that point on. I took about 10 minutes to write the rest of the lyric. I had set up the destination. He had set up the basis to the story. And I've always believed that next to the chorus—and sometimes even more than the chorus—the first two lines of the song are the most important in the whole song. You've got to hear enough to draw you in, but not so much that you don't want to hear the rest of the song."

WONDERWALL

Oasis

-

1995

"How do you tell your missus it's not about her once she's read it? It's a song about an imaginary friend who's gonna come and save you from yourself," Noel Gallagher said to BBC Radio 2 during a 2002 interview discussing what inspired his "Wonderwall." Gallagher said that the media ran with an assumption that the song's genesis was rooted in Noel's love for his then-girlfriend and current ex-wife Meg Matthews. "The meaning of that song was taken away from me by the media who jumped on it," he said.

It should be noted, of course, that Noel told *NME* that the song was "about my girlfriend, Meg Matthews" in a 1996 interview.

Oasis has often cited The Beatles as being one of their most important influences. Noel told *NME* as much in 1995, saying that "The Beatles are, to me, the be-all and end-all. Where it starts and where it finishes." That influence was made tangible in Noel's decision to refer to the potential savior in the song as a wonderwall, as the name of George Harrison's first solo album was *Wonderwall Music.*

So, what exactly is a wonderwall? "A wonderwall can be anything," vocalist Liam Gallagher told *Rolling Stone* in a 1996 interview. "It's just a beautiful word. It's like looking for that bus ticket, and you're trying to f*cking find it, that bastard, and you finally find it and pull it out, 'F*cking mega, that is me wonderwall.'"

"Wonderwall," like much of the genius put into the world by Oasis, became a source of frustration for the band, particularly for the Gallagher brothers. Perhaps best known for undermining their own success, if not their music, they grew tired of the song defining them. "I can't f*cking stand that f*cking song," Liam told MTV U.K. "Every time I have to sing it I want to gag. Problem is, it was a big, big tune for us. You got to America and they're like, 'Are you Mr. Wonderwall?' You want to chin someone." Noel said more of the same, telling NME.com that "outside of England, it's the one we're most famous for all over the world, and it annoys the f*ck out of me. It's not a f*cking rock and roll tune. There's quite a vulnerable statement to it."

KING KUNTA

Kendrick Lamar

-

2014

"It's just [Kendrick Lamar] expressing how he's feeling at the moment," producer Sounwave said. "And right now, he's mad."

The third single off his *To Pimp a Butterfly* album, Lamar named the song after Kunta Kinte, the main character in Alex Haley's novel *Roots: The Saga of an American Family*. Lamar turned the character into royalty, telling MTV: "I've been called many things growing up. In the state of just being a black man, I've been called many things. From my ancestors, they've been called many things. But it's taking that negativity and being proud of it and making it to your own. Saying I am a king no matter what you call me."

"It's taking that negativity and being proud of it and making it to your own. Saying I am a king no matter what you call me."

"No matter how many barriers you gotta break down, no matter how many escape routes you gotta run to tell the truth," he told *NME*. "That's what I think we can all relate to. Just being the most confident in the things that I wrote and the ideas that I have. Going back to the essence of being a true lyricist at heart."

I KISSED A GIRL

Katy Perry

-

2008

Katy Perry recently described the story behind her "I Kissed a Girl" at the 2017 Human Rights Campaign Gala, saying: "I speak my truths and I paint my fantasies into these little bite-size pop songs. . . .Truth be told, I did more than that. How was I going to reconcile that with a gospel-singing girl raised in youth groups that were pro-conversion camps? What I did know was I was curious and even then I knew sexuality wasn't as black and white as this dress. And honestly, I haven't always gotten it right, but in 2008 when that song came out I knew that I started a conversation and a lot of the world seemed curious enough to sing along, too. I found my gift and my gift introduced me to people outside my bubble and my bubble started to burst," she said. "These people were nothing like I had been taught to fear. They were the most free, strong, kind and inclusive people I have ever met. They stimulated my mind, and they filled my heart with joy, and they danced with joy while doing it. These people are actually magic, and they are magic because they are living their truth."

Before it became an anthem for the sexually curious, "I Kissed a Girl" was a risky pop song that Perry put on the shelf for over a year. "The chorus actually popped into my head when I woke up," Perry recalled. "It was one of those moments where you hear artists talking about songs they get in dreams or in the middle of the night. I was like 'Wow, what an interesting subject matter to kind of pop into the head.' and I didn't do anything with it for about a year-and-a-half. Then all of a sudden at the very, very end of making my album, I literally had two days left in the recording studio with my producer, Dr. Luke. We just said, 'We're gonna finish it—it's so catchy because it won't get out of our heads.'"

The song picked up steam after it was played for three straight days on 107.5 The River in Nashville, resulting in an uptick in popularity that then lead to speculation about who may have inspired the hit. It was reported that Scarlett

Johansson's lips played a part in Perry writing the song, while Miley Cyrus claims that the song is about her. "When she came out with 'I Kissed a Girl,' I was doing the *Hannah Montana* movie, and I heard her on the radio," Cyrus recalled to WKTU. "They said, 'Who did you write that about?' She said me! And I was on a four-wheeler, actually—my dad had this four-wheeler, this is how hillbilly we are, we had a radio attached to the four-wheeler—and I heard it, and I screamed and started freaking out." Perry said in an interview that a teenage friend also played a part in her being inspired, saying that "I did kiss her. I was totally obsessed with her. She was beautiful—porcelain skin, perfect lips."

DON'T STOP BELIEVIN'

Journey

1981

"The song began with the chorus," Jonathan Cain, the keyboardist for Journey, told *SongFacts*. "My father had coached me. I was in Hollywood, struggling with my career, kind of lost. I was asking him, 'Should I come back to Chicago and just give up on this dream?' And he said, 'No, son. Stay the course. We have a vision. It's gonna happen. Don't stop believin'.'"

Cain developed the idea to have the song set on Sunset Boulevard from there, which he later pitched to Journey singer Steve Perry. "I described the menagerie of people who would show up on a Friday night," he said. "All the dreamers that had dreams to become actors. Producers, artists, lawyers, anything . . .they were all there on a Friday night."

In the liner notes for their *Time*[3] compilation, we're offered the next step in the song's journey. "At the band's Oakland warehouse, this song bubbled out of a rehearsal. [Guitarist Neal] Schon developed the bass riff, the chugging guitar line and the sweeping chords on the chorus. Steve Smith [drummer] built the song around a pattern featuring a lot of tom-toms, anchoring the number to a rich drum figure. Perry and Cain drew from their experiences with the Sunset Strip street scene."

As for the song's intent, Cain said: "It was the first attempt to bring an audience into the band's world. We're singing for you. We're singing about your world now. So, it was a departure from what they had been doing before. What I wanted to do was get a little Bruce Springsteen going on. Bruce was the master of that, bringing his audience into his songs. I was a huge fan of Bruce's."

CHEESEBURGER IN PARADISE

Jimmy Buffett

-

1978

"The myth of the cheeseburger in paradise goes back to a long trip on my first boat, the Euphoria," Jimmy Buffet said of his hit "Cheeseburger in Paradise." "We had run into some very rough weather crossing the Mona Passage between Hispanola and Puerto Rico, and broke our new bowsprit. The ice in our box had melted, and we were doing the canned-food-and-peanut-butter diet. The vision of a piping hot cheeseburger kept popping into my mind. We limped up the Sir Francis Drake Channel and into Roadtown on the island of Tortola, where a brand new marina and bar sat on the end of the dock like a mirage. We secured the boat, kissed the ground, and headed for the restaurant. To our amazement, we were offered a menu that featured an American cheeseburger and piña coladas. Now, these were the days when supplies were scarce—when horsemeat was more plentiful than ground beef in the tiny stores of the Third World. Anyway, we gave particular instructions to the waiter on how we wanted them cooked, and what we wanted on them—to which very little attention was paid. It didn't matter. The overdone burgers on the burned, toasted buns tasted like manna from Heaven, for, they were the realization of my fantasy burgers on the trip. That's the true story. I've heard other people and places claim that I stopped or cooked in their restaurants, but that is the way it happened."

AQUALUNG

Jethro Tull

-

1971

Talking about why "Aqualung" was never released as a single, Jethro Tull front man Ian Anderson told *SongFacts*: "Because it was too long, it was too episodic, it starts off with a loud guitar riff and then goes into rather more laid back acoustic stuff. Led Zeppelin at the time, you know, they didn't release any singles. It was album tracks. And radio sharply divided between AM radio, which played the 3-minute pop hits, and FM radio where they played what they called deep cuts. You would go into [an] album and play the obscure, the longer, the more convoluted songs in that period of more developmental rock music. But that day is not really with us anymore, whether it be classic rock stations that do play some of that music, but they are thin on the ground, and they too know that they've got to keep it short and sharp and cheerful, and provide the blue blanket of familiar sounding music and get onto the next set of commercial breaks, because that's what pays the radio station costs of being on the air. So pragmatic rules apply."

"Short and sharp and cheerful" could hardly be used to describe "Aqualung," as Anderson wrote the song about the homeless men that his wife, the amateur photographer Jennie Anderson, was taking pictures of. "*Aqualung* wasn't a concept album, although a lot of people thought so," Anderson explained. "The idea came about from a photograph my wife at the time took of a tramp in London. I had feelings of guilt about the homeless, as well as fear and insecurity with people like that who seem a little scary. And I suppose all of that was combined with a slightly romanticized picture of the person who is homeless but yet a free spirit, who either won't or can't join in society's prescribed formats. So from that photograph and those sentiments, I began writing the words to 'Aqualung.' I can remember sitting in a hotel room in L.A., working out the chord structure for the verses. It's quite a tortured tangle of chords, but it was meant to really drag you here and there and then set you down into the more gentle acoustic section of the song."

"I had feelings of guilt about the homeless, as well as fear and insecurity with people like that who seem a little scary."

On what the song is actually about, Anderson said "It's about our reaction, of guilt, distaste, awkwardness and confusion, all these things that we feel when we're confronted with the reality of the homeless. You see someone who's clearly in desperate need of some help, whether it's a few coins or the contents of your wallet, and you blank them out. The more you live in that business-driven, commercially-driven lifestyle, you can just cease to see them."

CASEY JONES

Grateful Dead

-

1970

The name for the song comes from a railroad engineer by the same name, who worked for the Illinois Central Railroad. He was operating a passenger train early one morning at a speed of 75 miles per hour along a winding track, cutting off his view of an approaching station. Fireman Sim Webb, who was riding with Jones and had a more favorable vantage point, warned him that there was something on the main tracks ahead of them. Jones told Webb to jump, a leap he somehow lived to talk about, and Jones immediately activated the airbrakes. The speed of the train got down to about 35 miles per hour on impact, an effort that likely saved everybody on board other than Jones. As a Jackson, Mississippi newspaper put it: "The south-bound passenger train No. 1 was running under a full head of steam when it crashed into the rear end of a caboose and three freight cars which were standing on the main track, the other portion of the train being on a sidetrack. The caboose and two of the cars were smashed to pieces, the engine left the rails and plowed into an embankment, where it overturned and was completely wrecked, the baggage and mail coaches also being thrown from the track and badly damaged. The engineer was killed outright by the concussion. His body was found lying under the cab, with his skull crushed and right arm torn from its socket. The fireman jumped just in time to save his life. The express messenger was thrown against the side of the car, having two of his ribs broken by the blow, but his condition is not considered dangerous."

Jones' friend Wallace Saunders, an engineer wiper, first immortalized Casey's story to the tune of the song "Jimmie Jones." Travelers heard the song and sang it as they made their way; the story was used in vaudeville performances and sang on the front lines in World War I. That story would go on to inspire Jerry Garcia's and Robert Hunter's "Casey Jones," though it's unlikely that the man who inspired the song was actually on cocaine at the time.

MR. JONES

Counting Crows

1993

"It's really a song about my friend Marty and I," Adam Duritz said on an episode of VH1's *Storytellers*. "We went out one night to watch his dad play, his dad was a flamenco guitar player who lived in Spain (David Serva), and he was in San Francisco in The Mission playing with his old flamenco troupe. And after the gig we all went to this bar called the New Amsterdam in San Francisco on Columbus and we got completely drunk. And Marty and I sat at the bar staring at these two girls, wishing there was some way we could go talk to them, but we were too shy. We kept joking with each other that if we were big rock stars instead of such loser, low-budget musicians, this would be easy. I went home that night and I wrote a song about it. I joke about what it's about, that story. But it's really a song about all the dreams and all the things that make you want to go into doing whatever it is that seizes your heart, whether it's being a rock star or being a doctor or whatever. Those things run from 'All this stuff I have pent up inside of me' to 'I want to meet girls because I'm tired of not being able to.' It is a lot of those things, it's about all those dreams, but it's also kind of cautionary because it's about how misguided you may be about some of those things and how hollow they may be too. Like the character in the song keeps saying, 'When everybody loves me I will never be lonely,' and you're supposed to know that that's not the way it's gonna be. I knew that even then. And this is a song about my dreams."

"It's also kind of cautionary because it's about how misguided you may be about some of those things and how hollow they may be too."

FOLLOW YOU, FOLLOW ME

Genesis

-

1978

"I thought, 'F*ck, it can't be that easy.'" Mike Rutherford, one of the founding members of Genesis said while talking about "Follow You, Follow Me."

Faced with an audience that was primarily male, Rutherford was searching for a bit more balance, and found that writing a song which appealed to women might be a bit easier than he originally thought. "When I wrote the lyric, out came this lovely little song, catchy without being sloppy," he told *Mojo*. "It took ten minutes."

TURN IT ON AGAIN

Genesis

-

1980

Waste not want not, as you never know where you'll find your next hit. "Turn It On Again" rose to No. 8 on the U.K. Singles Chart, and is the result of bits Genesis had previously tossed aside. "Yeah, the second part of 'Turn It On Again,'. . .Mike [Rutherford, guitarist for Genesis] wrote the main riff on 'Turn It On Again,' which is really what is best about the song.

We kind of put that bit—the bit he didn't use on *Smallcreep's Day*, curiously enough—with the bit I didn't use on *A Curious Feeling*, and put these two together. We made it much more rocky. . .my bit was a bit more epic, and Mike's bit was a bit slower and a bit more heavy-metal," said front man Phil Collins.

The song was originally intended to be slower and provide much less commercial appeal than the released version. Rutherford recalls: "I had this riff, [plays riff] but at the time I was playing it like this, [plays slower] and Phil [Collins, front man for Genesis] said 'Why don't you try it in a faster speed?' and then he said to me 'Do you realize it is in 13/8?' and I said 'What do you mean it's in 13? It's in 4/4, isn't it?' 'No, it's 13,' Collins said. 'You can't dance to it. You see people trying to dance to it every now and again, they get on the off-beat but they don't know why.'"

BE MY BABY

Ronnettes

-

1964

In a 2015 piece for *The Guardian*, Ronettes lead vocalist Ronnie Spector recalled teaming up with producer Phil Spector to create "Be My Baby," saying, "I formed The Ronettes with my sister Estelle and cousin Nedra, but we couldn't get a hit. When we did shows, we'd be on the bill as 'and others.' It was an awful period. Then one day Estelle called Philles Records, which was run by Phil Spector. He was probably the hottest producer in America, but he answered the phone himself. The next night, we had an audition and he just freaked out. 'That's the voice I've been looking for,' he said. He went nuts over me from that moment. We went out to get sandwiches in his limousine and soon he was taking me for candlelit dinners. When I rehearsed songs at his penthouse, he'd keep me later and later. Things just got hotter and hotter. He was infatuated with my voice, my body, everything. It was mutual. 'Be My Baby'—which Phil wrote with [Brill Building writers] Jeff Barry and Ellie Greenwich—documents that initial explosion. Recording it took forever. I rehearsed in New York with The Ronettes, then I had to go to California on my own to sing the lead. My mom usually flew with me but because it was so far she said: 'Honey, you're 18. You can do this on your own now.' Phil picked me up at the airport and kept saying: 'This record is going to be amazing.' In the studio, I had to hide in the ladies' room so the musicians could get their work done—I was very pretty and they'd keep looking at me. While I was in there, I came up with all those [lines] inspired by my old Frankie Lymon records. It took three days to record my vocals, take after take. The recording captures the full spectrum of my emotions: everything from nervousness to excitement. When I came in with [the beginning line of the song], the band went nuts. I was 18 years old, 3,000 miles from home, and had all these guys saying I was the next Billie Holliday. After that, I wasn't allowed in the studio. There may have been a little jealousy thing going on. I had to stay in the hotel while Phil finished the record. The first time I heard it, The Ronettes were on tour. We were lying in bed watching—when he said: 'This is going to be the record of the century.' And it was us!"

VOGUE

Madonna

-

1990

Born out of the need for a successful B-side for her single *Keep It Together*, the hastily produced "Vogue" was deemed by studio executives as being too good to not release as a single. They were right.

The best-selling single in 1990, "Vogue" was instead included on her album *I'm Breathless*, which was built around songs and ideas from her Disney movie *Dick Tracy*. "I wrote it when I was making *Dick Tracy*," Madonna told *Rolling Stone*. "After we shot the movie, [then-boyfriend] Warren Beatty asked me if I could write a song that would fit my character's point of view, that she could have conjured up. She was obsessed with speakeasies and movie stars and things like that. The idea for the lyrics came through that request. Coincidentally, I was going to Sound Factory and checking out these dancers who were all doing this new style of dancing called vogueing. And Shep Pettibone, who co-produced 'Vogue' with me, used to DJ there. That's how it grew together."

Of course, the song had nothing to do with the film; rather, it inspired a David Fincher-directed music video that is considered by some to be more famous. The video introduced "vogueing," a dance craze popular in the New York City gay community in which you would strike a pose, to the masses. Shot in black-and-white in what may have been a nod towards Hollywood past, the list of names that Madonna rattles off near the end of the song consists of those who shaped the Golden Age of Hollywood.

AMERICAN PIE

Don McLean

1971

"For some reason I wanted to write a big song about America and about politics, but I wanted to do it in a different way," Don McLean said while appearing as a guest on the U.K. show *Songbook*. "As I was fiddling around, I started singing this thing about the Buddy Holly crash...I thought, 'Whoa, what's that?'... And I said, 'Oh, that is such a great idea.' And so that's all I had. And then I thought, 'I can't have another slow song on this record. I've got to speed this up.' I came up with this chorus, crazy chorus. And then one time about a month later I just woke up and wrote the other five verses. Because I realized what it was, I knew what I had. And basically, all I had to do was speed up the slow verse with the chorus and then slow down the last verse so it was like the first verse, and then tell the story, which was a dream. It is from all these fantasies, all these memories that I made personal. Buddy Holly's death to me was a personal tragedy. As a child, a 15-year-old, I had no idea that nobody else felt that way much. I mean, I went to school and mentioned it and they said, 'So what?' So I carried this yearning and longing, if you will, this weird sadness that would overtake me when I would look at this album, *The Buddy Holly Story*, because that was my last Buddy record before he passed away."

"All I had to do was speed up the slow verse with the chorus and then slow down the last verse so it was like the first verse, and then tell the story, which was a dream."

SULTANS OF SWING

Dire Straits

1978

The concept for "Sultans of Swing" came from Mark Knopfler's taking in a lousy band on a lousier night in Ipswich, where he entered a bar as a reprieve from the rain. As the band wrapped up their set, the singer said to the audience "Goodnight and thank you. We are the sultans of swing." As Knopfler recalled: "When the guys said 'Thank you very much, we are the Sultans of Swing,' there was something really funny about it to me because sultans, they absolutely weren't. You know they were rather tired little blokes in pullovers."

The singer, guitarist, and songwriter for Dire Straits, Knopfler recalls how the switch from a National Steel guitar to a Fender Stratocaster changed his outlook on the song, saying: "I thought it was dull, but as soon as I bought my first Strat in 1977, the whole thing changed, though the lyrics remained the same. It just came alive as soon as I played it on that '61 Strat which remained my main guitar for many years and was basically the only thing I played on the first album and the new chord changes just presented themselves and fell into place."

GET LUCKY

Daft Punk

-

2013

On the "deep hidden meaning" behind Daft Punk's "Get Lucky," co-writer Nile Rodgers told *The Village Voice*: "Well, it wasn't even that deep. It was how it all came together. . . . I had met [Daft Punk] 16 years prior. It was, instantly, mutual admiration society because they had this great song, 'Da Funk,' on their first record. I loved it a lot, and when we met, they told me how much they loved [my band] Chic and how influenced by Chic their music is. . . .We tried to get together after that on two subsequent occasions, and it didn't work out, for whatever reason. And it's probably good that it didn't work out because, by the time it did work out, they had already done the Tron soundtrack, and that was the first time they had ever gone into the studio with people—with real, live, human beings—and worked on a record. So [for this album] they'd decided they'd do a Daft Punk album, but now they would use humans."

He continued: "One of the people who was interested in working with them was Pharrell Williams. They finally got together when Pharrell was in Paris, and they asked him, 'What are you working on right now?' He said, 'Well, I'm actually working on these Nile Rodgers type of grooves.' And the guys from Daft Punk looked at each other and said, 'Really? Well, listen to this.' And I had already written with them. I had already recorded. So [Pharrell] got lucky. He didn't have to work on [the Nile Rodgers grooves] because, there it was. They just gave it right to him. So, in the case of the song 'Get Lucky,' it was really perfect. I mean, it was one of those situations where everybody got lucky."

MORE THAN A FEELING

Boston

1976

"Epic flat out rejected it-and sent me an insulting letter!" Boston founder Tom Scholz told *Maximum Guitar*. "I have that letter framed now, but it said that there was nothing new about this music, and they were in no way interested. Then later, someone went through the proper political channels with Epic and, all of a sudden, they were interested. Still, we didn't get signed until they heard 'More Than a Feeling'."

The song rose to No. 5 on the *Billboard* Hot 100 in 1976 and is now remembered as one of the catchiest hard rock songs of all time. "More Than a Feeling" was Boston's big break, but it represented more than that to Scholz, who spent five years writing a song that drew inspiration from his past. "There actually is a Marienne," Scholz says. "She wasn't my girlfriend, she was. . .when I was a little kid, I think I was maybe eight or nine, I had a much older cousin who I just thought was the most beautiful girl that I'd ever seen. Her name was Marienne . . .I was secretly in love with my cousin," he laughs. "But I was only eight or nine, so. . .and that's Marienne." He called the song "sort of a bittersweet ballad," as it represented an aching for the past that was emphasized when contrasted with his dissatisfaction for the present.

The song was also inspired by The Left Banke's tune "Walk Away Renee," so much so that its chord progression was lifted for "More Than a Feeling." When an interviewer pointed that out to Scholz, he broke up laughing, saying "Oh my God, you're right! It's right there in the song! You know, I never realized that! The Left Banke was one of my favorite groups at that time, and they were very classically inspired."

ROSALITA

Bruce Springsteen

1973

"The stuff I write is the stuff I live with," Bruce Springsteen said. "They're all true. Even the names—Big Balls Billy, Weak-Kneed Willie, all of 'em."

"Rosalita" presented a unique concept to the world: a show-stopping anthem that doubled as a love song. The subject? Though he's never confirmed it, all signs point to Springsteen's ex-girlfriend Diane Lozito, who he dated as he began to experience substantial success in the music business. The title of the song certainly lends itself to that theory, as Diane's grandmother's name was Rose Lozito, similar to "Rosalita" when said in succession.

The advance Springsteen referenced in the song came from Columbia Records, who gave him $25,000 when he signed his first record deal.

I DON'T LIKE MONDAYS

The Boomtown Rats

1979

"I was doing a radio interview in Atlanta with [Johnnie] Fingers and there was a telex machine beside me," said The Boomtown Rats lead singer Bob Geldof while talking about what inspired him to write his hit "I Don't Like Mondays," which deals with the news of a school shooting that came over that telex. "I read it as it came out. Not liking Mondays as a reason for doing somebody in is a bit strange. . . .And the journalists interviewing her said, 'Tell me why?' It was such a senseless act. It was the perfect senseless act and this was the perfect senseless reason for doing it. So perhaps I wrote the perfect senseless song to illustrate it. It wasn't an attempt to exploit tragedy."

"It was such a senseless act. It was the perfect senseless act and this was the perfect senseless reason for doing it."

The tragedy that Geldof refers to occurred at a playground at Grover Cleveland Elementary School in San Diego, California, on January 29, 1979, where teenager Brenda Ann Spencer opened fire on a group of students, killing two adults and injuring a police officer and eight children. When asked why she did it, Spencer responded "I don't like Mondays. This livens up the day." The song performed very well in the U.K. and was eventually released as a single in the U.S., despite an unsuccessful attempt to prevent its release by Spencer's family.

LIVIN' ON A PRAYER

Bon Jovi

-

1986

In a 2014 interview with *The Tennessean*, co-writer Desmond Child dives into how he started working with Jon Bon Jovi on the 1986 hit "Livin' on a Prayer," saying "I got a call from this kid in a rock band from New Jersey. His name was Jon Bon Jovi. And he had gotten my number from Paul Stanley, because they had been the opening act for KISS in Europe that year. This was 1985, I think. He talked me into coming out to Jersey, so I had to rent a car, drive out there to this little wooden house. It was like the last house on the last little block. Behind it was a gi-normous marsh, and at the end of the marsh, it was like Emerald City, it was an oil refinery. Healthy place to live, right? It was [guitarist] Richie Sambora's parents' house, and that's where he grew up. I walk in, and Richie comes to the door, shows me down the hallway. I look into his room: posters of Farrah Fawcett and KISS. Went into the kitchen, and Jon, with his big, giant mullet, was on the phone, [with] lots of rings, lots of torn jeans and stuff. There was no place to be, so Richie showed me downstairs. It [had] a little keyboard on a tottering Formica table. There was a space heater because it was kind of cold, and there were some buzzing amps. And I just sat down there for a long time, and Richie was trying to do his best, being Mr. Nice Guy, talking to me. Then Jon came down. I had brought a title with me. We sort of sat around, and I said, 'Well, I've got a title. It's called 'You Give Love a Bad

Name.' [Jon] loved that. He had a title he loved, which was on his previous record, a song called 'Shot Through the Heart.' That's how we opened it.

"We started writing this story song about Tommy and Gina. . . .I think that each person, there was something autobiographical—for Jon with his relationship with [wife] Dorothea, because they were high school sweethearts. In my case, I had a girlfriend that I started my first band [with], called Desmond Child & Rouge. Her name was Maria Vidal. I stayed home writing songs, and she worked as a waitress at a place called Once Upon a Stove. They called her Gina because she reminded them of [Italian actress] Gina Lollobrigida. So we started the song off with Johnny and Gina because Johnny was my original name. And [Jon] said, 'I can't be singing about Johnny. My name's Johnny.' It was like, 'OK. . .Tommy then. Tommy and Gina.' And that's where Tommy and Gina were born."

TURN THE PAGE

Bob Seger

1973

Written in 1972 while Bob Seger was on tour with Teegarden & Van Winkle, "Turn the Page" deals with the tumultuous life that comes with being a rock star on the road. As drummer David Teegarden recalled: "We had been playing somewhere in the Midwest, or the northern reaches, on our way to North or South Dakota. [Guitarist] Mike Bruce was with us. We'd been travelling all night from the Detroit area to make this gig, driving in this blinding snowstorm. It was probably three in the morning. Mike decided it was time to get gas. He was slowing down to exit the interstate and spied a truck stop. We all had very long hair back then—it was the hippie era—but Skip, Mike and Bob had all stuffed their hair up in their hats. You had to be careful out on the road like that, because you'd get ostracized. When I walked in, there was this gauntlet of truckers making comments—'Is that a girl or a man?' I was seething; those guys were laughing their asses off, a big funny joke. That next night, after we played our gig—I think it was Mitchell, S.D.—Seger says, 'Hey, I've been working on this song for a bit, I've got this new line for it. . . .It was 'Turn the Page.'"

GOODNIGHT SAIGON

Billy Joel

1982

"I wanted to do that for my friends who did go to 'Nam," Billy Joel said, in a town hall hosted by Howard Stern. "A lot of them came back from being in country and really had a hard time getting over it, and still to this day I think a lot of them are having a hard time. They were never really welcomed back, and whether you agreed with the war or not, these guys really took it on the chin. They went over there and they served, and they never really got their due."

That Joel, in "Goodnight Saigon," was writing a song for the soldier rather than to make any sort of political statement was clear from the onset; his tendencies didn't deal in politics, and his characterizations of the war were from the point of view of a brother amongst his family. His referencing *Playboy*, Bob Hope appearances, and general company names like "Charlie" and "Baker" served to broaden the scope of his narrative; as Stephen Holden of *Rolling Stone* puts it: "As the song unfolds, Joel's 'we' becomes every American soldier, living and dead, who fought in Southeast Asia."

Saigon, now known as Ho Chi Minh City, was the capital of South Vietnam before it fell to the People's Army of Vietnam (often referred to as the North Vietnamese Army) and the National Liberation Front of South Vietnam (often referred to as the Viet Cong) on April 30, 1975, marking the end of the Vietnam War. American forces had been heavily withdrawn at that point, though an airport attack killed servicemen Darwin Judge and Charles McMahon, the last two Americans to die in Vietnam. The city's capture resulted from a major failure in judgment by those placing faith in the South Vietnamese forces; much of the ground gained by American soldiers was lost almost immediately after they had withdrawn. On top of that, the artillery left by American forces was rendered all but useless due to an oil embargo in the Middle East. The resulting lack of optimism surrounding the North's advance on the capital allowed for a preceding evacuation known as Operation Frequent Wind, the largest helicopter evacuation in history. Such an event could have lent itself to Joel as inspiration, as his song starts with crickets chirping and helicopter blades whooshing and ends with those same noises in reverse order. Of course, if such is the case, the only responsible interpretation of the chirping is it representing an end to the warfare, as peace was never again found by the 300,000 South Vietnamese who were "reeducated" by way of torture.

Of course, the major inspirations for the song came from the periods of American engagement in the war efforts. "It was all about them depending on each other," Joel said. "When they were over there, they weren't thinking about mom, apple pie and the flag, they were doing it for each other—to try to help and save each other and protect each other. That really hit me."

WORKS CITED

Like a Rolling Stone
"Like a Rolling Stone." Songfacts.com. Web. Accessed 03 Nov. 2017.

Interviewed by Marvin Bronstein. "Bob Dylan." *CBC*. 20 Feb. 1966.

Interviewed by Nat Hentoff. "Bob Dylan." *Playboy*, March 1966.

Kozinn, Alan. "Dylan's Handwritten Lyrics to 'Like a Rolling Stone' to Be Auctioned." *The New York Times*. 30 Apr. 2014.

Siegel, Jules. "Well, What Have We Here?" *Saturday Evening Post*, 30 July 1966.

(I Can't Get No) Satisfaction
"(I Can't Get No) Satisfaction." Songfacts.com. Web. Accessed 03 Nov. 2017.

St. Michael, Mick. *Keith Richards—in His Own Words*. Omnibus Press, 1994. Print.

Imagine
Blaney, John. *Lennon and McCartney: Together Alone*. Jawbone Press, 2007. Print.

Sheff, David. *All We Are Saying: The Last Major Interview with John Lennon and Yoko Ono.* St. Martin's Griffin, 1981. Print.

Spizer, Bruce. *The Beatles Solo on Apple Records.* 498 Productions, LLC, 2005. Print.
Wenner, Jann. *The 500 Greatest Songs of All Time. Rolling Stone*, 2010. Print.

Hello
Hiatt, Brian. "Adele: Inside Her Private Life and Triumphant Return." Rollingstone.com. 03 Nov. 15. Web. Accessed 03 Nov. 2017.

McRady, Rachel. "Adele Reveals the Inspiration for 'Hello,' Jokes That Her Son Makes Her Act Like a D-Head." *US Magazine*. 28 Oct. 2015. Web. Accessed 03 Nov. 17.

Respect
"'Respect' Wasn't a Feminist Anthem Until Aretha Franklin Made It One.'" *NPR*. NPR, 14 Feb. 17. Accessed 03 Nov. 2017.

Black, Johnny. *Classic Tracks Back to Back: Singles and Albums.* Thunder Bay Press, 2008. Print.

Good Vibrations
"Good Vibrations." Songfacts.com. Web. Accessed 03 Nov. 2017.

Badman, Keith. *The Beach Boys, the Definitive Diary of America's Greatest Band on Stage and in the Studio.* Backbeat Books, 2004. Print.

Gaines, Steven. *Heroes and Villains: The True Story of the Beach Boys.* Da Capo Press, 1986. Print.

Johnny B. Goode
Taylor, Timothy D. and Middleton, Richard. *Reading Pop: Approaches to Textual Analysis in Popular Music.* Oxford University Press, 2000. Print.

Miller, James. *Flowers in the Dustbin: The Rise of Rock and Roll, 1947–1977.* Simon & Schuster, 1999. Print.

Hey Jude

"McCartney Speaks About the Inspiration Behind 'Hey Jude.' YouTube.com. Web. Accessed 03 Nov. 2017.

Smells Like Teen Spirit

"Smells Like Teen Spirit." Songfacts.com. Web. Accessed 03 Nov. 2017.

Interviewed by David Fricke. "Kurt Cobain, the *Rolling Stone* Interview: Success Doesn't Suck." *Rolling Stone*. 27 Jan. 1994. Web. Accessed 03 Nov. 2017.

Queenan, Joe. "Was 'Smells Like Teen Spirit' Really Named after a Deodorant?" *The Guardian*. 19 July 2007. Web. Accessed 03 Nov. 2017.

What'd I Say

Charles, Ray and Ritz, David. *Brother Ray: Ray Charles' Own Story*. Da Capo Press, 2004. Print.

Evans, Mike. *Ray Charles: The Birth of Soul*. Omnibus Press, 2007. Print.

Interviewed by Ben Fong-Torres. "The *Rolling Stone* Interview: Ray Charles." *Rolling Stone*. 18 Jan. 1973. Web. Accessed 03 Nov. 2017.

My Generation

Bernays, Paul. "Mose Allison: Director's Statement." Bbc.co.uk. 1 Dec. 2005. Web. Accessed 03 Nov. 17.

Cavanagh, David. "Interview with Pete Townshend." *Q Magazine*. 1999.
Wenner, Jann. *The 500 Greatest Songs of All Time. Rolling Stone*, 2010. Print.

Wilkerson, Mark. "Amazing Journey: The Life of Pete Townshend." Lulu.com. 2006. Web. Accessed 03 Nov. 2017.

London Calling

"London Calling." Songfacts.com. Web. Accessed 03 Nov. 2017.

"'London Calling,' Repurposed as a Tourism Jingle." NPR. NPR, 30 July 2011. Web. Accessed 03 Nov. 2017.

Guarisco, Donald A. "London Calling—The Clash—Song Review." Allmusic.com. Web. Accessed 03 Nov. 2017.

Purple Haze

McDermott, John, et al. *Ultimate Hendrix*. Backbeat Books, 2009. Print.

McDermott, John, et al. *Jimi Hendrix: Sessions*. Little Brown, 1995. Print.

Roby, Steven and Schreiber, Brad. *Becoming Jimi Hendrix*. Da Capo Press, 2010. Print.

Roby, Steven. *Black Gold: The Lost Archives of Jimi Hendrix*. Billboard Books, 2002. Print.

Shadwick, Keith. *Jimi Hendrix: Musician*. Backbeat Books, 2003. Print.

Earth Angel

"Earth Angel." Songfacts.com. Web. Accessed 03 Nov. 2017.

Black, Johnny. *Singles: Six Decades of Hot Hits and Classic Cuts*. Thunder Bay Press, 2006. Print.

Let It Be
"Let It Be." *Sold on Song*. BBC Radio 2, 2009.

McLeod, Jeffrey. "A Lesson on Text Criticism and the Beatles' *Let It Be*." Catholicstand.com. 30 July 2013. Web. Accessed 03 Nov. 2017.

Spitz, Bob. *The Beatles*. Little Brown, 2005. Print.

Born to Run
"Born to Run." Songfacts.com. Web. Accessed 03 Nov. 2017.

Hiatt, Brian. "Bruce Springsteen on Making 'Born to Run': 'We Went to Extremes.'" *Rolling Stone*. 25 Aug. 2015. Web. Accessed 03 Nov. 2017.

Lose Yourself
Interviewed by Zane Lowe. "Eminem." *Beats 1 Radio*. Youtube.com. 27 Aug. 2015. Web. Accessed 03 Nov. 2017.

It Wasn't Me
Gebreyes, Rahel. "Shaggy's Hit Song 'It Wasn't Me' Didn't Come from Firsthand Experience." Huffingtonpost.com. 16 Oct. 2014. Web. Accessed 03 Nov. 2017.

Layla
Interviewed by Bobby Whitlock. "Layla's 40th: The Where's Eric! Interview with Bobby Whitlock." Whereseric.com. 26 Apr. 2011. Web. Accessed 03 Nov. 2017.

Gundersen, Edna. "Clapton doesn't sing the blues in autobiography. *USA Today*. 10 April 2007.

Leopold, Todd. "Harrison, Clapton and their muse." *CNN*. CNN, 03 Feb. 2005. Web. Accessed 04 Nov. 2017.

Schumacher, Michael. *Crossroads: The Life and Music of Eric Clapton*. Citadel Press, 2003. Print.

I Walk the Line
"I Walk the Line." Songfacts.com. Web. Accessed 03 Nov. 2017.

Grant, Marshall. *I Was There When It Happened: My Life with Johnny Cash*. Cumberland House Publishing, 2006. Print.

Horstman, Dorothy. *Sing Your Heart Out, Country Boy*. Country Music Foundation, 1976. Print.

Schlenker, Bob. "I Walk the Line – Reverse Speech." Theopenscroll.com. Web. Accessed 03 Nov. 2017.

Stairway to Heaven
Interviewed by Terry Gross. "Guitar Legend Jimmy Page." *NPR*. NPR, 02 June 2003. Web. Accessed 03 Nov. 2017.

Llewellyn, Sian. "Stairway to Heaven." *Total Guitar*. December 1998.

Sutcliffe, Phil. "Bustle in the Hedgerow." MOJO. April 2000.

Welch, Chris. *Led Zeppelin*. Orion Books, 1994. Print.

Sympathy for the Devil
"Sympathy for the Devil." Songfacts.com. Web. Accessed 03 Nov. 2017.

Interviewed by Jann Wenner. "Mick Jagger Remembers." *Rolling Stone*. 14 Dec. 1995.

Light My Fire

"American single certifications – Light My Fire." Riaa.com. Web. Accessed 03 Nov. 2017.

"Light My Fire." Songfacts.com. Web. Accessed 03 Nov. 2017.

"Set the Night On Fire: Behind the Doors' 'Light My Fire.'" *NPR*. NPR, 28 Aug. 2000. Web. Accessed 03 Nov. 2017.

One

"The 500 Greatest Songs Since You Were Born." *Blender*. October 2005.

From the Sky Down. Directed by Davis Guggenheim, performance by U2, BBC Worldwide Canada, 2011.

Jaeger, Barbara. "One Small Step for Mankind." *The Record*. 13 Mar. 1992.

McCormick, Neil. *U2 by U2*. HarperCollins, 2006. Print.

Stokes, Niall. *U2: Into the Heart: The Stories Behind Every Song*. Thunder's Mouth Press, 2005. Print.

Closer

"Closer." Songfacts.com. Web. Accessed 03 Nov. 2017.

"The Chainsmokers Reveal the Inspiration for 'Closer' + More." Siriusxm.com, 24 Sep. 2016. Web. Accessed 03 Nov. 2017.

The Weight

Bowman, Rob. "Life Is a Carnival." *Goldmine*. 26 July 1991. Theband.hiof.no. Web. Accessed 10 Nov. 2017.

Ebert, Roger. "Great Movie: *Un Chien Andalou*." Rogerebert.com. 16 Apr. 2000. Web. Accessed. 10 Nov. 2017.

Flint, Peter B. "Luis Bunuel Dies at 83; Film Maker for 50 Years." *The New York Times*. 30 July 1983. Web. Accessed 10 Nov. 2017.

Margolis, Lynne. "No False Bones: The Legacy of Levon Helm." Americansongwriter.com. 30 Aug. 2012. Web. Accessed 10 Nov. 2017.

Livin' la Vida Loca

"Livin' la Vida Loca. Songfacts.com. Web. Accessed 10 Nov. 2017.

Heroes

"Heroes." Songfacts.com. Web. Accessed 10 Nov. 2017.

"Uncut Interviews Tony Visconti on Berlin; The Real 'Uncut' Version." Bowiewonderland.com. Web. Accessed 10 Nov. 2017.

DeMain, Bill. "The Sound and Vision of David Bowie." *Performing Songwriter*. Sep./Oct. 2003. Web. Accessed 10 Nov. 2017.

Fisher, Max. "David Bowie at the Berlin Wall: The Incredible Story of a Concert and Its Role in History." Vox.com. 11 Jan. 2016. Web. Accessed 10 Nov. 2017.

O'Grady, Siobhan. "Germany to David Bowie: Thank You for Helping to Bring Down the Berlin Wall." Foreignpolicy.com. 11 Jan. 2016. Web. Accessed 10 Nov. 2017.

Bridge Over Troubled Water

"Across America Promotional CD Interview with Art." Artgarfunkel.com. Web. Accessed 26 Nov. 2017.

Eliot, Marc. *Paul Simon: A Life*. John Wiley and Sons, 2010. Print.

"The 500 Greatest Songs of All Time." *Rolling Stone*. 07 Apr. 2011. Web. Accessed 10 Nov. 17.

Hotel California

Crowe, Cameron. "Conversations with Don Henley and Glenn Frey." Liner notes for *The Very Best of the Eagles*, 2003.

Don Felder interviewed by Howard Stern. *The Howard Stern Show*. 17 July 2008.

Interviewed by Joe Bosso. "Interview: Don Felder on The Eagles' classic song, Hotel California. Musicradar.com. 21 Aug. 2012. Web. Accessed 10 Nov. 2017.

Savage, Mark. "Glenn Frey: How Hotel California destroyed The Eagles." *BBC*. BBC, 19 Jan. 2016. Web. Accessed 10 Nov. 2017.

History of the Eagles. Directed by Allison Ellwood. 2013.

The Message

"Rapper Melle Mel: Delivering 'The Message.'" *NPR*. NPR, 29 Aug. 2005. Web. Accessed 10 Nov. 2017.

When Doves Cry

"When Doves Cry." Songfacts.com. Web. Accessed 10 Nov. 2017.

Coryat, Karl. "His Highness Gets Down." *Bass Player*. November 1999.

Mr. Brightside

Cooper, Leonie. "The Killers' Brandon Flowers: 'We're a Bunch of Strong Personalities.'" *NME*. 17 Aug. 2012. Web. Accessed 10 Nov. 2017.

Patterson, Silvia. "Artists of the Century: Brandon Flowers." *Q Magazine*, 2009.

Van Luling, Todd. "The History of 'Mr. Brightside' by The Killers, 10 Years Later. Huffingtonpost.com. 12 July 2013. Web. Accessed 10 Nov. 2017.

Paul Revere

"Adrock Goes Back to School." YouTube.com. 04 Oct. 2007. Web. Accessed 10 Nov. 2017.

Kaufman, Gil. "Beastie Boys' Adam Horowitz Talks MCA Death: 'I Don't Believe Adam Was Afraid.'" MTV.com. 24 May 2012. Web. Accessed 10 Nov. 2017.

Kryptonite

Interviewed by Shawna Ortega. "Brad Arnold from 3 Doors Down." Songfacts.com. 20 Mar. 2009. Web. Accessed 10 Nov. 2017.

Whiter Shade of Pale

"Whiter Shade of Pale." Songfacts.com. Web. Accessed 10 Nov. 2017.

Thriller

"John Landis–Biography." Imdb.com. Web. Accessed 10 Nov. 2017.

"Thriller." Songfacts.com. Web. Accessed 10 Nov. 2017.

Edwards, Gavin. "12 Thrilling Facts About Michael Jackson's 'Thriller' Video." *Rolling Stone*. 29 Oct. 2013. Web. Accessed 10 Nov. 2017.

The Times They Are a-Changin'
Crowe, Cameron. Liner notes in Biograph, 1985.

Scaduto, Anthony. *Bob Dylan: A Biography*. Helter Skelter, 1972. Print.

For What It's Worth
Browne, David. "'For What It's Worth:' Inside Buffalo Springfield's Classic Protest Song." *Rolling Stone*. 11 Nov. 2016. Web. Accessed 10 Nov. 2017.

Jailhouse Rock
Interviewed by Marc Myers. "Interview: Mike Stoller." Jazzwax.com. 30 May 2012. Web. Accessed 10 Nov. 2017.

Chandelier
Renshaw, David. "Sia says her new song 'Chandelier' could have gone to Beyoncé or Rihanna." NME.com. 18 Mar. 2014. Web. Accessed 10 Nov. 2017.

Whole Lotta Love
"Whole Lotta Love." Songfacts.com. Web. Accessed 10 Nov. 2017.

"Whole Lotta Love." Kramerarchives.com. 25 Mar. 2009. Web. Accessed 10 Nov. 2017.
Wall, Mick. *When Giants Walked the Earth: A Biography of Led Zeppelin*. St. Martin's Griffin, 2010. Print.

Young, Charles M. "Robert Plant's manic persona." *Musician*. June 1990.

Mr. Tambourine Man
Kreps, Daniel. "Bruce Langhorne, Bob Dylan's 'Mr. Tambourine Man' Inspiration, Dead at 78." *Rolling Stone*. 17 Apr. 2017. Web. Accessed 10 Nov. 2017.

You Really Got Me
"You Really Got Me." Songfacts.com. Web. Accessed 10 Nov. 2017.

Hinman, Doug. *The Kinks: All Day and All of the Night: Day by Day Concerts, Recordings, and Broadcasts, 1961-1996*. Backbeat Books, 2004. Print.

Jovanovic, Rob. *God Save The Kinks: A Biography*. Album Press Ltd., 2014. Print.

Every Breath You Take
"Every Breath You Take." *BBC Radio 2*. Web. Accessed 10 Nov. 2017.

Buskin, Richard. "Classic Tracks: The Police 'Every Breath You Take.'" *Sound on Sound*. March 2004. Web. Accessed 10 Nov. 2017.

Davies, Hunter and Smith, Giles. "Interview: Sting." *Independent*. 30 Apr. 1993. Web. Accessed 10 Nov. 2017.

Garbarini, Vic. "Police Reunion!" *Revolver*. Spring 2000. Sting.com. Web. Accessed 10 Nov. 2017.

Ring of Fire
Cash, Vivian and Sharpsteen, Ann. *I Walked the Line: My Life with Johnny*. Scribner, 2007. Print.

Miller, Stephen. *Johnny Cash: The Life of an American Icon*. Omnibus, 2003. Print.

My Girl

Blair, Elizabeth. "'My Girl.'" *NPR*. NPR, 04 June 2000. Web. Accessed 10 Nov. 2017.

Blitzkrieg Bop

"Blitzkreig Bop." Songfacts.com. Web. Accessed 10 Nov. 2017.

Laitio-Ramone, Jari-Pekka. *Ramones: Soundtrack of Our Lives*. Tmi Ramoniac, 2009. Print.

I Still Haven't Found What I'm Looking For

Austin, Dave, et al. *Songwriting for Dummies*. Wiley Publishing, 2002. Print.

McCormick, Neil. *U2 by U2*. HarperCollins, 2006. Print.

O'Hare, Colm. "The Secret History of 'The Joshua Tree.'" Atu2.com. 2007. Web. Accessed 26 Nov. 17.

Fortunate Son

Fogerty, John and McDonough, Jimmy. *Fortunate Son: My Life, My Music*. Little, Brown and Company, 2015. Print.

"The Battles Premiere." *The Voice*, NBC, 12 Oct. 2015.

Crazy

Interviewed by Jan Blumentrath. "Interview with Josh Deutsch, A&R for Gnarls Barkley." Hitquarters.com. 04 Sep. 2006. Web. Accessed 10 Nov. 2017.

You Can't Always Get What You Want

"You Can't Always Get What You Want." Songfacts.com. Web. Accessed 10 Nov. 2017.

"You Can't Always Get What You Want." Timeisonourside.com. Web. Accessed 10 Nov. 2017.

Loewenstein, Dora and Dodd, Philip. *According to the Rolling Stones*. Chronicle Books, 2003. Print.

The Boxer

"The Boxer." Songfacts.com. Web. Accessed 10 Nov. 2017.

Kienzle, Rich. "Hired Gun." *Fretboard Journal*. Issue No. 12, 2008.

Brown Eyed Girl

Appel, Rich. "Revisionist History, Valentine's Day Edition: Captain & Tennelle Crunches Aerosmith, Van Morrison Boots Lulu." Billboard.com. 14 Feb. 2015. Web. Accessed 10 Nov. 2017.

Heylin, Clinton. *Can You Feel the Silence? Van Morrison: A New Biography*. Chicago Review Press, 2003. Print.

Interviewed by Tim Morrison. "Time Magazine Interviews: Van Morrison." *Time*. 27 Feb. 2009. Youtube.com. Web. Accessed 10 Nov. 2017.

Halo

"Halo." Songfacts.com. Web. Accessed 10 Nov. 2017.

Balls, David. "Tedder: 'Halo wasn't written for Leona.'" Digitalspy.com. 01 Dec. 2009. Web. Accessed 10 Nov. 2017.

Hampp, Andrew. "Ryan Tedder Reveals the Stories Behind His Songs for Beyoncé, Adele, Ellie Goulding & More." Billboard.com. 19 Mar. 2014. Web. Accessed 10 Nov. 2017.

Kheraj, Alim. "Beyoncé: The REAL Stories Behind Six of Her Biggest Songs." Digitalspy.com. 13 Aug. 2016. Web. Accessed 10 Nov. 2017.

Shout (Parts 1 and 2)

Myers, Marc. *Anatomy of a Song: The Oral History of 45 Iconic Hits That Changed Rock, R&B and Pop*. Grove/Atlantic, 2016. Print.

Go Your Own Way

"Lindsay Buckingham & Stevie Nicks Talk Fleetwood Mac's Go Your Own Way–Anatomy of a Song." Accesshollywood.com. 11 Feb. 2013. Web. Accessed 10 Nov. 2017.

Stand by Me

"Good Rockin' Tonight." *The History of Rock n' Roll*. Warner Bros. Domestic Television Distribution, PTEN, Time-Life Video. 1995.

"Stand by Me." Songfacts.com. Web. Accessed 10 Nov. 2017.

Interviewed by Marc Myers. "Interview: Mike Stoller." Jazzwax.com. May 2012. Web. Accessed 11 Nov. 2017.

House of the Rising Sun

Marshall, Ray. "The Rise of Supergroup." *Newcastle Evening Chronicle*. 17 Aug. 2005.

Matteson, Jr., Richard L. and Matteson, Richard. *Bluegrass Picker's Tune Book*. Mel Bay Publications, 2006. Print.

Sullivan, Steve. *Encyclopedia of Great Popular Song Recordings, Volume 2.* Scarecrow Press, 2013. Print.

Burdon, Eric. *I Used to Be an Animal, But I'm All Right Now*. Faber and Faber, 1986. Print.

Peggy Sue

Conradt, Stacy. "Who Was Buddy Holly's 'Peggy Sue.'" Mentalfloss.com. 03 Feb. 2016. Web. Accessed 11 Nov. 2017.

"Buddy Holly and 'The Day the Music Died.'" *NPR*. NPR, 03 Feb. 2009. Web. Accessed 11 Nov. 2017.

Born to be Wild

Horowitz, Hal. "Steppenwolf–Born to Be Wild." Allmusic.com. Web. Accessed 11 Nov. 2017.

Maggie May

"Maggie May." Songfacts.com. Web. Accessed 11 Nov. 2017.

Stewart, Rod. *Rod: The Autobiography*. Three Rivers Press, 2013. Print.

In the Midnight Hour

"In the Midnight Hour." Songfacts.com. Web. Accessed 11 Nov. 2017.

Purple Rain

Daley, Dan. "Classic Tracks: Prince and the Revolution's 'Purple Rain.'" *Mix*. 2009.

Jones, Lucy. "20 Things You Didn't Know About 'Purple Rain.'" NME.com. 10 Dec. 2012. Web. Accessed 11 Nov. 2017.

Raftery, Brian. "Prince: The Oral History of 'Purple Rain.'" *Spin*. July 2009. Web. Accessed 11 Nov. 2017.

Rock Lobster

"Rock Lobster." Songfacts.com. Web. Accessed 11 Nov. 2017.

Lust for Life

"Lust for Life." Songfacts.com. Web. Accessed 11 Nov. 2017.

Boilen, Bob. "Old Music Tuesdays: The Lust for Life Beat." *NPR*. NPR, 15 Jan. 2008. Web. Accessed 11 Nov. 2017.

"Interview with Iggy Pop." *Q Magazine*, Vol. 321. 2013.

Pareles, Jon. "Iggy Pop on David Bowie: 'He Resurrected Me.'" *The New York Times*. 13 Jan. 2016. Web. Accessed 11 Nov. 2017.

Foxy Lady

Campion, Chris. "Lithofayne Pridgon: Jimi Hendrix's Original 'Foxy Lady.'" *The Guardian*. 22 Mar. 2015. Web. Accessed 11 Nov. 2017.

Shapiro, Harry and Glebbeek, Cesar. *Jimi Hendrix: Electric Gypsy*. St. Martin's Press, 1990. Print.

Redding, Noel. Liner notes for *Are You Experienced?*, 1993.

I'm Waiting for the Man

"I'm Waiting for the Man." Songfacts.com. Web. Accessed 11 Nov. 2017.

Shout

"Shout." Antiwarsongs.org. Web. Accessed 11 Nov. 2017.

"Shout." Songfacts.com. Web. Accessed 11 Nov. 2017.

Comaratta, Len. "Tears for Fears' Curt Smith: Back in the Big Chair." Consequenceofsound.net. 06 Nov. 2014. Web. Accessed 11 Nov. 2017.

Bohemian Rhapsody

Black, Johnny. "The Greatest Songs Ever!" *Blender*. Dec. 2001/Jan. 2002.

Corn, John. *Britain Since 1948*. Folens Publishers, 2005. Print.

McAlpine, Fraser. "10 Things You May Not Know About Queen's 'Bohemian Rhapsody.'" Bbcamerica.com. 2015. Web. Accessed 11 Nov. 2017.

Queen: Days of Our Lives. Directed by Matt O'Casey. BBC, 2011.

Losing My Religion

Black, Johnny. *Reveal: The Story of R.E.M.* Backbeat Books, 2004. Print.

Buckley, David. *R.E.M.: Fiction: An Alternative Biography*. Virgin, 2002. Print.

Mettler, Mike. "R.E.M.: Radio Songs." *Guitar School*. September 1991.

99 Problems

Interviewed by Paul Holdengraber. "Jay-Z and Cornel West in Conversation with Paul Holdengraber." 15 Nov. 2010. Fora.tv. Web. Accessed 11 Nov. 2017.

Grow, Kory. "How Chris Rock and Ice-T Inspired Jay Z's '99 Problems.'" *Rolling Stone*. 25 Mar. 2014. Web. Accessed 11 Nov. 2017.

Dream On

"Dream On." Songfacts.com. Web. Accessed 11 Nov. 2017.

Interviewed by David Fricke. "Talk This Way." *Rolling Stone*. 03 Nov. 1994. Web. Accessed 11 Nov. 2017.

Interviewed by Bruce Pollock. "Steven Tyler of Aerosmith." Songfacts.com. 1984. Web. Accessed 11 Nov. 2017.

Masley, Ed. "Interview: Steven Tyler of Aerosmith on Going Country and Why 'Dream On' Kind of Freaked Him Out." *The Republic*. 13 July 2016. Azcentral.com. Web. Accessed 11 Nov. 2017.

Wild Thing

"Billboard Hot 100." *Billboard*. 02 July 1966.

Mastropolo, Frank. "'Wild Thing'—The First Punk Rock Song?" *Pop(ular) Culture Elective*. November 2012.

Sutcliffe, Phil. "The Troggs: The Missing Links." *MOJO*. July 2011.

Billboard Magazine. Vol. 78, No. 27. Nielson Business Media, Inc., 1966.

Dancing Queen

"ABBA: Dancing Queen (Royal Swedish Opera 1976)." Youtube.com. 21 June 2010. Web. Accessed 11 Nov. 17.

"ABBA—Dancing Queen—The Missing Verse/Lost Lyric." Youtube.com. 14 Nov. 2007. Web. Accessed 11 Nov. 2017.

Gatward, Cheryl. "Abba – Dancing Queen." Creation.com. 09 Apr. 2015. Web. Accessed 11 Nov. 2017.

Free Fallin'

Olson, Cathy Applefeld. "Tom Petty Originally Wrote 'Free Fallin'' Just to Make Jeff Lynne Laugh." Billboard.com. 07 June 2016. Web. Accessed 11 Nov. 2017.

Hey Ya!

"Hey Ya!" Songfacts.com. Web. Accessed 11 Nov. 2017.

Moss, Corey. "Road to the Grammys: The Making of OutKast's 'Hey Ya!'" Mtv.com. 30 Jan. 2004. Web. Accessed 11 Nov. 2017.

Van Luling, Todd. "The History of 'Hey Ya!', As Explained By André 3000." Huffingtonpost.com. 12 Sep. 2013. Web. Accessed 11 Nov. 2017.

Hells Bells

Elliot, Paul. "AC/DC: The Epic Inside Story of *Back in Black*." Teamrock.com. 05 May 2016. Web. Accessed 11 Nov. 2017.

Stayin' Alive

Bilyeu, Melinda, et al. *The Ultimate Biography of the Bee Gees: Tales of the Brothers Gibb*. Omnibus Press, 2011. Print.

Hughes, Andrew Mon. *The Bee Gees: Tales of the Brothers Gibb*. Omnibus Press, 2009. Print.

Small, Mark. "On the Watchtower–Albhy Galuten '68." *Berklee Today*. Summer 2002. Berklee.edu. Web. Accessed 11 Nov. 2017.

Free Bird

"Lynyrd Skynyrd—The Story Behind 'Free Bird.'" Alanpaul.net. 20 Oct. 2015. Web. Accessed 11 Nov. 2017.

Rehab

"Rehab." Songfacts.com. Web. Accessed 11 Nov. 2017.

Irwin, Lew. "Amy Winehouse's Dad Reveals Meaning Behind 'Rehab' Song." Contactmusic.com. 27 June 2012. Web. Accessed 11 Nov. 2017.

Sweet Child O' Mine

Gallucci, Michael. "The Story Behind Every Song—'Sweet Child O' Mine.'" Ultimateclassicrock.com. 26 July 2017. Web. Accessed 11 Nov. 2017.

"The Story Behind the Song—Guns N' Roses 'Sweet Child O' Mine.'" *Q Magazine*. December 2005. Heretodaygonetohell.com. Web. Accessed 11 Nov. 2017.

Fight the Power

"Fight the Power." Songfacts.com. Web. Accessed 11 Nov. 2017.

Myrie, Russell. *Don't Rhyme for the Sake of Riddlin: The Authorized Story of Public Enemy*. Grove Press, 2010. Print.

Simpson, Janice C. "Music: Yo! Rap Gets on the Map." *Time*. 05 Feb. 1990. Web. Accessed 11 Nov. 2017.

Loser

Black, Johnny. "The Greatest Songs Ever!" *Blender*. Dec. 2001/Jan. 2002.

Palacios, Julian. *Beck: Beautiful Monstrosity*. Boxtree, 2000. Print.

Schoemer, Karen. "The Last Boy Wonder." *Elle*. December 1999.

Come Together

"100 Greatest Beatles Songs." *Rolling Stone*. 19 Sep. 2011. Web. Accessed 11 Nov. 2017.

"Come Together." Beatlesebooks.com. Web. Accessed 11 Nov. 2017.

"Something/Come Together." Everyhit.com. 18 July 2007. Web. Accessed 11 Nov. 2017.

Interviewed by Jann S. Wenner. "Lennon Remembers." *Rolling Stone*. 21 Jan. 1971. Web. Accessed 11 Nov. 2017.

Miles, Barry. *Many Years From Now*. Seeker & Warburg, 1997. Print.

Sheff, David. *All We Are Saying: The Last Major Interview with John Lennon and Yoko Ono*. St. Martin's Press, 2000. Print.

Wallgren, Mark. *The Beatles on Record*. Simon & Schuster, 1982. Print.

Rockin' in the Free World

"Rockin' in the Free World." Songfacts.com. Web. Accessed 11 Nov. 2017.

"Rockin' in the Free World." Thrasherswheat.org. Web. Accessed 11 Nov. 2017.

McDonough, Jimmy. *Shakey: Neil Young's Biography*. Random House, 2002. Print.

... Baby One More Time

"E! Entertainment Special: Britney Spears." E!, 14 Mar. 2004.

"The 500 Greatest Songs Since You Were Born." *Blender*. Sep. 2005.

Taylor, Chuck. "Jive's Britney Spears Sets Top 40 Abuzz with Rhythm-Leaning 'Baby One More Time.'" *Billboard*. 24 Oct. 1998.

Sorry

Howard, Tom. "Justin Bieber: The Full NME Cover Story." *NME*. 13 Nov. 2015. Web. Accessed 11 Nov. 2017.

Kawashima, Dale. "Young Pop Songwriter Julia Michaels Co-Writes Big Hits for Justin Bieber and Selena Gomez." Songwriteruniverse.com. 16 Nov. 2015. Web. Accessed 11 Nov. 2017.

Tanzer, Myles. "Producer BLOOD Breaks Down His Work on Justin Bieber's 'Sorry.'" Thefader.com. 27 Oct. 2015. Web. Accessed 11 Nov. 2017.

Walk on the Wild Side

"Joe Dallesandro: The Warhol-Era Sex Symbol Talks." *LA Weekly*. 17 Jan. 2014.

"Walk on the Wild Side." Songfacts.com. Web. Accessed 11 Nov. 2017.

Klemm, Michael D. "Warhol on the Beach." CinemaQueer.com. June 2014. Web. Accessed 11 Nov. 2017.

McCourt, James. "Warhol's Brainy Goddess." *Gay City News*. 23 June 2005.

Moynihan, Colin. "From the Archives, a Portrait of a Pop-Art Muse." *The New York Times*. 24 Feb. 2009.

Simpson, Dave. "Bet You Think This Song Is about You." *The Guardian*. 12 Dec. 2008.

Paper Planes

Interviewed by Alex Wagner. "Interview with M.I.A." *Fader*. 07 Aug. 2007. Web. Accessed 11 Nov. 2017.

Rocket Man

"Rocket Man: The Inspiration." Youtube.com. 12 Dec. 2016. Web. Accessed 11 Nov. 2017.

Jump

Crouse, Richard. *Who Wrote the Book of Love?* Doubleday Canada, 2012. Print.

Wilkening, Matthew. "Did a Bad Hot Dog Inspire Eddie Van Halen to Write 'Jump?'" Ultimateclassicrock.com. 12 Aug. 2012. Web. Accessed 11 Nov. 2017.

All the Young Dudes
Buckley, David. *Strange Fascination—David Bowie: The Definitive Story*. Virgin Books, 2001. Print.

Copetas, Craig. "Beat Godfather Meets Glitter Mainman: William Burroughs Interviews David Bowie." *Rolling Stone*. 28 Feb. 1974. Web. Accessed 11 Nov. 2017.

Goddard, Simon. *Ziggyology*. Random House, 2013. Print.

Jesus Walks
"Jesus Walks." Songfacts.com. Web. Accessed 11 Nov. 2017.

Seven Nation Army
Martin, Daniel. "20 Things You Might Not Know About 'Seven Nation Army.'" NME.com. 13 May 2013. Web. Accessed 11 Nov. 2017.

Webb, Robert. "Story of the Song: Seven Nation Army—The White Stripes." *Independent*. 24 June 2010. Web. Accessed 11 Nov. 2017.

Stan
Total Request Live. Eminem interviewed by Dave Holmes. MTV, 2000. Youtube.com. Web. Accessed 11 Nov. 2017.

She's Not There
"She's Not There." Songfacts.com. Web. Accessed 11 Nov. 2017.

Simpson, Will. "The Story Behind The Song: She's Not There by The Zombies." Teamrock.com. 02 Apr. 2008. Web. Accessed 11 Nov. 2017.

Rock the Casbah
Interviewed by Spike Webb. "Topper Headon (The Clash) Talks about 'Mad, Bad and Dangerous.'" Youtube.com. 03 May 2012. Web. Accessed 11 Nov. 2017.

Waterfalls
Thomas, Rebecca. "TLC's Left Eye Remembered: 10 Years Later." MTV.com. 25 Apr. 2017. Web. Accessed 11 Nov. 2017.

Wish You Were Here
Leahey, Andrew. "Behind the Song: Pink Floyd's 'Wish You Were Here.'" Americansongwriter.com. 30 Aug. 2012. Web. Accessed 12 Nov. 2017.

Manning, Toby. *The Rough Guide to Pink Floyd*. Rough Guides, 2006. Print.

We Will Rock You
"We Will Rock You." Songfacts.com. Web. Accessed 12 Nov. 2017.

Interviewed by Tom Browne. "Interview with Brian May." *BBC Radio One*. 24 Dec. 1977.

Spirit in the Sky
"Spirit in the Sky." Christianorder.com. February 2011. Web. Accessed 12 Nov. 2017.

Billie Jean
"Billie Jean." Songfacts.com. Web. Accessed 12 Nov. 2017.

Jones, Lucy. "30 Cool Facts You Didn't Know About 'Billie Jean.'" Nme.com. 02 Jan. 2013. Web. Accessed 12 Nov. 2017.

Baba O'Riley

"Baba O'Riley." Songfacts.com. Web. Accessed 12 Nov. 2017.

Semi-Charmed Life

"Semi-Charmed Life." Songfacts.com. Web. Accessed 12 Nov. 2017.

Elfman, Doug. "Musical Diversity—Third Eye Blind's influences range from Lou Reed to Queen." *Las Vegas Review-Journal.* 15 Feb. 2002.

Watching the Detectives

Harrington, Richard. "Elvis Costello's (Really) Big Band." *Washington Post.* 14 Apr. 2016.

Hutchinson, Lydia. "Happy Birthday, Elvis Costello." Performingsongwriter.com. 25 Aug. 2011. Web. Accessed 12 Nov. 2017.

Tears in Heaven

"Exclusive: Mother of 'Tears in Heaven' Inspiration Shares Story." Abcnews.go.com. 07 Sep. 2007. Web. Accessed 12 Nov. 2017.

"Tears in Heaven." Songfacts.com. Web. Accessed 12 Nov. 2017.

Sweet Dreams (Are Made of This)

"Sweet Dreams (Are Made of This)." Songfacts.com. Web. Accessed 12 Nov. 2017.

Farber, Jim. "Dave Stewart: 'What Annie Lennox and I Went through Was Insane.'" *The Guardian.* 13 Feb. 2016. Web. Accessed 12 Nov. 2017.

White Room

"White Room." Songfacts.com. Web. Accessed 12 Nov. 2017.

Fake Plastic Trees

"Fake Plastic Trees." Songfacts.com. Web. Accessed 12 Nov. 2017.

Black, Johnny. "The Greatest Songs Ever!" *Blender.* Dec. 2001/Jan. 2002. Archive.li. Web. Accessed 12 Nov. 2017.

Bitter Sweet Symphony

"Bitter Sweet Symphony." Songfacts.com. Web. Accessed 12 Nov. 2017.

"Bitter Sweet Symphony: The Controversy." Thevervelive.com. 01 May 2005. Web. Accessed 12 Nov. 2017.

"Rolling Stones' Manager Derides The Verve." Nme.com. 07 Oct. 2008. Web. Accessed 12 Nov. 2017.

"The Last Time." Songfacts.com. Web. Accessed 12 Nov. 2017.

Prato, Greg. "The Verve—Bitter Sweet Symphony." Allmusic.com. Web. Accessed 12 Nov. 2017.

Turner, Gustavo. "Song Authorship Controversies, from George Harrison to Oasis." *Los Angeles Times.* 27 Jan. 2015. Web. Accessed 12 Nov. 2017.

Tiny Dancer

Bessman, Jim. "Elton John—30 Years of Music with Bernie Taupin." *Billboard.* 04 Oct. 1997.

Beviglia, Jim. "Behind the Song: 'Tiny Dancer' by Elton John." Americansongwriter.com. 23 Dec. 2013. Web. Accessed 12 Nov. 2017.

Rock Around the Clock
"Bill Haley and the Comets record 'Rock Around the Clock.'" History.com. Web. Accessed 12 Nov. 2017.

Chilton, Martin. "Rock Around the Clock: How Bill Haley's Song Became a Hit." *The Telegraph*. 17 Apr. 2016. Web. Accessed 12 Nov. 2017.

Eye of the Tiger
Paulson, Dave. "Story Behind the Song: 'Eye of the Tiger.'" *The Tennessean*. 14 Feb. 2015. Web. Accessed 12 Nov. 2017.

(Don't Fear) The Reaper
"(Don't Fear) The Reaper." Songfacts.com. Web. Accessed 12 Nov. 2017.

"The 100 Greatest Singles of All Time." *MOJO*. 1997.

Hutchinson, Lydia. "(Don't Fear) The Reaper." Performingsongwriter.com. 25 Oct. 2011. Web. Accessed 12 Nov. 2017.

Enter Sandman
"Enter Sandman." Songfacts.com. Web. Accessed 12 Nov. 2017.

Divita, Joe. "Kirk Hammett: Soundgarden Inspired the Riff Behind Metallica's 'Enter Sandman.'" Loudwire.com. 14 Sep. 2017. Web. Accessed 12 Nov. 2017.

Umbrella
Rosen, Jody. "Song of the Year." *Blender*. 25 Dec. 2007.

In Bloom
"In Bloom." Songfacts.com. Web. Accessed 12 Nov. 2017.

Barker, Emily. "Nirvana—The Secret Story of Every Album Track Explained." Nme.com. 01 Apr. 2014. Web. Accessed 12 Nov. 2017.

The Boys of Summer
Cooke, R. "Bumper Sticker!" *NME*. 23 Feb. 1985.

Interviewed by Mikal Gilmore. "Don Henley." *Rolling Stone*. Nov. 1987/ Dec. 1987.

Newton, Steve. "Meet Mike Campbell, the Underrated Guitar Genius Behind all Those Tom Petty Hits." Straight.com. 14 Aug. 2014. Web. Accessed 12 Nov. 2017.

Piano Man
"An Evening of Questions and Answers—Billy Joel at Harvard University." 03 Oct. 1994. Youtube.com. Web. Accessed 12 Nov. 2017.

American Idiot
"American Idiot." Songfacts.com. Web. Accessed 12 Nov. 2017.

DiPerna, Alan. *Guitar Legends*. Future US, 2005. Print.

Pappedemas, Alex. "Green Day: The 2004 'American Idiot' Cover Story." *Spin*. November 2004. Web. Accessed 12 Nov. 2017.

The World Is Yours
Isenberg, Daniel. "Pete Rock Tells All: The Stories Behind His Classic Records." Complex.com. 09 June 2011. Web. Accessed 12 Nov. 2017.

Creep
"Creep." Songfacts.com. Web. Accessed 12 Nov. 2017.

Daly, Rhian. "Radiohead: 10 Geeky Facts About 'Creep.'" Nme.com. 08 Apr. 2015. Web. Accessed 12 Nov. 2017.

English, Tim. *Sounds Like Teen Spirit: Stolen Melodies, Ripped-Off Riffs, and the Secret History of Rock and Roll*. iUniverse Star, 2006. Print.

Marzorati, Gerald. "The Post-Rock Band." *The New York Times*. 01 Oct. 2000. Web. Accessed 12 Nov. 2017.

Randall, Mac. *Exit Music: The Radiohead Story*. Delta, 2000. Print.

I Wanna Be Your Dog

"I Wanna Be Your Dog." Songfacts.com. Web. Accessed 12 Nov. 2017.

"Interview with Iggy Pop." *The Howard Stern Show*, WWOR, 1990.

Pink Houses

"John Mellencamp: My Life in 15 Songs." Rollingstone.com. 23 Dec. 2013. Web. Accessed 12 Nov. 2017.

Abbott, Jim. "John Mellencamp Art Exhibit Set to Open in DeLand." *Orlando Sentinel*. 08 Oct. 2014. Web. Accessed 12 Nov. 2017.

I Shot the Sheriff

Colagrande, J.J. "Bob Marley's Ex-Girlfriend Brings Her Own Marley Documentary to Miami." *Miami New Times*. 19 Apr. 2012.

Surrender

"Surrender." Songfacts.com. Web. Accessed 12 Nov. 2017.

"The 500 Greatest Songs of All Time." *Rolling Stone*. 07 Apr. 2011. Web. Accessed 12 Nov. 2017.

Welcome to the Jungle

Elliott, Paul. "Guns N' Roses: The Story Behind 'Welcome to the Jungle.'" Teamrock.com. 10 July 2015. Web. Accessed 12 Nov. 2017.

Spitz, Marc. "Just a Little Patience." *Spin*. July 1999. Heretodaygonetohell.com. Web. Accessed 12 Nov. 2017.

Last Nite

"Last Nite." Songfacts.com. Web. Accessed 12 Nov. 2017.

"Interview with Tom Petty." *Rolling Stone*. 28 June 2006. Web. Accessed 12 Nov. 2017.

I Wanna Know What Love Is

"I Wanna Know What Love Is." Songfacts.com. Web. Accessed 12 Nov. 2017.

Yates, Henry. "The Story Behind the Song: 'I Wanna Know What Love Is' by Foreigner." Teamrock.com. 17 Oct. 2007. Web. Accessed 12 Nov. 2017.

I Want It That Way

"I Want It That Way." Songfacts.com. Web. Accessed 13 Nov. 2017.

Westhoff, Ben. "What the Hell Is Backstreet Boys' 'I Want It That Way' About? UPDATE: Mind-blowing Shit Has Come to Light." Laweekly.com. 15 Dec. 2011. Web. Accessed 13 Nov. 2017.

White Rabbit

Hughes, Rob. "The Story Behind the Song: 'White Rabbit' by Jefferson Airplane." Teamrock.com. 29 Oct. 2016. Web. Accessed 13 Nov. 2017.

I Love Rock 'N' Roll

"I Love Rock 'N' Roll." Songfacts.com. Web. Accessed 13 Nov. 2017.

Sharell, Jerry J. "The Recording Academy Announces 2016 Grammy Hall of Fame Inductees." Grammy.com. 18 Nov. 2015. Web. Accessed 13 Nov. 2017.

Whitburn, Joel. *The Billboard Book of Top 40 Hits, 8th Edition*. Billboard Publications, 2004. Print.

Time to Pretend

"Time to Pretend." Songfacts.com. Web. Accessed 13 Nov. 2017.

Ignition/Remix

Heath, Chris. "The Confessions of R. Kelly." *GQ*. 20 Jan. 2016. Web. Accessed 13 Nov. 2017.

Loughrey, Clarisse. "R. Kelly Wrote 'Ignition (Remix)' Five Years before 'Ignition.'" *Independent*. 02 Mar. 2016. Web. Accessed 13 Nov. 2017.

Everlong

"Foo Fighters' Dave Grohl on the Story Behind 'Everlong' and Its Unforgettable Music Video." Youtube.com. 17 July 2015. Web. Accessed 13 Nov. 2017.

Buddy Holly

Domball, Ryan. "Buddy Holly: How Four LA Rockers Created the Definitive Hipster-Doofus Battle Cry." *Blender*. Nov. 2008.

Luerssen, John D. *Rivers' Edge: The Weezer Story*. ECW Press, 2004. Print.

Wake Me Up

"Avicii: 'Aloe Blacc Wrote "Wake Me Up" Lyrics in Two Hours.'" Mtv.co.uk. 30 July 2013. Web. Accessed 13 Nov. 2017.

Doyle, Patrick. "How Avicii Helped Aloe Blacc Wake Up and Break Out." Rollingstone.com. 28 Aug. 2013. Web. Accessed 13 Nov. 2017.

December, 1963 (Oh, What a Night)

"December, 1963 (Oh, What a Night)." Songfacts.com. Web. Accessed 13 Nov. 2017.

Hagwood, Rod Stafford. "Gaudio Put Words in Valli's Mouth." *Sun-Sentinel*. 15 Feb. 2011. Web. Accessed 13 Nov. 2017.

It Was a Good Day

"It Was a Good Day." Songfacts.com. Web. Accessed 13 Nov. 2017.

Anderson, Kyle. "Ice Cube Finally Resolves 'It Was a Good Day' Theories: 'It's a Fictional Song.'" Ew.com. 05 Mar. 2012. Web. Accessed 13 Nov. 2017.

I Gotta Feeling

"I Gotta Feeling." Songfacts.com. Web. Accessed 13 Nov. 2017.

Reuter, Annie. "Black Eyed Peas Talk New Album, Performing on 'American Idol' Finale." *Marie Claire*. 19 May 2009.

September

"September." Songfacts.com. Web. Accessed 13 Nov. 2017.

Dean, Maury. *Rock N' Roll Gold Rush*. Algora, 2003. Print.

Whitburn, Joel. *Top R&B/Hip-Hop Singles: 1942–2004*. Record Research, 2004. Print.

Mad World

Interviewed by Dave Simpson. "Tears For Fears: How We Made 'Mad World.'" *The Guardian*. 10 Dec. 2013. Web. Accessed 13 Nov. 2017.

You Can Call Me Al

"You Can Call Me Al." Songfacts.com. Web. Accessed 13 Nov. 2017.

Buskin, Richard. "Classic Tracks: Paul Simon 'You Can Call Me Al.'" *Sound On Sound*. September 2008. Web. Accessed 13 Nov. 2017.

McNoldy, Kelly. "An Artistic Conversation of Brilliance." *The Sandspur*. 17 Oct. 2008. Web. Accessed 13 Nov. 2017.

Day 'N' Nite

"Day 'N' Nite." Songfacts.com. Web. Accessed 13 Nov. 2017.

Ahmed, Insanul. "Soundtrack to My Life: Kid Cudi's 25 Favorite Albums." Complex.com. 02 Mar. 2012. Web. Accessed 13 Nov. 2017.

Interviewed by Joe La Puma. "Kid Cudi." *Complex*. 03 Aug. 2009.

One Dance

"Drake brakes down how Skepta introduced Wizkid to him and how 'One Dance' was created." Youtube.com. 19 Feb. 2017. Web. Accessed 13 Nov. 2017.

What's Up

"What's Up." Songfacts.com. Web. Accessed 13 Nov. 2017.

Zombie

"Zombie." Songfacts.com. Web. Accessed 13 Nov. 2017.

This Charming Man

"This Charming Man." Songfacts.com. Web. Accessed 13 Nov. 2017.

Snow, Mat. "Ello 'Andsome." *MOJO*. March 2008.

Are You Gonna Go My Way

"Are You Gonna Go My Way." Songfacts.com. Web. Accessed 13 Nov. 2017.

Oh, Pretty Woman

"Oh, Pretty Woman." Songfacts.com. Web. Accessed 13 Nov. 2017.

Mallernee, Ellen. "The Story Behind The Song: How Roy Orbison Wrote '(Oh) Pretty Woman.'" Gibson.com. 09 Dec. 2009. Web. Accessed 13 Nov. 2017.

Goodbye Horses

Garvey, William. "Goodbye Horses—The Garvey Remixes." Garveymedia.com. 2008. Web. Accessed 13 Nov. 2017.

Hallelujah

Barton, Laura. "Hail, Hail, Rock 'n' Roll." *The Guardian*. 18 Dec. 2008. Web. Accessed 13 Nov. 2017.

Evil Woman

Greene, Andy. "ELO's Jeff Lynne: My Life in 15 Songs." Rollingstone.com. 21 Jan. 2016. Web. Accessed 13 Nov. 2017.

Since U Been Gone

"Since U Been Gone." Songfacts.com. Web. Accessed 13 Nov. 2017.

Irwin, Lew. "Kelly Clarkson Initially Unsure About 'Since U Been Gone.'" Contactmusic.com. 25 Oct. 2011. Web. Accessed 13 Nov. 2017.

Good Riddance (Time of Your Life)

"Good Riddance (Time of Your Life). Songfacts.com. Web. Accessed 13 Nov. 2017.

"Good Riddance (Time of Your Life). *Top 100 Songs of the '90's*. VH1.

Hare, Breeanna. "That Song Doesn't Mean What You Think." Cnn.com. 01 May 2017. Web. Accessed 13 Nov. 2017.

Spitz, Marc. *Nobody Likes You: Inside the Turbulent Life, Times, and Music of Green Day*. Hyperion, 2006. Print.

Where Is My Mind

"Where Is My Mind." Aleceiffel.free.fr. Web. Accessed 13 Nov. 2017.

"Where Is My Mind." Songfacts.com. Web. Accessed 13 Nov. 2017.

You Oughta Know

"You Oughta Know." Songfacts.com. Web. Accessed 13 Nov. 2017.

Carter, Nicole. "Dave Coulier admits Alanis Morissette's 'You Oughta Know' is about him." *New York Daily News*. 14 Aug. 2008. Web. Accessed 13 Nov. 2017.

Galindo, Brian. "You Oughta Know There's More to Dave Coulier than 'Full House.'" Buzzfeed.com. 04 June 2014. Web. Accessed 13 Nov. 2017.

Interviewed by Jean-Francois Méan. "Interview with Scott Welch, manager for Alanis Morissette." Hitquarters. com. 06 Aug. 2002. Web. Accessed 13 Nov. 2017.

Trust, Gary. "Rewinding the Charts: In 1995, We Got To 'Know' Alanis Morissette." Billboard.com. 22 July 2015. Web. Accessed 13 Nov. 2017.

Electric Feel

"Electric Feel." Songfacts.com. Web. Accessed 13 Nov. 2017.

Poker Face

"Lady GaGa Entertains Thousands At Palm Springs White Party." Nbcbayarea.com. 17 July 2009. Web. Accessed 13 Nov. 2017.

McKay, Hollie. "Lady Gaga Opens Up About Her Preference for Boys That Look Like Girls." Foxnews.com. 22 May 2009. Web. Accessed 13 Nov. 2017.

Scaggs, Austin. "Lady Gaga Worships Queen and Refuses to Wear Pants." Rollingstone.com. 19 Feb. 2009. Web. Accessed 13 Nov. 2017.

Remedy

Interviewed by Greg Prato. "Chris Robinson of the Black Crowes." Songfacts.com. 10 Dec. 2013. Web. Accessed 13 Nov. 2017.

Pumped Up Kicks

"Single Pumps up Foster the People." *The Columbian*. 21 June 2012. Web. Accessed 13 Nov. 2017.

"Band Talks 'Pumped Up Kicks' Post School Shooting." Cnn.com. 21 Dec. 2012. Web. Accessed 13 Nov. 2017.

Somebody That I Used to Know

"Gotye Interview: Find Out Why He Wrote 'Somebody That I Used to Know.'" Metrolyrics.com. 30 Apr. 2012. Web. Accessed 13 Nov. 2017.

Jones, Nicholas. "Kimbra Replacement After First Choice Cancelled Reveals Gotye." Tonedeaf.com.au. 15 Feb. 2012. Web. Accessed 13 Nov. 2017.

Tingen, Paul. "Mixing Gotye's 'Somebody That I Used to Know'—Francois Tétaz." *Sound On Sound.* July 2012. Web. Accessed 13 Nov. 2017.

Bat Out of Hell

"Bat Out of Hell." Songfacts.com. Web. Accessed 13 Nov. 2017.

Jim Steinman, performer. *Classic Albums: Meat Loaf Bat Out of Hell.* Directed by Bob Smeaton, 1999.

Loaf, Meat and Dalton, David. *To Hell and Back: An Autobiography.* Virgin Publishing, 2000. Print.

Yorke, Ritchie. "The Julia Child of Rock 'N Roll." *Sounds.* June 1978.

Royals

"Lorde—Lyrical Influences (VEVO LIFT)." Youtube.com. 27 Nov. 2013. Web. Accessed 13 Nov. 2017.

Iris

"Iris." Songfacts.com. Web. Accessed 13 Nov. 2017.

Black Hole Sun

Anderson, Kyle. "Chris Cornell tells stories behind classic 'Superunknown' songs." Ew.com. 03 June 2014. Web. Accessed 13 Nov. 2017.

Santeria

"Santeria." Songfacts.com. Web. Accessed 14 Nov. 2017.

Delgado, Ray. "Band's singer found dead in motel." *San Francisco Examiner*. 27 May 1996. Web. Accessed 14 Nov. 2017.

Come Sail Away

Wright, Jeb. "Dennis Deyoung: Speaking the Truth." Classicrockrevisited.com. Web. Accessed 14 Nov. 2017.

Wrecking Ball

"Wrecking Ball." Songfacts.com. Web. Accessed 14 Nov. 2017.

Drewett, Meg. "Miley Cyrus's 'Wrecking Ball' written in session meant for Beyoncé." Digitalspy.com. 03 Jan. 2014. Web. Accessed 14 Nov. 2017.

Two Princes

"Two Princes." Songfacts.com. Web. Accessed 14 Nov. 2017.

Aizlewood, John, et al. "Run for Your Life! It's the 50 Worst Songs Ever." *Blender*. May 2004.

Today

Black, Johnny. "The Greatest Songs Ever!" *Blender*. Dec. 2001/Jan. 2002.

Corgan, Billy. "Guitar Geek USA." *Guitar World*. August 1995.

Trendell, Andrew. "Billy Corgan opens about feeling suicidal due to Nirvana's success." Nme.com. 28 Feb. 2017. Web. Accessed 14 Nov. 2017.

Tom Sawyer

Infantry, Ashante. "New home a place to sing praises of our songwriters." Thestar.com. 20 Jan. 2010. Web. 14 Nov. 2017.

Elliott, Paul. "Rush: The story behind Tom Sawyer." Teamrock.com. 23 Apr. 2014. Web. Accessed 14 Nov. 2017.

Girls Just Wanna Have Fun

Parker, Lyndsey. "The Unusual Story of Cyndi Lauper's 'Girls Just Wanna Have Fun.'" Yahoo.com. 25 Mar. 2014. Web. Accessed 14 Nov. 2017.

Under the Bridge

Kiedis, Anthony and Sloman, Larry. *Scar Tissue*. Hyperion, 2004. Print.

Fricke, David. "The Naked Truth." *Rolling Stone*. 25 June 1992.

Swann, Jennifer. "The Red Hot Chili Peppers' Bridge Is Not Where You Think." Blogs.citypages.com. 30 Dec. 2014. Web. Accessed 14 Nov. 2017.

"Report: Bridge from Chili Peppers' 'Under the Bridge' Identified in L.A." *Rolling Stone*. 25 May 2012. Web. Accessed 14 Nov. 2017.

Under Pressure

May, Brian. "Brian May tells how David Bowie and Queen wrote the legendary track 'Under Pressure.'" Mirror.co.uk. 11 Jan. 2016. Web. Accessed 14 Nov. 2017.

In the Air Tonight

Collins, Phil, et al. *Genesis: Chapter and Verse*. St. Martin's Griffin, 2007. Print.

Greene, Andy. "Phil Collins: My Life in 15 Songs." Rollingstone.com. 29 Feb. 2016. Web. Accessed 14 Nov. 2017.

Solsbury Hill

Easlea, Daryl. *Without Frontiers: The Life & Music of Peter Gabriel*. Music Sales Group, 2013. Print.

Greene, Andy. "Peter Gabriel: Story That Bruce Springsteen Was Inspiration for 'Solsbury Hill' Is 'Hogwash.'" Rollingstone.com. 10 Oct. 2011. Web. Accessed 14 Nov. 2017.

Alive

Crowe, Cameron. "Five Against the World." *Rolling Stone*. 15 June 2006. Web. Accessed 14 Nov. 2017.

Better Man

Hilburn, Robert. "Working Their Way Out of a Jam." *Los Angeles Times*. 22 Dec. 1996. Fivehorizons.com. Web. Accessed 14 Nov. 2017.

Marks, Craig. "Let's Get Lost." *Spin*. Dec. 1994.

We Belong

Paulson, Dave. "Story Behind the Song: 'We Belong.'" *The Tennessean*. 25 June 2014. Web. Accessed 14 Nov. 2017.

Wonderwall

Beaudoin, Kate. "The Story Behind Oasis' 'Wonderwall' Will Make You Like It Even More." Mic.com. 29 Apr. 2015. Web. Accessed 14 Nov. 2017.

Beviglia, Jim. "Behind The Song: Oasis, 'Wonderwall.'" Americansongwriter.com. 04 Aug. 2015. Web. Accessed 14 Nov. 2017.

King Kunta

Hillyard, Kim. "Kendrick Lamar on new single 'King Kunta:' 'I studied James Brown.'" Nme.com. 05 June 2015. Web. Accessed 14 Nov. 2017.

"King Kendrick." Mtv.com. Web. Accessed 14 Nov. 2017.

I Kissed a Girl

"Katy Perry." *Talking Shop*, BBC, 26 Aug. 2008.

Curti, Jesse. "Scarlett Johansson Is Flattered She Inspired 'I Kissed a Girl.'" People.com. 17 Nov. 2008. Web. Accessed 14 Nov. 2017.

Elizabeth, De. "Miley Cyrus Says Katy Perry Wrote 'I Kissed a Girl' About Her." Teenvogue.com. 17 May 2017. Web. Accessed 14 Nov. 2017.

French, Megan. "Katy Perry on 'I Kissed a Girl:' 'Truth Be Told, I Did More Than That.'" *US Magazine*. 19 Mar. 2017. Web. Accessed 14 Nov. 2017.

Interviewed by Jan Blumentrath. "Interview with Chris Anokute, A&R for Katy Perry, Joss Stone." Hitquarters.com. 18 Oct. 2010. Web. Accessed 14 Nov. 2017.

Don't Stop Believin'

"Don't Stop Believin'." Songfacts.com. Web. Accessed 14 Nov. 2017.

Cheeseburger in Paradise

"Cheeseburger in Paradise." Songfacts.com. Web. Accessed 14 Nov. 2017.

"Where Did Jimmy Get the Real 'Cheeseburger in Paradise'?" Margaritaville.com. Web. Accessed 14 Nov. 2017.

Aqualung

"Aqualung." Songfacts.com. Web. Accessed 14 Nov. 2017.

Casey Jones

Browne, David. "Robert Hunter on Grateful Dead's Early Days, Wild Tours, 'Sacred' Songs." *Rolling Stone*. 09 Mar. 2015. Web. Accessed 14 Nov. 2017.

Mr. Jones

"Mr. Jones." Songfacts.com. Web. Accessed 14 Nov. 2017.

Follow You, Follow Me

"Follow You, Follow Me." Songfacts.com. Web. Accessed 14 Nov. 2017.

Turn It on Again

Genesis. *The Genesis Songbook*, Eagle Rock Entertainment, 2001.

Interviewed by Helmut Janisch. "Tony Banks—Interview." Genesis-news.com. 30 Sep. 2009. Web. Accessed 14 Nov. 2017.

Be My Baby

Interviewed by Dave Simpson. "How We Made the Ronettes' 'Be My Baby.'" *The Guardian*. 17 Nov. 2015. Web. Accessed 14 Nov. 2017.

Vogue

"Vogue." Songfacts.com. Web. Accessed 14 Nov. 2017.

Iaboni, Rande. "With passing of Bacall, all Madonna's 'Vogue' icons have died." Cnn.com. 13 Aug. 2014. Web. Accessed 14 Nov. 2017.

Interviewed by Austin Scaggs. "Madonna." *Rolling Stone*. 29 Oct. 09.

American Pie
"American Pie." Songfacts.com. Web. Accessed 14 Nov. 2017.

Sultans of Swing
"Sultans of Swing." Songfacts.com. Web. Accessed 26 Nov. 17.

"100 Greatest Guitar Solos: No. 22 'Sultans of Swing' (Mark Knopfler)." *Guitar World*. 21 Oct. 2008.

Get Lucky
Leseman, Linda. "Nile Rodgers Explains the 'Deep Hidden Meaning' of 'Get Lucky.'" Villagevoice.com. 25 Sep. 2013. Web. Accessed 14 Nov. 2017.

More Than a Feeling
Interviewed by Paul Riario. "Tom Scholz interview—Boston/'More Than a Feeling.'" Youtube.com. 10 Oct. 2015. Web. Accessed 14 Nov. 2017.

Rosalita
Goldiner, Dave. "Meet Springsteen's Rosalita and rock muses Rikki and Sharona, too." *New York Daily News*. 19 Apr. 2008.

Hiatt, Brian, et al. "100 Greatest Bruce Springsteen Songs of All Time." *Rolling Stone*. 16 Jan. 2014. Web. Accessed 14 Nov. 2017.

I Don't Like Mondays
Clarke, Steve. "The Fastest Lip on Vinyl." *Smash Hits*. 18–31 Oct. 1979.

Livin' on a Prayer
Paulson, Dave. "Story Behind the Song: 'Livin on a Prayer.'" *The Tennessean*. 20 June 2014. Web. Accessed 14 Nov. 2017.

Turn the Page
McCollum, Brian. "A Definitive Oral History of Seger's Early Years." *Detroit Free Press*. 14 Mar. 2004.

Goodnight Saigon
"Goodnight Saigon." Songfacts.com. Web. Accessed 14 Nov. 2017.

Bordowitz, H. *Billy Joel: The Life & Times of an Angry Young Man*. Random House, 2006. Print.

INDEX

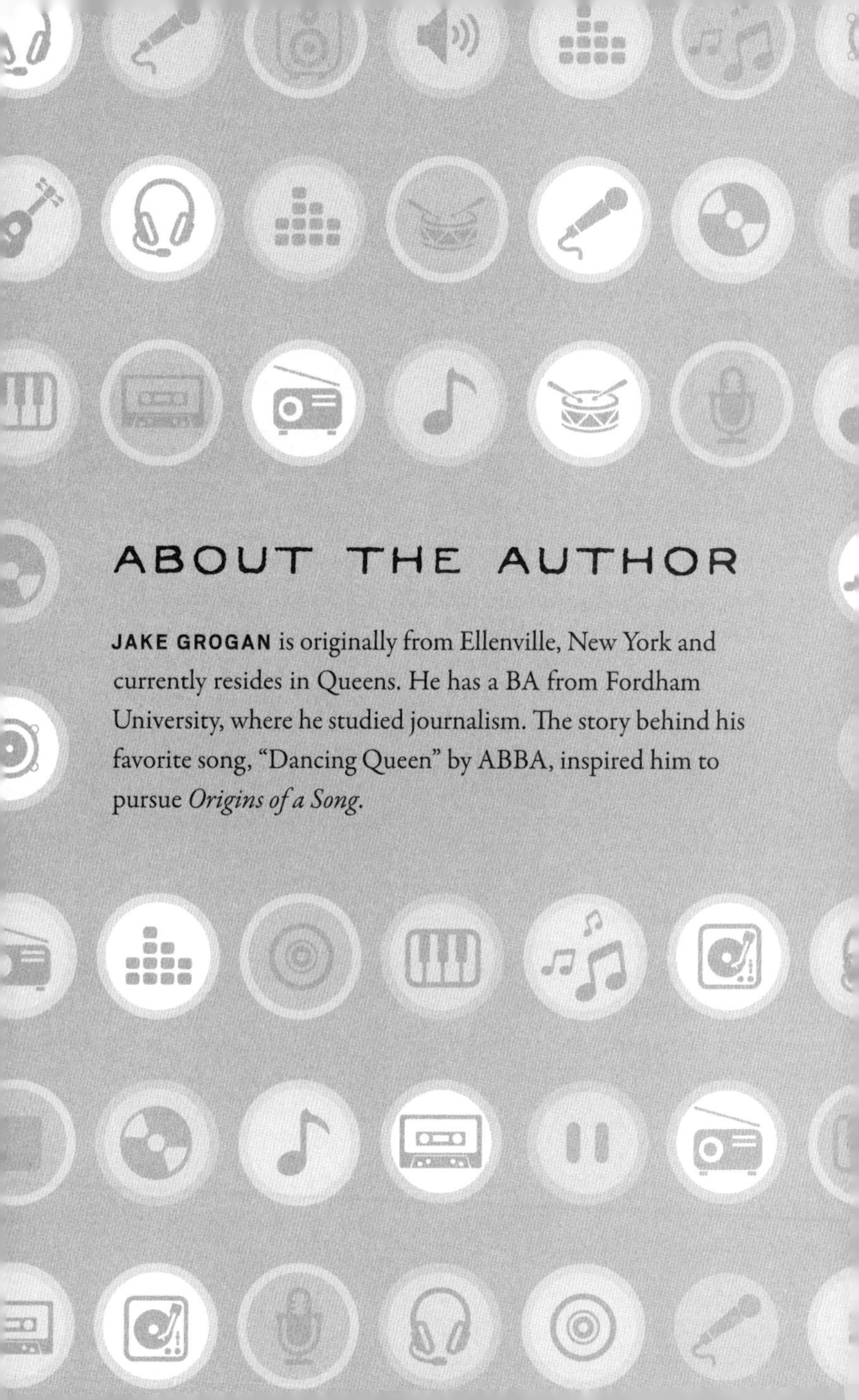

ABOUT THE AUTHOR

JAKE GROGAN is originally from Ellenville, New York and currently resides in Queens. He has a BA from Fordham University, where he studied journalism. The story behind his favorite song, "Dancing Queen" by ABBA, inspired him to pursue *Origins of a Song*.

"Where Good Books Are Ready for Press" Good ideas ripen with time. From seed to harvest, Cider Mill Press brings fine reading, information, and entertainment together between the covers of its creatively crafted books. Our Cider Mill bears fruit twice a year, publishing a new crop of titles each spring and fall.

Visit us online at
www.cidermillpress.com
or write to us at
PO Box 454, 12 Spring St.
Kennebunkport, Maine 04046

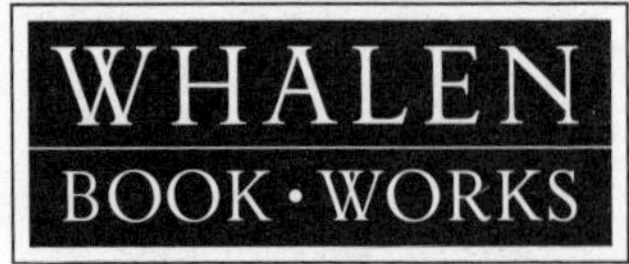

NEW YORK CITY, NEW YORK

Whalen Book Works is a book packaging company that combines top-notch design, unique formats, and fresh content to create truly innovative gift books. We plant one tree for every 10 books we print, and your purchase supports a tree in the Rocky Mountain National Park.

Visit us online at
www.whalenbooks.com
or write to us at
338 E 100 Street, Suite 5A
New York, NY 10029

BOSTON

NIRVANA
NEVERMIND
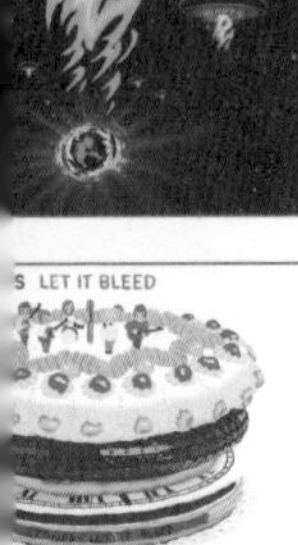
LET IT BLEED

"HEROES" DAVID BOWIE

BEASTIE BOYS

Andy Warhol

FLEETWOOD MAC
RUMOURS

Who's next

DEREK & THE DOMINOS · LAYLA

STYX